The German Navy in World War Two

A Reference Guide to the Kriegsmarine, 1935-1945

JAK P. MALLMANN SHOWELL

NAVAL INSTITUTE PRESS

This book is dedicated to *U-boat 377* and particularly to her first commander, Kpt.z.S. a.D. Otto Köhler without whose help and encouragement it would never have been written. *U377*, with my father on board, vanished into the North Atlantic in January 1944, three months before I was born. She was recorded as "lost by unknown cause: no survivors". Over a quarter of a century has passed before the facts of her disappearance have come to light. In 1977, I learned that *U377* was accidentally sunk by a German acoustic torpedo fired from another German submarine; *U972* suffered a similar fate. Otto Köhler left the boat to become commander of the T5 Training School shortly before that fateful 13th war cruise, and a few other members of the crew were also promoted to other posts. My father had completed his tour of duty as well, and was on his way to engineering officers' school only to be recalled because his opposite number had been taken ill and it would have been too hazardous to risk offensive action with two new men in the engine room.

Library of Congress Catalog Card Number 79-84933
ISBN 0-87021-933-2
Published and distributed in the United States of America by the Naval Institute Press, Annapolis, Maryland 21402.

British Library Cataloguing in Publication Data:
Showell, Jak Peter Mallmann
The German Navy in World War Two.
1. World War, 1939-1945—Naval operations, German
2. Germany. Kriegsmarine—History   I. Title
359'.00943   D771   ISBN 0-85368-093-0

Edited and indexed by Tessa Rose. Designed by David Gibbons. Maps and diagrams by Anthony A. Evans. Typeset by Trade Linotype Limited, Birmingham. Camerawork by Photoprint Plates Limited, Rayleigh. Printed by T. & A. Constable Limited, Edinburgh. Bound by Hunter & Foulis Limited, Edinburgh.

Photograph captions, page 1:
Top left: Informal dress on a sunny day. The man on the left is wearing the sport shirt with eagle and swastika printed on the front. Naval *Schiffchen* or forage caps are visible. (The second from the left is not wearing his correctly, but this way helps to keep the ears warm.) See pages 153 and 162-4.
Top right: The Ensign of the Kriegsmarine, which consisted of a black and white pattern on a red background—see the jacket illustration. Flags are discussed on page 9.
Below left: Otto Köhler (left) as commander of minesweeper *M18* with Obersteuermann Herbert Warner. (Photos: Author's Collection)
Below right: The man on the right is wearing a fully inflated Dräger Lung, the German equivalent of the British Davis Submarine Escape Apparatus, for getting out of submerged submarines. An ordinary life jacket, as used in U-boats and on surface ships, can be seen on the left. (Photo: Imperial War Museum)
Title spread: Motor torpedo-boats were known as Schnellboote or S-boote in Germany. *S19*, seen here, was commissioned during October 1938 and survived the war to be sold, by Britain, in 1947/48. (Photo: Bundesarchiv, Koblenz)

Below: *U377* surfacing off Norway. The framework forward of the 88mm gun is a cradle for taking on torpedoes. (Photo: Author's Collection)

Contents

Major Aspects of German Naval History

The birth of the Navy

Before the unification of Germany, each of the small states paid for its defence alone. Among the poorest of these states were the coastal regions, which could not afford to build fleets on the scale of the larger powers. Instead, they maintained small ships intended to combat piracy rather than fend off organized, armed aggression. Indeed, the first real German navy was not created until almost fifty years after the Battle of Trafalgar, so it is a relatively young force.

The decision to found a navy was taken at Frankfurt-am-Main in 1848—during the war against Denmark—after the Danes had declared their intention of blockading German sea ports. This first German Navy was but a modest affair, although there were a few individual efforts of note, such as the construction of Germany's first submarine—*Brandtaucher*. Designed by Wilhelm Bauer, a Bavarian artillery officer, she was launched at Kiel on 18 December 1850—an event that caused the blockading Danish ships to leave the bay and anchor farther out in the Baltic. But, on balance, the maritime force, or Bundesmarine (Federal Navy, the same as today) achieved very little and was disbanded again in 1852. The ships were handed over to the Royal Prussian Navy— also founded in 1848—and Germany's first great admiral, Rudolf Brommy (original spelling Bromme), who had been the driving force behind the fleet's development, was dismissed (without even a pension).

The first autonomous naval command, or admiralty, of the Royal Prussian Navy was founded during 1853. A year later it came under the command of Prince Adalbert of Prussia, who held the title 'Admiral of the Prussian Coast'. There was still no battle fleet, and the main function of the Navy was still seen as a transport vehicle for the Army. The next major change came in 1866, after Austria's withdrawal from the German Alliance and Prussia had founded the North-German Federation. This resulted in the Navy being renamed Nord-Deutsche Bundes-marine (North-German Federal Navy) during October 1867. But, although this move was a step in the right direction, the basic problem remained: the Federation's membership still comprised small, independent kingdoms and principalities between which there was little love lost. Indeed, the twenty-five Germanic states had a long history of conflict, not only between themselves but also with neighbouring nations.

The unification of Germany came about quite unexpectedly in 1870, after France had declared war on the largest of these Germanic kingdoms, Prussia. The French hoped that the Catholic princes in the south would help them supress the Protestant economic development in the north. But this did not happen. Surprisingly, Bavaria, Baden and Württemberg took up arms in support of Prussia, and soon the three armies were heading west, singing as one "Lieb Vaterland magst ruhig sein, fest und treu steht die Wacht am Rhein" ("Dear fatherland, be peaceful, the guard is standing firm and faithful at the Rhine"). They did not stop at the Rhine, but fought their way to Paris, surrounded the city and crushed all opposition.

The dramatic success of this campaign created a deep feeling of unity among the German people, with even the Catholics of the south calling for King Wilhelm I of Prussia to become emperor of all the German states. For the first time in Germany's history the majority of those who held the reins of government also wanted a united nation. Their wish was granted on 18 January 1871, when the German Empire was born in the Galerie des Glaces in Versailles. The Navy was then appropriately renamed Kaiserliche Marine (Imperial Navy).

The creation of a unified Germany sparked off a chain reaction of reforms, and developments in science and technology were especially rapid. The accession in 1888 of Kaiser Wilhelm II, who had a special interest in ships, brought about a new approach to the Navy. During his reign, it graduated from being a mediocre collection of coastal craft to a powerful battle fleet capable of challenging that of any other nation. The fleet was constructed along the same lines as the British Navy, with powerfully-armed battleships forming the backbone of the force. One of the basic problems of this set-up was that officers and men were trained to come to terms with the rapid technological developments, without too much thought going into how best the monstrous weapons might be used. It was this sort of thing that prompted Grand Admiral Alfred von Tirpitz —the architect of the German Navy—to make the justifiable comment: "Germany does not understand the sea."

Kaiserliche Marine, Reichsmarine and Kriegsmarine

Battleships, the Kaiser's greatest symbols of power, played no decisive role in the First World War. Instead, the main burden of the fighting was carried by torpedo-boats, minesweepers, submarines and similar vessels—many of which were developed and built under harsh war conditions. Most of the hard fighting was conducted by young men, not by the admirals, and the fact that many of these sailors were at odds with their High Command was made quite clear by a breakdown of discipline, especially in the larger units. The peak of human obedience to authority had been reached during the early part of the war, when thousands of men, on both sides, faced certain death without questioning the orders of their superiors. But as the war drew to a close, attitudes in the German armed forces changed to such a degree that, rather than face more futile blood-baths, many men preferred to mutiny.

The Navy found itself in a strange situation after the war, for it had not really suffered a great defeat, but neither had it scored any decisive victory. In addition, many of the ships were still afloat and in fighting condition, although by the terms of the Treaty of Versailles these had to be handed over to the Allies. Despite the ill-feeling against authority, several young officers found this clause humiliating, and wanted to sail into the British surrender ports with guns ablaze and fight to the death. However, this extreme element must have been a small minority, for the Fleet entered the Royal Navy anchorage at Scapa Flow peace-fully. It was not until later, while lying at anchor in deep water, that the war flags fluttered once more from the mast heads—an indication that the ships were being scuttled and were on their way to the sea bed. German morale may have been at an extremely low ebb, but the Imperial Navy's old tradition of sinking one's ship before surrendering it was still alive. So, with nearly all ships lost, 1919 saw the end of the Kaiser's Navy. Those not sunk at Scapa Flow were either sunk elsewhere or handed over to the Allies, and the few remaining in German hands were already obsolete.

The foundation day of the new Navy (Reichs-marine) is considered to be 1 January 1921, for by that time Germany had reduced her strength sufficiently to meet the requirements of the peace treaty. The Kaiser's flag* was officially hauled

Below: Grosser Hafen, Wilhelmshaven, in 1918 with the units of Germany's first, powerful High Seas Fleet. (Photo: Druppel)
Bottom of page: When the Imperial Navy came to an end and was replaced by the Reichsmarine, most of the Fleet had either been sunk or handed over to the Allies, leaving the fitting-out basin of Wilhelmshaven Naval Dockyard completely empty, with a 'ghost town' atmosphere. Coal stocks are visible on the right, where the ship is moored, and sea locks leading to the tidal River Jade can be seen in the background. (Photo: Author's Collection)

Left: Officers and officials of the Naval Command Office in 1924. (Photo: Bundesarchiv, Koblenz)
Below left and this page: The early Reichsmarine Ensign was made up of black, white and red stripes, with a small canton of black, red and gold stripes in the upper (black) band. The canton was removed in March 1933. The left-hand photograph was taken aboard the light cruiser *Karlsruhe* during Sunday service, while the ship was passing through the English Channel; in the photograph below, *Karlsruhe* is at anchor. (Photos: Author's Collection)

down for the last time on 31 December 1921—some two years after the end of the war. However, new laws relating to the Navy were not finalized until later. The new Reichsmarine flag was hoisted for the first time on 11 April 1921. It consisted of black, white and red horizontal stripes with a large iron cross in the middle, and had a small canton of black, red and gold horizontal stripes in the top left-hand corner. (Later, on 14 March 1933, the canton was removed by order of President Paul von Hindenburg—shortly after Hitler's elevation to chancellor. Unfortunately, this useful aid for determining dates of photographs was rather small, occupying only a minute part of the upper black stripe, and it is often not distinguishable.) The Reichsmarine was renamed Kriegsmarine on 21 May 1935, its new identity being underlined five months later by the introduction of a new flag bearing a large swastika. When this flag was first hoisted on 9 November 1935, only those with psychic powers could have recognized what the swastika would come to represent for millions of people. This flag was used until it, and all it came to represent, was finally torn down in May 1945.

The old imperial flag was used to commission at least one ship in the war years. During *M18*'s commissioning ceremony, a rolled up flag bearing the printed name 'war flag' was attached to the flag staff. The commander then gave the order to hoist the flag, whereupon the royal eagle and cross unfurled itself to flutter in the light breeze! After the initial panic had died down, a correct flag was hurriedly found and the ceremony continued. Luckily, *M18* had sufficient drinks on board to help make the press and publicity men forget the incident, but the German High Command did eventually learn of the slip-up when it was reported, in depth, by a Swedish newspaper.

A prefix, like HMS, was also used for ships during the emperor's time: SMS for Seine Majestäts Schiff. In later years, warships were distinguished from merchant vessels by the words Reichsmarine Schiff or Kriegsmarine Schiff. However, the abbreviations RMS and KMS were rarely, if ever, used by the Navy. In the Kriegsmarine it was far more common to prefix warships

*When using flags to date photographs, it should be remembered that during Hitler's era the old imperial flag was also flown on special occasions. This should not cause any problem because the swastika flag often appeared with it, and most of the ships on which it was flown were commissioned after the First World War. However, it may lead to some confusion if it appears on its own on one of the earlier ships.

with their class, for example: Panzerschiff *Deutschland*, Schlachtschiff *Tirpitz* or Torpedoboot *Möwe*.

The Treaty of Versailles

The end of the First World War and the imposition of harsh peace terms forced drastic changes upon the German Navy; perhaps hardest of all was coming to terms with the Treaty of Versailles, the conditions of which were dictated by the Allies. It was a hefty political document with far-reaching effects on the German economy and armed forces. The Navy was affected as follows:

1. a. National conscription had to be abolished.
b. The armed forces were restricted to volunteers. The Navy was to be restricted to a total of 15,000 men, including 1,500 officers. This figure included crews for all ships, coastal defence forces and staff for shore stations.
c. There was to be no naval reserve force.
d. Volunteers had to sign on for at least twenty-five years in the case of officers and twelve years for other ranks.
e. Personnel leaving the Navy were not permitted to serve in any capacity in any armed force. Those remaining had to commit themselves to serve until the age of forty-five.
f. Members of the merchant navy were not allowed to receive military training.
2. a. The number of ships had to be limited to:
6 Battleships plus 2 reserve
6 Cruisers plus 2 reserve
12 Destroyers plus 4 reserve
12 Torpedo-boats plus 4 reserve
Additional small craft were also limited.
b. Germany was not permitted to build or own submarines (including merchant submarines), aircraft carriers, heavy artillery or military aircraft.
3. Displacements of replacement ships were limited to:

Battleships	10,000 tons
Small cruisers	6,000 tons
Destroyers	800 tons
Torpedo-boats	200 tons

Ships sunk or destroyed could be replaced, but otherwise, ships had to be between fifteen and twenty years old before a new ship could be built as a replacement. (Neither was Germany permitted to sell a fairly new warship and then build another in its place.) All armament was limited and determined by the Allies.

4. Germany had to maintain ships for clearing mines.
5. All German warships not in German ports ceased to belong to Germany and all rights to them had to be renounced.
6. a. No fortifications could be erected near the Baltic shipping lanes. Existing defence installations had to be removed. All information about these fortifications, including hydrographic details, had to be made available to the Allies.
b. All fortifications and naval installations (except Heligoland) within 50km (approximately 30 miles) of the German coast or from the German islands were allowed to remain in their end-of-war condition. New fortifications were not permitted within that zone. Armament, both total number of guns and calibre, could not be increased from their 1918 state.
7. The German government had to hand over documents and information to the Allied Naval Control Commission. These included plans, specifications and other details of armaments and of radio communication equipment.
8. Germany had to agree that Germany and her Allies were responsible for all war losses and all war damage.

The main aim of the Treaty was to limit the power of the German nation, whose meagre obsolete fleet was only permitted to meet a possible attack from the East, where the revolution in Russia was still showing signs of political unrest. But, whilst the Treaty severely limited the material aspects, it was a complete failure on the psychological side. Indeed, these harsh terms sowed the seeds of their own undoing, and were a major factor in the events that led to the Second World War. The German Emperor was forced to abdicate, leaving his position of Head of State free for anyone to climb into. And the Treaty of Versailles provided the National Socialists with the ideal ladder. The hatred for authority shown by German soldiers at the end of the war, the general unrest and the strikes were quickly given direction. Both the Allies and the German government became objects at which the masses could vent their anger and frustration; the former were loathed as suppressors, while the latter were despised for agreeing to the terms of the Treaty.

The sailors' main grudges were not against the material impositions, but the order to hand over the Fleet to the Allied navies, not being permitted a free German defence constitution, and having national defence controlled by an international commission. The majority also disagreed with the clause whereby German soldiers had to face Allied military tribunals; and there was total rejection of the clause by which the men had to consider themselves guilty of all war damage. The Navy did not, as the Allies might have expected, sit down on its wilted laurels and devote the following years to polishing the remains of the Fleet. Germans work well under pressure, and the Treaty of Versailles presented a suitable stimulus to get together and work hard.

Selection for the German Navy was rigorous, with only the best men from the old Imperial Navy accepted. In the 1920s there were thirty to forty applicants for every post available, so it was possible to pick and choose. Only candidates with the highest qualifications were admitted to the ranks, making the Navy into an élite fighting force. This pool of concentrated talent was put to work finding ways around the restrictions imposed by the Treaty, and a very great deal was achieved. For example, submarines were not permitted, so in 1922 a 'Submarine Development Bureau'—employing the cream of German submarine designers—was set up in Holland, where it cleverly concealed its true purpose by posing as an ordinary Dutch shipbuilding firm. Although guns were limited in size, the problem was neatly side-stepped with the perfection of quick-firing guns and the development of rockets. Radar was invented as a radio direction-finder, in order to make heavy artillery more effective. Germany had a working radar set before Britain started work on the project, yet the idea was never developed to its full potential. As battleships were restricted to 10,000 tons, it was probably expected that Germany would build smaller dreadnoughts, but she went one better and developed the pocket battleship—a new concept in naval warfare. The first product of this idea, Panzerschiff *Deutschland*, was much admired by foreign navies, with some naval experts heralding her as the warship of the future.

So, step by step, the small naval force of the Reichsmarine slowly and unobtrusively made its limited power much more effective. And some measure of its success can be gauged if one considers that this modestly-sized navy, often with less than fifty operational units in the Atlantic per

month, was to keep the world's most powerful fleet on the defensive for some four years. Apart from enjoying a numerical advantage, the British were also in the enviable position of being able to decipher a fair proportion of German secret radio signals. Add to this the support they received from the rapidly expanding United States Navy, and one can see that theirs was no mean achievement.

The Washington Naval Treaty

There was very little naval development of significance in Germany during the 1920s. However, meetings of the major maritime powers, on 12 August 1921 and during the following autumn, saw the formation of a new international treaty, which indirectly affected the German Navy. This Washington Treaty limited armaments at sea. It was agreed that battleships should have their guns restricted to 16in calibre and that cruisers should be no larger than 10,000 tons with 8in guns.

The tonnage under this treaty was measured with the United States ton, which is slightly heavier than the British or Imperial ton, used in the Treaty of Versailles. In Germany, people became quite enthusiastic about these developments when they saw the possibility of sidestepping the peace treaty in favour of the Washington Treaty. By this ploy, German ship sizes laid down at the end of the First World War could be increased by up to 15% without changing the tonnage numbers.

In fact, Germany was now in a unique position among maritime nations, as her naval planners were quick to perceive. Although the limitations of Versailles meant that battleships with 16in guns were completely out of the question, the cruiser figures were very interesting: the international limitation on the displacement of cruisers coincided with the maximum tonnage laid down for German battleships. So the German designers came up with the idea of building a ship that would be too fast for any enemy battleship and much superior to a cruiser. This concept, the so-called 'pocket battleship', was by no means easy to develop. One of the biggest problems was that of propulsion and, in the end, it was decided to use powerful diesel engines. It was essential to test the design before it was installed in a major warship, so the prototypes were eventually fitted into the artillery training ship *Bremse*, which was launched in January 1931. The first pocket battleship, Panzerschiff *Deutschland*, splashed into the water

on 19 May 1931 and was completed two years later, to be commissioned on 1 April 1933. Her powerful diesel engines gave her a top speed of 26 knots, a range of 10,000 nautical miles, and she carried six 11in guns. (The designers cheated with her displacement figures, making her a little heavier than she should have been: when empty she displaced 11,700 tons and when fully loaded almost 16,000.) Her high top speed enabled her to run away from an enemy battleship; but she could blast a cruiser out of the water from outside the range of the cruiser's guns.

Hitler and the Anglo-German Naval Agreement

In the early 1930s, the naval leadership was still labouring under extreme difficulties and could not finance all the schemes it would have liked. Many of their clandestine projects were paid for by overcharging on permitted developments and then filtering off the excess money to pay for the illicit plans. The first real boost came after Hitler had been appointed chancellor, for he was not only in favour of rearmament, but strongly encouraged it.

Adolf Hitler made his famous proclamation in which he repudiated the Treaty of Versailles and re-introduced national conscription on 16 March 1935. The words he used, however, were not his own. Parts of this famous speech were word for word those of one written seven years earlier by Defence Minister Groener—Hitler appears to have been the first front line politician prepared to stand up and present it. He certainly expected some repercussions from the Allies, but they were too busy with their own internal affairs and took no notice. It is curious that the Versailles Treaty, which was meant to effectively clip the wings of German power, was allowed to be thrown out by the very people it was designed to control. So, with no trouble at all, Hitler was left free to lay the foundation stone of his mighty war machine. At the same time, he made every effort to maintain good relations with Britain, partly because he expected her to present the biggest problems should difficulties arise. This consideration led to the next major milestone in the development of the German Navy: The Anglo-German Naval Agreement, which was signed on 18 June 1935 by Sir Samuel Hoare for Britain and by Special Envoy Joachim Ribbentrop for Germany. With this agreement, Hitler hoped to show that he had no

desire to conduct a war against Britain. Germany volunteered to restrict her maritime strength to thirty-five per cent of that of the Royal Navy; however, submarines were considered as a separate case, and a forty-five per cent ratio was agreed. Parity in submarines was also agreed in principle, but in that event Germany would have to sacrifice tonnage in other categories, and Britain would have to approve the move.

Although the political intrigues and manoeuvrings that took place at this time are somewhat beyond the scope of this book, a few observations should be made. There were several reasons for Britain's apparent capitulation to German demands. For various domestic reasons, the British government of the day was not prepared to take a hawkish stance, and the Admiralty were convinced that the British Fleet would not be strong enough to take on both Japan and the foremost European naval power simultaneously. Therefore, until terms with Japan could be agreed, they were keen to reach an agreement with Germany that would preclude the possibility of another arms race. Reactions to the Agreement

were like sighs of relief. Earl Beatty, the British Fleet Commander during the latter part of the First World War, stated that, as a result of the Agreement, Britain had at least one country with which they need not conduct an armaments race. And Hitler told Admiral Erich Raeder, Commander-in-Chief of the German Navy, that the day the Agreement was signed was the happiest of his life—quite understandably, since he had thrown out the Versailles Treaty and had now apparently received international approval for doing so! Raeder himself told his officers they could not have hoped for better conditions during the coming decade. He went on to say that the Agreement ruled out the possibility of Germany having to fight another war against Britain. Later, he prohibited any theoretical studies of a conflict with Britain. And the next set of routine battle orders circulated to the High Command on 27 May 1936 made no mention of Britain—France and Russia were considered as the potential enemies.

The Anglo-German Naval Agreement permitted Germany to build and own previously prohibited ship groups, such as submarines and aircraft

Below: This early photograph of the light cruiser *Leipzig* shows three aircraft from the 'Naval Air Arm' operating under civilian flying club registration because military aircraft were still prohibited by the Treaty of Versailles. This flying club was founded during the 1920s, when pilots received their early naval training at the Hanseatic Yacht School in Neustadt, Schleswig-Holstein. (Photo: Author's Collection)

Right: *Prinz Eugen*'s Arado 196 seaplane. (Photo: Imperial War Museum)

carriers. The first aircraft carrier, Hull 'A' (*Graf Zeppelin*), was launched on 8 December 1938, but never completed. Hull 'B' was laid down at Germania Works in Kiel and later scrapped at an early stage of construction. The third one, not due to be launched until about 1940, was never started.

The Naval Air Arm

In 1935, aircraft—also prohibited under the Versailles Treaty—were no longer considered to be auxiliary weapons, but fully integrated tools for naval warfare. Thoughts of engaging aeroplanes had been in the minds of the higher commanders since the First World War, and plans for building a naval air arm were considered long before 1935. A 'private' flying club, with aeroplanes capable of landing on water, had been in existence for some years before Germany was permitted to own military aircraft.

The Naval Air Arm, Luftkreis IV, which was later renamed Luftwaffenkommando See, was founded by the Luftwaffe to work in cooperation with the Navy for coastal defence. In the event of a war, one of its branches, the Marine-luftstreitkräfte (later Seeluftstreitkräfte), under the command of Generalmajor Geissler (Führer der Marineluftstreitkräfte or FdL) was to come under the direct command of the Fleet Commander.

It was considered important to have good naval minds commanding aircraft at sea, so personnel were selected exclusively from the Navy. The training was rigorous, and only a fraction of the men who embarked upon it were accepted for flying duties. The majority returned to ship-based work. In 1935 it was planned to create some 25 squadrons with a grand total of about 300 aircraft. These squadrons were planned to be equipped with various types of aircraft:

a. Land-based aircraft—long-range, short-range, multi-purpose and fighters.
b. Carrier-based: fighters, dive-bombers and general purpose aircraft.
c. Ship-based reconnaissance aircraft.

The Luftwaffe became more interested in ships, docks and other naval targets as time progressed, and a true naval air arm never materialized. Hermann Göring, Commander-in-Chief of the Luftwaffe and, early on in the war, a close friend of Adolf Hitler, always maintained "Everything

17

which flies belongs to me!'' Nevertheless, small
naval air groups did exist, but there were too few in
number to have any significant impact on the
overall war picture.

Submarines

Germany was able to build submarines much
faster than new cruisers because she had kept
abreast of modern technological trends through
her 'Development Bureau' in Holland. This
'private' enterprise had built several submarines
for foreign countries, whose new vessels—
unbeknown to them—were taken on long sea trials
by German submarine experts before being
delivered. So, by 1935, Germany had not only the
technology to construct modern submarines, but
the necessary core of trained men to operate them.

Several submarines had been partly constructed
during 1934, put into a top secret store in Kiel, and
were only waiting to be assembled. This advanced
state of readiness enabled the first new submarine,
U1, to be launched two days before the signing of
the Anglo-German Naval Agreement. *U1* was
commissioned a fortnight later, after which she
joined the submarine school's flotilla. Her
commander was Kptlt. Klaus Ewerth. The first
new 'Front' (operational) U-boat, *U7*, was
commanded by Kptlt. Kurt Freiwald and commissioned on 8 August. All operational submarines were grouped together in one flotilla—
named 'Weddigen', after the First World War
submarine hero—and were commanded by
Kapitän zur See Karl Dönitz.

Dönitz has often been described as a ''successful
First World War U-boat commander'', which is
most misleading since he had many strings to his
bow and was successful at most jobs he tackled.
Destiny must have given him a glimpse of what his
future held, for he was given the nickname 'diva'
(meaning star or prima donna) by his fellow cadets
at training school. By 1935 Dönitz had spent most
of his 25 years' service in the surface Navy—his
experience as a submariner only amounting to two
and a half years. So, on that score, there were
certainly many others better qualified for the
position of Flag Officer for Submarines. When
asked after the war why Dönitz had been chosen,
Grand Admiral Raeder replied that there had been
no prime reason, but, looking back, he was
convinced he had done the right thing. At first,
Raeder had thought Hitler would be unsuccessful

Below: Training Flotilla Salzwedel in the locks at Wilhelmshaven during 1936. (The flotilla, commanded by Fregkpt. Werner Scheer, was earlier based in Kiel.) The submarines are of Type VIIA, which can easily be determined because this was the only type with rear torpedo tubes above the waterline: these are clearly visible here. Only ten experimental Type VIIA boats were built before they were modified and replaced by VIIB from 1938 onwards. The design was further changed after the start of the war, and Type VIIC became the most important submarine in the Battle of the Atlantic. (Photo: Druppel)

with the Anglo-German Naval Agreement, and he therefore made no plans to develop a special submarine arm. In 1934, when Germany started to think seriously about building underwater craft, Raeder thought the Navy might be permitted a handful of submarines, but these would be attached to some existing unit. Then, out of the blue, he was faced with the prospect of creating an autonomous submarine arm, for which there was no obvious leader. It was at about this time that Karl Dönitz—who was returning from a successful tour 'showing the flag' in the Far East aboard the light cruiser *Emden*—sailed into the reckoning. This small, energetic commander had served in submarines, albeit briefly, and had twice before successfully commissioned new units: firstly, the 4. Torpedoboots Halbflottille, and secondly *Emden*—which had been de-commissioned for a lengthy refit and then re-commissioned with a brand new crew.

That Dönitz's appointment as Flag Officer for Submarines was a hasty and temporary move on Raeder's part is indicated by several factors. Firstly, before docking at Wilhelmshaven at the end of her tour of the Far East, *Emden* had called in at Vigo, where the German naval representative had given Dönitz several documents including orders from the Supreme Naval Command instructing him to go ahead with plans for another cruise to the Far East in the autumn. So Raeder had not yet made his decision, although it was only a short time after this that *Emden* reached Wilhelmshaven and Dönitz was informed of his new post. Secondly, in 1936 it was planned that Dönitz would return to cruisers as a flotilla commander and take a squadron on a world tour. As a result, his successor, Hans-Georg von Friedeburg, was appointed a few years later in the autumn of 1938 to start the necessary training. But the war came too soon, and it was decided to keep Dönitz as head of U-boats and give von Friedeburg command of the large and complex Organization Department.

Surface ships

After the Anglo-German Naval Agreement, there was no similar expansion in the construction of surface ships as there had been in the field of submarines. Germany still had several design problems to overcome, the largest of which was, without doubt, the propulsion question. One school of thought argued for diesel engines, as used in the pocket battleships, and the other was in favour of superheated high-pressure steam turbines. In the end, the German Navy decided to use the latter in battleships and heavy cruisers—a move considered by many to have been *the* catastrophe in battleship construction. The main disadvantage with superheated high-pressure steam turbines was their limited range. Pocket battleships could be employed in the South Atlantic or even in the Indian Ocean, but the large battleships could only operate in the North Atlantic near their German bases. However, at that time there were no great thoughts about conducting a battleship war in the Atlantic. Equally out of the question was a blockade of either French or British ports by German surface ships. The prime function of battleships was considered to be the prevention of a blockade of German ports by enemy warships. So their limited range was not thought critical, as they would only be required to operate at relatively short distances from home.

The construction programme of June 1936, therefore, only met the requirements for the immediate future, and there were no plans to build up to the limits of the Anglo-German Naval Agreement. The following proposed launching dates were circulated to departments of the Supreme Naval Command during June 1936:

Dec 1937	Pocket battleship 'E'
June 1938	Pocket battleship 'D'
July 1938	Cruiser 'H'
Sept 1938	Cruiser 'G'
April 1939	Aircraft carrier 'A'
May 1939	Cruiser 'I'
Nov 1939	Aircraft carrier 'B'
Dec 1939	Cruiser 'K'
March 1940	Pocket battleship 'F'
April 1940	Pocket battleship 'G'
End of 1940	Cruiser 'L'
May 1941	Pocket battleship 'H'
Dec 1936 to October 1938	Destroyers *Z1* to *Z22*
Aug 1936 to May 1938	U-boats *U21* to *U44*
Nov 1937 to February 1938	Torpedo-boats 1 to 8
Aug 1938 to December 1939	Minesweepers 1 to 9
Oct 1936 to January 1937	Fleet Escorts *F7* to *F10*
Oct 1937 and the end of that year at the earliest	Submarine escorts 1 and 2

Below: *Scharnhorst's* two forward 280mm-gun turrets, a photograph taken in the Polar Seas during 1940. (Photo: Bundesarchiv, Koblenz)

Plan 'Z'

Thus far, construction plans had been conceived in an atmosphere of 'no war with Britain'. But this ideal was given a severe jolt a year later, when, on 5 November 1937, Hitler made a dramatic speech to high-ranking government officials and military leaders, in which he re-stated his case for the forcible acquisition of territory in Eastern Europe. Prior to the meeting, Admiral Raeder, Commander-in-Chief of the Navy, had been taken aside by Hermann Göring and told that the Führer's speech would be rather strong, but he was not to take any notice, as Hitler was trying to launch the Army's armament plan. Afterwards, Werner von Blomberg, Commander-in-Chief of the OKW, told Raeder roughly the same thing. So, as naval development was proceeding quite well, Raeder ignored the implications of Hitler's speech and took no steps to speed up the naval planners.

Raeder informed Hitler on several occasions that Germany's naval development was not sufficient to cope with a war against a major sea power, and that production should be increased. But each time the Führer replied by saying there would be no war against Britain because such an act would signal the end of the Reich. Not until early 1938 did Hitler tell Raeder that the Kriegsmarine would have to consider meeting the Royal Navy on a war footing. Even then, he stressed that it would not be until the late 1940s at the earliest.

By 1937, warship development had progressed sufficiently for the first long-term planning policy to be effected. The plan was intended to remain in force from 1938 until 1948, and would see the fleet develop to the limits of the Anglo-German Naval Agreement. All the original demands and suggestions for new warships were evaluated by Kpt.z.S. Werner Fuchs, and put down on paper as Plan 'X'. This was an immense document and could not be considered under the terms of the Naval Agreement, so he modified the details and reduced the plan to a practical size. His tailored version was designated 'Plan Y', and was laid before the Supreme Commander-in-Chief of the Navy, who modified the ideas still further. The final version then became known as 'Plan Z'.

Plan 'Z' had been conceived under the ideal of 'no war with Britain', but matters had to be re-considered after Hitler told Raeder that they might have to fight the Royal Navy after all. As roughly half of Britain's naval forces were employed in

foreign waters, it was thought that Plan 'Z' fleet would be able to hold its own against the remaining Home Fleet. So, it was decided to go ahead with the plan, the idea being to speed up production at a later date, should the political situation demand it. There were two distinct opinions on naval warfare in the German Navy at the time Plan 'Z' was formulated. One idea, which received the backing of the Supreme Naval Command, was to build a powerful surface fleet consisting of mainly battleships and cruisers. The other idea was to develop a navy centred around submarines and small craft such as torpedo-boats.

Plan 'Z' was strongly opposed by Kpt.z.S. Karl Dönitz, who could only muster a long list of foul adjectives to describe the decision. Another opponent of Plan 'Z' was Fregkpt. Hellmuth Heye who, acting on an instruction from Raeder,

Table 1: Plan 'Z' —ship construction plans for 1938 to 1948.

Type of ship:	Total number to be built by 1948:	Ultimate total to be built:	Under construction at the start of the war:	Completed or almost completed at the start of the war:
Aircraft carrier	4	8	Design 'B'	Graf Zeppelin
Battleship	4	4	–	Gneisenau
				Scharnhorst
				Bismarck
				Tirpitz
Battleship, Type H	6	6	–	–
Pocket battleship, early type[1]	3	3	–	Deutschland
				Admiral Scheer
				Admiral Graf Spee
Pocket battleship, later type	10	12	–	–
Heavy cruiser	5	5	–	Admiral Hipper
				Blücher
				Prinz Eugen
				Seydlitz[2]
				Lützow[3]
Light cruiser	12	24	'M', 'N', 'O', 'Q' and 'R' designs	Emden
				Königsberg
				Karlsruhe
				Köln
				Leipzig
				Nürnberg
Scout cruiser[4]	20	36	–	–
Destroyer	58	70	Several	22
Torpedo-boat	90	90	About 15	About 20
Submarines (all types)	241[5]	241	Several	57

1. Pocket battleships were all based on the original *Deutschland* design. It was planned to build new versions later.
2. *Seydlitz* was launched at Deschimag in Bremen on 19 January 1939. She was about three-quarters complete when work was stopped and the hull converted to that of an aircraft carrier. This plan was cancelled during 1943 and the uncompleted hull towed to Königsberg during the spring of 1944. It was scuttled towards the end of the war.
3. *Lützow* was sold to Russia, and the pocket battleship *Deutschland* was later renamed *Lützow*.
4. Scout cruisers were about half way between

destroyers and cruisers in size.

5. 241 submarines may appear to be an impressive number, especially when one considers Dönitz's request for 300, but these boats only represented a small fraction of the total expenditure; roughly the same cost as four battleships and amounting to approximately ten per cent of the total force. The total of 241 boats included huge submarine cruisers carrying heavy artillery.

produced a thesis on the subject of war with Britain. He concluded that it would not be possible to defeat Britain by pitting German battleships against her merchant shipping. But it appears that nobody took much notice of Heye during the summer of 1938. Perhaps this was because he was an individualist with unconventional and "quite mad ideas"—which he fully demonstrated towards the end of the war by building up the Midget Weapons Unit to a fantastically high standard, against terrific odds and in an incredibly short time. In addition to Heye there were several other submarine supporters in the Supreme Naval Command: Hermann Boehm, Fleet Commander, and Hermann Densch, Commander-in-Chief of Reconnaissance Forces, were both in favour of U-boats. In fact, Densch had a pet-saying: "We must build submarines on every meadow, in every shed and on every stream—it is our only hope of winning."

But theirs were only faint cries in the wilderness, for the majority were in favour of a battleship navy. Many in the Supreme Naval Command kept repeating their stereotype views that there would be no war with Britain, and that, under war conditions, Dönitz's submarine tactics would be found wanting. Several powerful men in the High Command maintained their belief that only the mightiest and heaviest battleships would penetrate the shipping lanes of the Atlantic. They considered submarines to be outdated and obsolete weapons. The High Command also had some knowledge of Britain's asdic, which, it was thought, might prevent a successful submarine war. Similarly, they pointed to the Prize Ordinance Regulations (page 200), which imposed numerous operational limitations on submarines and further restricted their effectiveness.

The final decision on the type of construction policy to adopt was made by Hitler. The Naval High Command gave him two alternatives: either a battleship fleet or a U-boat dominated navy. Hitler chose the surface fleet outlined in the 'Z' Plan and, on 27 January 1939, gave the programme top priority—just over six months before the outbreak of the Second World War.

The new capital ships were to be equipped with eight 406mm (16in) and twelve 150mm (6in) guns; they would carry four aeroplanes, have a top speed of thirty knots, and a range of over 12,000 nautical miles at a cruising speed of just under twenty knots. (Construction of *Bismarck* and *Tirpitz* had, of course, already started when the plan was formulated.) The Chiefs of Staff also examined what had been Germany's main weakness during the First World War—that of trying to operate far out in the Atlantic from bases in the German Bight. This problem was solved by planning to put the new battleships into the South Atlantic, where they would be serviced by supply and repair ships, the idea being to seek out remote spots in the Southern Ocean for more lengthy repairs.

The end of the treaties
In 1939 came the final break. Firstly, on 27 January 1939, Germany informed the British government that they wished to increase their submarine strength to equal that of the Royal Navy. And then, on 28 April during a speech to the German government, Hitler cancelled the Anglo-German Naval Treaty.

The German Navy had been on full war alert since early August 1939, and many ships had been sent to their war stations. But this in itself was nothing new, because full war alert had been ordered on several previous occasions, such as the re-occupation of the demilitarized Rhineland, the Austrian Anschluss and the crisis in the Sudetenland. Even at this late stage, few people in the German High Command seriously thought there would be a war with Britain—least of all Admiral Raeder, who was still telling his officers that the German Navy did not have sufficient ships for such a conflict, and that, in the event of a war, all they could show was how to die with dignity.

During the morning of 3 September 1939, Raeder was handed a note informing him of Britain's declaration of war on Germany. Raeder then faced his High Command and sent them into battle with these words: "Meine Herren, wir haben keine Wahl. Voller Einsatz. Mit Anstand Sterben!" ("Gentlemen, we have no choice. Total engagement. Die with dignity!")

Early wartime surface vessels
The pre-war ship construction plan was abandoned shortly after the war started; ships nearing completion were finished, others were scrapped, and there was no significant development of large surface warships during the war years. All of the ships launched henceforth had been designed long before the start of the conflict, and the naval

Below: Invitation to the 'Commissioning of the first R-boats built in Norway'. The badge on the front of the cover is the private insignia of Hans Bartels minesweeping unit in Norway. Finding himself a little short of suitable ships, Bartels decided to build his own. He then sent an invitation and the bill to the Supreme Naval Command—hence the question mark over the bank notes in the bottom right-hand corner. (Photos: Author's Collection)

Bottom: Bartels unofficially issued a 'Tiger Pin' award to the men who served with him; each was awarded this certificate. Below right: Two views of *M1* in her famous role as 'Tiger of the Fjords'. She was fitted with cycloidal propellers, making it possible for her to rotate on the spot and travel sideways. (Photos: Author's Collection)

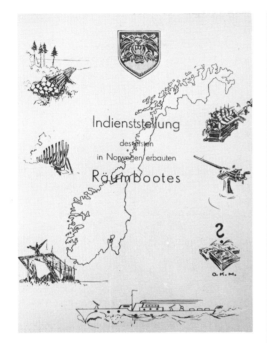

designers concentrated on building small surface boats capable of operating in coastal waters under air protection.

Some of the boats built during the war were created in quite astonishing circumstances. Probably one of the wildest projects was the construction, in Norway, of the Navy's smallest minesweepers. These Zwerge (dwarfs) were the brainchild of Kptlt. Hans Bartels, who commanded the minesweeper *M1* at the start of the war. After taking part in the invasion of Norway, *M1* developed mysterious engine trouble and was unable to return to Germany with the rest of the flotilla. By the time the fault had been traced and repaired, the other ships were too far away for her to catch up, so Bartels reported to the senior German naval commander, who was only too pleased to use *M1*'s services.

Bartels distinguished himself by carrying out several extraordinary feats: he managed to capture a destroyer, together with an entire torpedo-boat flotilla; and, later, he even captured an Allied convoy and took it into a German-held port. The men of *M1* also 'defended' several small Norwegian ports from possible enemy attacks from the sea, by making mock mines—ingeniously devised by welding spikes onto empty petrol cans—and then mooring them in the harbour approaches. This charade was given an air of reality when the British laid a few mines of their own! Unfortunately for Bartels, these were rather inconveniently placed—right in the German shipping lanes running in and out of the ports. Undaunted, Bartels and *M1*, together with several modified fishing boats, tried to clear them. Three of the fishing boats were lost in quick succession, making it quite clear that existing craft were unsuitable for sweeping mines in shallow fjord waters. It was apparent to Bartels that he needed an easily manoeuvrable craft with a shallow draught, capable of passing over the mines without detonating them. Such boats did not exist, so Bartels decided to build his own. While looking for suitable designs, he found a Norwegian fishing vessel with all the necessary requirements. Unfortunately, the engines (which were almost certainly purchased from Sweden) did not fit, until someone struck on the idea of turning the plans around and putting the propeller in the bows. It worked. The bows were flattened, a new point added at the stern and, in the end, everything fitted together quite well.

Twelve such Zwerge were constructed, and the Supreme Commander-in-Chief of the German Navy was invited to the commissioning ceremony —and to pay the necessary bills. But Grand Admiral Raeder did not take up this offer and, in the end, Bartels moved one of them to Berlin, moored it in the canal outside Naval Headquarters and Raeder inspected it there. Raeder took a dim view of Bartels independence, however, and promoted him to the rank of First Officer of the destroyer *Z34*, in the hope that he might re-learn some naval discipline. Later in the war, Bartels returned to his unorthodox way of life when he worked under the equally unconventional Admiral Hellmuth Heye in the Midget Weapons Unit.

Magnetic mines

Accounts of events at the start of the war tend to highlight the sinking of the aircraft carrier HMS *Courageous*; the sinking of the battleship HMS *Royal Oak* in Scapa Flow; the Battle of the River Plate, when the pocket battleship *Admiral Graf Spee* was scuttled; and the Norwegian Campaign of spring 1940. But these famous actions give a slightly false picture of the war, because the majority of German ships were not sent out to hunt British warships. The main burden of the fighting at sea was carried by small vessels, such as U-boats, destroyers, torpedo-boats and minesweepers, which conducted numerous successful mining operations in British sea lanes. Mines, especially the magnetic variety, were certainly the

most important weapon in the German naval armoury during the winter of 1939/40.

The magnetic mine was not a German invention, for Britain had developed it before the end of the First World War—although with little success. By 1939, the German Navy had perfected the weapon, which Raeder, certain there would be no war with Britain until 1945 at the earliest, carefully locked away in a top-secret store. With this ace up their sleeve, the Germans sat back, convinced that the Royal Navy were unaware of the mine's presence in Hitler's arsenal. But, in the event, it was they who were caught out: for, when war broke out, the few existing models were still lying in cold storage and, until mass production of the magnetic type could be organized, the Navy had to make do with old percussion mines.

The German Naval Command were well aware that, once they realized magnetic mines were being used, the British would find the means to neutralize their effect. It would be necessary for them to find out how the detonation system worked, but after that it would be a simple matter of generating strong magnetic fields that would cause the mines to explode short of their target. The de-magnetizing of merchant ships would also

be possible. But, in a way, the German Navy was helped by having so few magnetic mines: ordinary mines were cleared by minesweepers, after which the channel was declared open to merchant shipping, while magnetic mines were not cleared during such sweeps. They remained on the sea bed, only rising as the first large iron ship passed over. The German Navy took great care to deposit these mines in areas where they would have maximum effect and where they were not likely to be washed ashore. Ironically, it was an aircraft of the Luftwaffe that finally rendered this most deadly weapon ineffectual, by dropping one on the mud flats near Shoeburyness late in November 1939.* The pilot could not have chosen a better place for presenting this valuable trophy to the Royal Navy, for it landed without damage, without the safety destruct mechanism for shallow water switched on and only a short distance from a fully-equipped workshop. A British naval specialist simply walked out to it during the hours of darkness, took rubbings of the screw and nut heads, and then returned in daylight with specially made tools for

*Incidentally, the Luftwaffe further distinguished itself during those early months of the war by attacking a group of German destroyers and causing the sinking of *Maass* and *Schultz*; see page 118.

opening the mine. He thus defuzed one of the war's most valuable prizes.

The torpedo crisis of 1939/40
During the early days of the war, it was realized that U-boats could get close to British harbours and ships without being detected, and that they were usually only discovered when their torpedoes failed to explode at the target. When this happened, the 'eels' (German slang for 'torpedoes') either detonated early or passed underneath the target, blowing up harmlessly on the other side. This often resulted in serious consequences for the firer, because the old G7a torpedoes—which were still being used—left a noticeable wake of small bubbles as they passed through the water, thus revealing the U-boat's position.

The G7a torpedo worked quite simply by compressed air helping to burn fuel in a six-cylinder combustion engine. The later G7e torpedoes were fully electric, with batteries and an electric motor. Although these did not leave a wake, they had the disadvantage of requiring much more maintenance and had to be withdrawn from the tubes for battery charging about once every three days.

Initially, most of the torpedo failures were attributed to war nerves on the part of the U-boat crews. It was thought that the men acted too hastily and did not complete the firing procedure. But the facts pointed to quite a different reason: only about one-third of the total of torpedoes fired detonated on target. By the end of October 1939, Karl Dönitz, head of the U-boat arm, was certain the fault did not lie with his men. Indeed, he was constantly being innundated with complaints from his commanders, of which the following are but a few examples.

Kptlt. H. Schultze had come into port with *U48* and reported that half of the ten torpedoes he had fired had been duds. Less than a week later, Kptlt. Wilhelm Zahn had had several battleships lined up in front of *U56*'s three tubes—it was a Type IIC U-boat—and had fired a salvo at HMS *Rodney*. The crew had heard the torpedoes strike her hull, but there had been no detonation. After stopping a merchant ship, Kptlt. Viktor Schütze decided to sink it with a torpedo, but found that four had to be fired from very close range before one detonated. Shortly afterwards, Kptlt. Herbert Sohler 'flew off the handle' at this de-briefing, telling Dönitz that on three occasions he had managed to get within point-blank range of a convoy: each time, it was like shooting at a solid wall of ships, yet his torpedoes seemed to achieve nothing. All he heard were two premature explosions.

Stories like these abounded throughout 1939 and well into the following year before the reasons for the failures were discovered. The situation during the Norwegian Campaign of spring 1940 was appalling: out of a total of forty-eight U-boats, forty-two engaged the enemy, but over thirty of these attacks failed because the torpedoes did not work. At least twenty-five Allied warships were attacked but only one Allied submarine was sunk.

However, the first two U-boats sunk by enemy action were lost as a result of premature explosions alerting the escorts. The first casualty, *U39*, commanded by Korvkpt. Gerhard Glattes, went down on 14 September 1939 after attacking the aircraft carrier HMS *Ark Royal*. *U39*'s torpedoes were of the old-fashioned compressed air variety that left a tell-tale wake. Escorts were alerted and some men in HMS *Foxhound* actually spotted the U-boat's dark shadow beneath the surface of the water. *Foxhound* raced over to the spot and dropped several well-placed depth charges. *U27*, commanded by Korvkpt. Hans Franz, was the second boat to go down. Again, a salvo of three torpedoes detonated short of their target and two escorts, HMS *Forester* and HMS *Fortune*, darted over to the suspected position. And again, well-placed depth charges brought the U-boat to the surface. Some of the crew managed to get out before it sank and, through letters sent back to Germany from prisoner-of-war camps, at least the details of *U27*'s fate reached Dönitz's desk. (Such information was written in code and sent to close relatives, who had instructions to forward all mail to the Naval High Command.)

During November 1939, Dönitz recorded in his diary: "The Torpedo Inspectorate has perpetrated a real blunder." Fortunately, Grand Admiral Raeder had reached the same conclusion and hastily appointed Professor E. A. Cornelius to find out what had gone wrong and to eliminate the fault. Cornelius had worked as a torpedo specialist at Eckernförde before the war, and his knowledge in this field spanned some twenty years. However, it was not until about mid-1940 that the fault was run to earth and the sordid details were brought to light at a court martial.

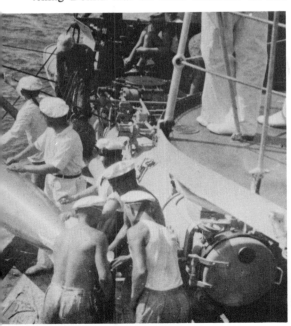

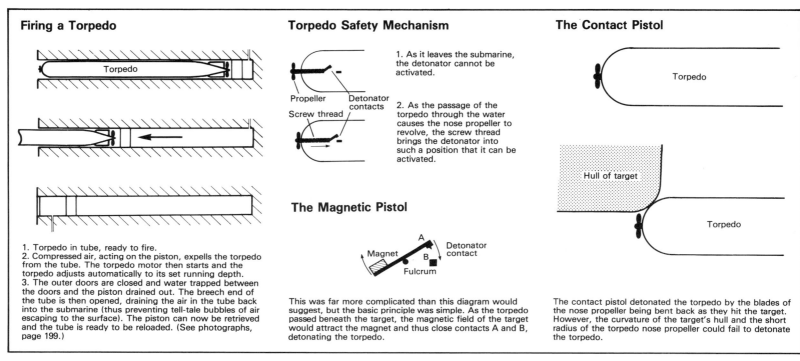

Firing a Torpedo

Torpedo

1. Torpedo in tube, ready to fire.
2. Compressed air, acting on the piston, expels the torpedo from the tube. The torpedo motor then starts and the torpedo adjusts automatically to its set running depth.
3. The outer doors are closed and water trapped between the doors and the piston drained out. The breech end of the tube is then opened, draining the air in the tube back into the submarine (thus preventing tell-tale bubbles of air escaping to the surface). The piston can now be retrieved and the tube is ready to be reloaded. (See photographs, page 199.)

Torpedo Safety Mechanism

1. As it leaves the submarine, the detonator cannot be activated.

Propeller   Detonator contacts
Screw thread

2. As the passage of the torpedo through the water causes the nose propeller to revolve, the screw thread brings the detonator into such a position that it can be activated.

The Magnetic Pistol

A
Magnet   Detonator contact
B
Fulcrum

This was far more complicated than this diagram would suggest, but the basic principle was simple. As the torpedo passed beneath the target, the magnetic field of the target would attract the magnet and thus close contacts A and B, detonating the torpedo.

The Contact Pistol

Torpedo

Hull of target

Torpedo

The contact pistol detonated the torpedo by the blades of the nose propeller being bent back as they hit the target. However, the curvature of the target's hull and the short radius of the torpedo nose propeller could fail to detonate the torpedo.

There were three major faults which, to make matters more complex, did not affect every torpedo. Some of these problems were not recognized until the end of the war. This, understandably, clouded the problem, for as one fault was isolated and rectified another would crop up. The three major faults were:

1. Peacetime experiments had not accurately simulated the rigours of war. Torpedoes had simply been put on board a ship and, a few hours later, fired at a target—hardly an adequate test when one considers that under war conditions torpedoes were tossed about by rough seas for days, sometimes even weeks, before being used. This was especially detrimental to torpedoes used by submarines. Air pressure inside a submarine was very variable, and would usually increase slightly the longer the boat remained submerged. Torpedoes were expelled from the tubes by compressed air, which would then escape from the machinery into the interior of the boat. (A special free-running piston would be fitted behind the torpedo and, when the order to fire was given,

compressed air would be released into the space behind the piston. This worked in a similar way to an air gun: the piston was pushed forward along the torpedo tube, pushing the torpedo in front of it. The piston would stop at the end of the tube and the compressed air be allowed to escape into the interior of the boat, thus preventing it from sending tell-tale bubbles to the surface.) Such increases in pressure affected the controls of the torpedoes and made them run erratically. The depth mechanism, especially, was affected.

2. The explosive could be detonated by two different methods, the necessary adjustment for whichever detonation was required having to be made before the torpedo was fired. This was no great problem because it could be carried out while the torpedo was in the tube, waiting to be fired. The commander had the choice of either exploding the torpedo on impact, using the so-called contact pistol, or the detonation could take place magnetically. By the latter method, the torpedo would swim deep under the target and blow up beneath it. This had far greater impact than a

torpedo exploding at the side, for such an explosion could easily break a merchant ship in two. The problem with the magnetic detonator was that too little was known about the earth's magnetic fields. This was especially evident during the Norwegian Campaign, where it was thought the proximity of the North Pole and the abundance of iron ore (magnetic magnetite) could affect the torpedo mechanism. After the Norwegian Campaign the torpedoes were mainly used with the contact pistol.

3. Torpedoes had a safety mechanism to prevent them from exploding too close to the firer. This device worked quite simply with the aid of a small propeller at the front of the torpedo. The propeller would spin around when the torpedo travelled through the water, and this turned a screw that pushed the two contacts of the detonator together so that, if activated, they could touch. This safety mechanism made it impossible for the torpedo to explode accidentally until it had travelled at least 300m (a little over 320yds) through the water. The blades of this propeller also acted as a trigger for

Below: The bridge of *U532* showing the torpedo-aimer in action. (See also page 189.) When shooting from a surfaced position, it was always the First Officer's responsibility to fire torpedoes. He had full control of the boat, and the commander only looked on to keep an eye on the overall situation. In this case, the aimer is being tried out by Admiral Sir Max Horten, who inspected the boat shortly after it docked in Liverpool at the end of the war. A speaking tube and radar detector aerial are visible between the two men. (Photo: Imperial War Museum)

the contact pistol. But this was where the major fault lay, for each blade was marginally shorter than the radius of the torpedo. As a result, the explosives were detonated when the torpedo hit a flat target, such as those used for practice or when the torpedo hit the side of a merchant ship with a deep draught; but it was also possible for the torpedo to hit a curved hull without the triggers being pushed back to activate the contact pistol. In those instances, the torpedo would bounce off, slide under the target and often carry on swimming. The contact pistol worked quite well against merchant ships, but the same problem cropped up in later years when U-boats started attacking small warships escorting convoys.

Experiments with new magnetic pistols had started in 1927, as a result of irregularities discovered during the First World War. These tests had been carried out using the very old G7v torpedoes, which were an earlier type to the G7a compressed air variety. The new pistol, consisting of a modified magnetic pistol, had been tested during the autumn of 1928 by firing torpedoes at

an iron plate suspended in water. The torpedoes missed their target, and hit the framework instead, but the detonators went off, suggesting that the pistols were functioning.

At that time, there was no independent body for testing new torpedo developments, and all the work—designing, building, testing and evaluating—was carried out by the Torpedoversuchsanstalt (TVA). This arrangement was not changed until almost the end of the Spanish Civil War, when Admiral Raeder ordered the establishment of an independent testing command to find out why torpedoes used off the Spanish coast were not functioning properly. This body, called the Torpedoerprobungskommando (TEK), subsequently appeared, and was considered by many people to be in direct competition with the TVA. Consequently, there was considerable friction between the two.

The TEK carried out several tests, including firing torpedoes at the raised hull of the old sailing ship *Niobe*, and discovered several irregularities. But their findings were channelled back to the

Supreme Naval Command through the TVA, where some people were of the opinion that the torpedoes were functioning perfectly and anyone could make them fail if they tried hard enough. Apparently, some of the test results were not passed on to the Supreme Naval Command, and it was not until after the war had started that one of the TVA's junior officers took matters into his own hands and complained directly to the admirals about the nature of some of his duties. He felt he could no longer tolerate the irregularities in the administration. After this, Raeder dismissed several top officials and, in the summer of 1940, ordered a full inquiry—by which time the Norwegian Campaign was over.

At a court martial held later, it was revealed that the trouble had been caused by the TVA, which had been responsible for what was described as "criminal negligence". But, apparently, they were not solely to blame, for several of their engineers had requested ships for torpedo-testing in rough weather. Unfortunately, they had received little support, and often had to make do with small boats not capable of going far out to sea.

Submarine tactics

In 1935, there existed three important but diverse schools of thought on submarine warfare: the views of the Admiralty in London, those of the Oberkommando der Marine in Berlin and the ideas of Karl Dönitz.

Powerful battleships and fast cruisers formed the backbone of the Royal Navy's fleet. Submarines, on the other hand, had no place in this pattern. They were too slow to operate alongside battleships and cruisers, and were more easily affected by bad weather conditions. Some people at the Admiralty saw uses for submarines in theatres of war where the Royal Navy was numerically inferior, but on the whole they were considered unimportant weapons. This attitude is borne out by looking at the total number of ships in the British Navy at the start of the Second World War: it was the largest fleet afloat, yet it only had fifty-seven submarines.

After the First World War, Britain had perfected an ultrasonic detection device for finding submerged submarines. As a submerged submarine was totally blind and fairly immobile, it was easy to destroy once it had been detected. Experiments with this device, called 'asdic' (now known as sonar) together with new submarine defence methods led the British Shipping Defence Advisory Committee to state in 1937 that the submarine would never again present the problems faced in the Great War, when Britain's supply routes had been almost cut off by U-boats. This statement helped confirm the opinion that submarines were obsolescent.

Such negative ideas were also fairly widespread in Berlin, although they did not cut any ice with Karl Dönitz. On the contrary, he could see a terrific future for underwater weapons and was convinced the sceptics were wrong. In 1935, he started to revolutionize the submarine's role by introducing four new basic ideas.

1. Short-Range Attack. U-boat officers receiving secret training at the Submarine Defence School in Kiel before 1935 had been instructed to keep at least three kilometres (one and three quarter miles) away from their target; otherwise they risked detection by the 'secret weapon' (asdic). The British Advisory Committee probably also assumed that submarines would attack from similar ranges. In practice, it meant that a submarine would have to fire a salvo of torpedoes; even then, there was a good chance of missing because of the difficulty in judging speed, range and direction at such distances.

Dönitz changed these conventional tactics by instructing his commanders to attack from half a kilometre (550 yards). From such a short distance, he could almost guarantee a hit with one torpedo. Dönitz told his men to adopt the short-range method of attack until the exact performance of the 'secret weapon' was known. He added that the German Navy was not even certain it existed, but that, if it did, the device would be affected by wave action, salinity and noise from the vessel in which it was fitted, and so would offer the hunter no significant advantage.

The short-range method of attack was far more effective than might at first be imagined. It was not just a case of making every torpedo a possible hit— the submarine's role was changed from one of mere nuisance value to a most deadly weapon capable of tearing a convoy to pieces. Take the following example. Type VII, the most important U-boat class, had one stern and four bow torpedo tubes carrying about fourteen torpedoes. It took at least twenty minutes to reload one tube, and that had to be done away from wave action. In the

Atlantic, this meant that the boat would have to dive, slow down to a few knots and remain there for well over an hour: by the time the boat resurfaced, it would have lost sight of the convoy. And the time required for reloading was not the only problem, for sometimes the amount of manoeuvring needed to get into an attacking position further reduced the chances of getting even one hit in a convoy. But at short range there would be five potential sinkings. This short-range attack plan was later modified by U-boat commanders, especially Otto Kretschmer, who actually sailed into convoys and picked out the best targets at point-blank range.

2. Surface Attacks at Night. Submariners from many countries had been looking for ways of perfecting submerged attacks. Obviously, the early submarines still spent a great deal of time on the surface, either recharging batteries and air cylinders or travelling to their war stations. On the

whole, however, commanders avoided surfacing in daylight or during attacks.

Karl Dönitz changed such views by purposely putting his U-boats on the surface. They were to live and fight on the surface and only dive to avoid the enemy or heavy seas. This way, submarine performance could be improved considerably. Top speed, for example, could be increased from eight knots to seventeen. The cruising speed while submerged was four knots or less, but on the surface the boats could easily manage about ten knots. A surfaced submarine had a minute silhouette, and Dönitz felt certain he could find successful night-time methods of attack, when surface ships would stand out well on the horizon and the submarine would be barely visible to enemy lookouts.

3. Tirpitz's Dream. Dönitz also realized that submarines were the ideal tools for implementing the ideas of Grand Admiral Alfred von Tirpitz.

During the 1880s, Tirpitz had forecast a revolution in naval warfare, and he had predicted that the big guns of the battleships would be replaced by torpedoes. He had also advocated the use of small, fast torpedo-boats for night attacks. During Tirpitz's lifetime, designers lacked the necessary technology to build such craft and, when the idea became more feasible, they lacked the necessary imagination, which resulted in the concept being modified to increase armament, action radius and to carry greater loads. When the boats were eventually finished, they looked like small destroyers, and did not bear even a vague resemblance to Tirpitz's original idea!

Now, in 1935, Dönitz knew he had the answer: an easily manoeuvrable torpedo-carrier, almost undectable at night and capable of operating in the Atlantic. The word 'torpedo' is very important: Dönitz saw it as the most effective weapon so far devized for submarines. He regarded artillery as a secondary armament, to be used on targets that could not retaliate. One puncture in the delicate hull of a submarine would render it helpless. A surface ship, on the other hand, could take numerous hits without affecting its firepower. (This fact was not appreciated by some influential members of the Supreme Naval Command, who laid plans to build huge 2,000-ton cruisers, capable of engaging destroyers in artillery combat. These Type XI U-cruisers never progressed beyond the drawing-board stage. Plans were made to build four at Deschimag Works in Bremen, but the war came too soon and they were never laid down.)

4. *Wolf Packs.* It has often been said that 'wolf pack', or Rudel tactics, were dreamed up by Dönitz while in a prison camp during the First World War, but this is not so. The idea had been suggested by Kommodore Hermann Bauer, Flag Officer for Submarines of the High Seas Fleet, back in 1917—about the time that Dönitz first went into submarines. However, Dönitz was the first to put the theory into practice. The plan evolved slowly. By 1939, the technique called for a group of U-boats to spread out across the path of the anticipated convoy. During daylight, all boats would sail at an economical speed (roughly 10 knots) towards the expected ships. At dusk, they would sail in the convoy's direction, to make it more difficult for the enemy to slip through the net during the night. The first boat to spot the convoy would report to headquarters (see page 100), send

out homing signals to the rest of the group, and continue shadowing the merchant ships until the pack was assembled and could attack together. Each commander was usually free to decide the best way of intercepting the convoy. Those nearby had an easy task, for they only needed to head towards the homing signals. But boats farther away had the more difficult task of anticipating where the merchant ships would be in a few days time and heading for that spot.

The combination of close range attack and wolf pack tactics raises the question of collisions. Although these operations resulted in several U-boats milling about in relatively confined areas, there were surprisingly few accidents. The first one did not occur until 8 December 1942, when *U221*, commanded by Kptlt. Hans Trojer, ran into the stern of *U254*, commanded by Kptlt. Hans Gilardone. *U221* managed to return to France, but the other boat, unable to dive, was later sunk by

aircraft from 120 Squadron of the RAF. The U-boat Command realized it had been impossible for Trojer's lookouts to spot *U254* in the bad conditions prevailing at the time, and the incident was dismissed as an unfortunate accident.

Submarine construction

Several publications have either given the impression or stated that Karl Dönitz was responsible for building submarines before the war, but this is a misconception. In reality, Dönitz did not manage to influence U-boat construction until after the war had begun. The U-Bootsamt, a department in the Supreme Naval Command with no direct link with the U-boat arm, had been responsible for construction policies before the war. Because of this organizational division, Dönitz was completely unaware of the large quantities of material compiled by this department; nor did he realize that the plans he submitted

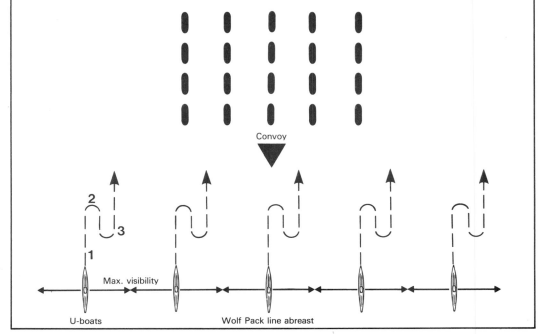

The Principle of the 'Wolf Pack' Attack

1. During daylight hours, all U-boats of the group sail at an economical cruising speed towards the anticipated convoy.
2. During the hours of darkness, the U-boats reverse direction to sail very slowly in the same direction as the convoy, thus maintaining their position relative to the convoy.
3. At daybreak, the U-boats resume cruising towards the oncoming convoy.

Convoy

Max. visibility

U-boats   Wolf Pack line abreast

between 1936 and 1939 had been largely disregarded. Before the end of 1939, Dönitz was unable to make any real impression on U-boat construction policies.

Dönitz laid his first emergency war plans before Grand Admiral Raeder on 8 September 1939. This memorandum, outlining the requirements for a battle in the Atlantic, made the following recommendations.

1. To build torpedo-carrying U-boats, concentrating on Types VII and IX.
2. To build large minelaying U-boats with longer range than existing submarine types.
3. To build large, long-distance supply submarines. Speed would not be important, as long as they could remain at sea for long periods and cover vast distances.
4. For the long term also, to build long-range torpedo-carrying submarines.

This eventually resulted in the construction of Types VIIC and IXC, Type XB, Type XIV supply submarines and Type IXD$_2$.

The British declaration of war caught the German Navy by surprise, and some of its higher officials suddenly realized that their previous priority of having sufficient deck space for parades was no longer of any use. Drastic new measures had to be taken. Existing plans were scrapped and, during that first autumn, new policies were devized. The Navy's first wartime construction plans stated: "Future U-boat types will be decided by the Flag Officer for Submarines." (At the start of the war, the head of the U-boat arm held the status of Flag Officer. Dönitz was not made Commander-in-Chief until October 1939.)

This new programme was laid before Hitler on 10 September 1939. He agreed to it, but, because at that time Hitler did not want a war with Britain, he did not give authorization for the necessary raw materials to be delivered to naval dockyards until 8 December 1939.

The general situation regarding submarine construction was quite astonishing. On average, there were sixteen U-boats in the Atlantic during each month of 1939. The number fell to thirteen during the winter of 1939/40, and it remained at that low ebb until mid-1941, when the average increased to about thirty-five. This means that only about sixteen boats were in the Atlantic at any one time during the U-boats' 'First Happy Time'—when

they all but defeated the world's most powerful maritime nation. One wonders what might have happened if Germany had more submarines during that fateful period.

Quoting numbers and averages, as has been done here, is a favourite occupation of many historians, but it can be most misleading and sometimes does not show the true picture. When one examines the details behind the statistics, one can find quite chaotic situations. Take January of 1942 as an example. Dönitz's war diary gives the following situation.

There were 91 operational submarines. 23 were in the Mediterranean and the Supreme Command had issued orders to send another 2, bringing the total to 25; 6 boats were stationed just west of Gibraltar, and 4 more were in Norwegian waters. This left a total of 56 boats for the important convoy battles in the North Atlantic. Some historians have quoted a total of 85 boats in the Atlantic—but such figures are misleading. About half of the operational boats would have been in dock because the U-boat arm was lacking in the materials, tools and skilled men to repair them!

Table 2: Phases of the Battle of the Atlantic

Approx. average no. U-boats in N. Atlantic		Losses to U-boats in N. Atlantic (tons)	Losses per U-boat in N. Atlantic (tons)
June-Aug. 1940	14	815,000	58.000
Sept.-Nov. 1940	12	764,000	64,000
Dec. 1940-Feb. 1941	10	502,000	50,200
March-May 1941	19	510,000	27,000
Dec. 1941-Feb. 1942	39	286,000	7,000
March-May 1942	53	125,000	2,000
June-Aug. 1942	72	350,000	5,000
Sept.-Nov. 1942	100	518,000	5,000
Dec. 1942-Feb. 1943	102	475,000	4,500
March-May 1943	115	620,000	5,000

There were three major phases in U-boats successes during the Second World War. These were:
1. 'The First Happy Time' (June 1940 to May 1941) when U-boats were fighting in the Western Approaches, close to the United Kingdom.
2. 'The Second Happy Time' (February to October 1942) when U-boats were fighting in American coastal waters.
3. The heavy convoy battles of spring 1943, when U-boats were fighting the biggest convoy battles of the Second World War in the middle of the North Atlantic.
The spring of 1943 looked especially grim for Allied shipping, and one tends to get the impression of this period being the climax of the U-boat war. However, this is superficial: there was no hope of the U-boats' gaining the upper hand at that stage. They had already lost the campaign before they crossed the Atlantic to fight in American waters. The only time they were in a position of 'almost' defeating Britain was during 'The First Happy Time', as is shown quite clearly by the table.

The Walter U-boat

U-boats commissioned up to 1942 were not submarines in the true sense of the word. It would be more correct to call them submersibles. (Today they are often referred to as 'conventional' submarines.) They operated mostly on the surface and only dived to evade the enemy or rough seas. Occasionally, should the enemy be in the right position, it was possible to deliver a deadly attack while submerged, but such action required great skill and, more important, a lot of luck, because their speed submerged was not equal to that of a surface ship. Once submerged, the submarines were more or less stationary, only able to move at the equivalent of a moderate walking pace, for their top speed of about eight knots could not be maintained for long periods.

The story of the Walter U-boat starts in 1934, a year after Hitler came to power and a year before the Anglo-German Naval Treaty—in other words, at a time when Germany was not allowed to build submarines. Helmuth Walter, an unknown and minor employee at the Germania Works in Kiel, approached the Supreme Naval Command with plans for a new type of submarine. Like many inventors who offered their services, he was given a file reference number and his documents were carefully locked in a safe. Walter was just one of many. But about a year later, when Germany started to build submarines again, Walter returned to the Supreme Command and reminded them of his project. Finding them uninterested and realizing that he was making no progress, he turned to Dönitz, who was a flotilla commander at the time. Walter told Dönitz that his design would be capable of maintaining a submerged speed of about twenty-five knots for quite considerable periods. (This speed was faster than most surface submarine-hunters.) He went on to explain how he had met blank apathy at the Supreme Naval Command and how no one seemed interested in his idea. As Dönitz sardonically remarked later, "Of course it's of no use to the Supreme Command— you can't parade a band on the upper deck!"

Walter's plans were eventually accepted and a small boat was built, although it had to be partly financed by the Germania Works. Resources were somewhat limited and, as a result, it took a long time to develop the project and the boat was not launched until 1940. However, it proved quite successful, being something of an impressive

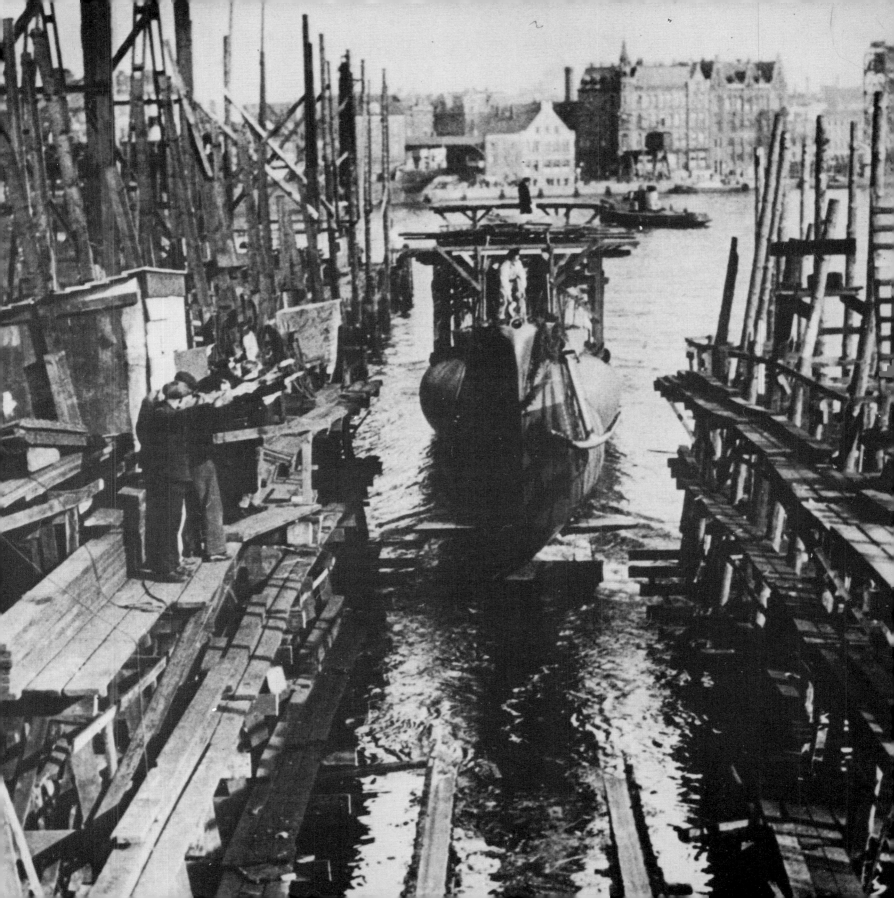

achievement, especially when one considers that Walter was no submariner and that he had no experienced full-time engineers to help him; and, despite the difficulties, two naval advisers eventually suggested that the boat should be mass-produced. Initially, this recommendation was rejected by the Supreme Naval Command, who gave Dönitz a dose of his own medicine by telling him that he had asked for Type VIIC; now, when he got his way, was he changing his mind and asking for something completely different? Eventually, Grand Admiral Raeder personally gave the go-ahead for the new project. He also agreed to enlarge research facilities, so that more fast underwater boats could be built.

Many sceptics were still not convinced of the new wonder boat's superior performance, even after it had completed trials. For the benefit of several high-ranking officials, it was planned for *U792*, one of the experimental boats, to cruise submerged at various speeds over a measured mile. A powerful searchlight, like that used on trial torpedoes, was fitted to the front of the boat, enabling the observers in a fast launch to watch the progress below the water. The first run at ten knots was completely satisfactory. Unfortunately, no

one appeared to have taken into account that the U-boat could turn in under 200 yards, which was about half the distance required for the launch's tightest turn. Consequently, the observers lost sight of *U792* and the day ended with suggestions of the trials having been rigged. The group from the Supreme Naval Command returned to Berlin with an indifferent impression. The leaders of the U-boat arm were the next to see *U792* in action, and, this time, there was no formality, speedboats or fancy lights. Admiral Dönitz collared the leaders of the testing team, took them into a quiet corner, away from other ears, and asked them point-blank: "Is that thing of any use?" "Use! Herr Admiral, it's not only useful, it's a revolution." Dönitz came away from the trials with his characteristic enthusiasm fired by the project. The next step was to get approval from the Supreme Naval Command to mass-produce the boats. But time was running out and Germany had lost many valuable weeks.

The electro-boat
The Walter project gave birth to another new idea in 1942, when it became clear that the old methods of submarine attack were becoming less effective.

Dönitz, wanting the Walter boat at the front and not as an additional novelty in the Baltic, called a meeting during November 1942 in Paris, to discuss the project's future. Walter could offer no prospect of the new boats being ready in the immediate future for, as he explained to the admirals, everything about them was new and untried—everything from the engines and the fuel they needed to the tanks in which it was stored. (The highly dangerous hydrogen peroxide fuel was stored inside a special pressure hull, situated under the hull, in a figure of eight pattern.) Two submarine construction officers suggested that it might be quicker to build a Walter U-boat as a conventional submarine and use the lower hull to accommodate additional batteries, which should produce a much faster underwater speed. Initially, Dönitz liked this suggestion, but he came to the conclusion that the boat would still have to surface to charge the batteries with its diesel engines, and it would have to remain on the surface even longer than existing boats because there would be more batteries to charge. Dönitz emphasized that the submarines should spend as little time as possible on the surface, at which point Walter came up with the idea of fitting a flexible air-pipe to a small float and towing it behind the submerged submarine. Such a float could be made so small as to be hardly visible at night.

All these ideas were made 'off the cuff' at the meeting, so it was necessary to consider them in detail and calculate whether they were feasible. The resulting work on the electric submarine was most encouraging. A top speed of about twenty knots, or even more, was foreseen. Walter's assistants also considered the flexible breathing-pipe, but Dip.Ing. Heep thought a rigid air pipe might be better. Ulrich Gabler (now a professor and a leading ship designer) further modified the idea by drawing on knowledge gained from Dutch boats captured earlier in the war. He wanted to build the pipe in such a way that it could also be used in rough weather, when waves would frequently wash over the top.

The results of these calculations were laid before Dönitz shortly after he took overall command of the Navy during January 1943, and he suggested that the electro-submarine be built immediately, while research continued on the Walter turbine project. The Construction Bureau at the Supreme Naval Command was approached, and they

Below: A large ocean-going electro-submarine of Type XXI in Kiel after the war, seen from the conning-tower of a Type VIIC. The twin 20mm anti-aircraft guns of both boats are clearly visible. The large hole in the foreground accommodated a Hohentwiel radar aerial, which looked like a bedstead. (See page 187.) (Photo: Imperial War Museum)

Below: Side view of a Type XXI electro-submarine. (Photo: Author's Collection)
Bottom of page: The large electro-boats, as seen here, were prefabricated and only needed to be assembled at riverside construction yards. A hydroplane blade, for controlling depth, can be seen in the foreground. (Photo: Imperial War Museum)

calculated that it would be 1946 before the first operational boats could be completed. Apparently, the Bureau did not agree to their immediate mass-production, saying they could not take responsibility for building a new and untried craft in such large numbers. It was emphasized that the date '1946' could only be a rough estimate, since Hitler's support had to be gained and the calculation did not allow for any possible disruption by air raids. But, for the U-boat Command, 1946 was too late, and they approached Dr. Albert Speer who was head of the Military Armaments Department in the government.

Negotiations paid off and, shortly afterwards, Speer's department came back to U-boat Command with new suggestions.

One of the directors suggested pre-fabricating the new boats; if they could be built in sections and assembled at a river-side shipyard, production time could be halved, and the first boats would be ready by 1944. Furthermore, the engineers saw no difficulty in starting mass-production without first building a prototype. These plans were laid before Hitler on 8 July 1943, and it was agreed that Speer should build forty new boats per month. Such expectations were never achieved, although the boats were constructed at an incredibly fast rate—especially when one considers the valuable labour lost producing the Type VIIC U-boats. Autumn 1943 saw a marked increase in Allied air raids and, as a direct consequence of the Allied leaders decision at the Yalta Conference to make defeating the U-boats one of their main aims, U-boat bases

and building yards were singled out for heavy bombing.

The few electro-boats that were used on operational missions before the end of the war proved enough to make their crews realize they were the weapons of the future—weapons that could have turned the tide of war in the Atlantic, had they arrived in time. It is interesting to speculate what might have happened in the Battle of the Atlantic if the boats had been ready in the summer of 1942 or even 1943, for the Allied navies would have had no countermeasures ready. The Allies were certainly surprised when they unearthed this new design in the German building yards at the end of the war.

U-boat construction and Dr. Albert Speer

Until 1943, the absence of a central office for submarine armament meant that construction was an uncommonly long-winded procedure. The initial ideas usually started at the Marine-kommandoamt I (Naval Command Office I), which considered the strategic requirements for new projects. Then, the military and technical aspects were considered by the Marinekonstruk-tionsamt (Naval Construction Office) and also by the Marinekommandoamt A IV a. The latter employed numerous experts in the major technical fields. These two departments then decided on the details of the new ship, and their resulting plans only had to be approved by the Supreme Naval Command before construction could begin. The Naval Construction Office was also responsible for all stages of ship construction, including submarines. There was an additional specialist office for U-boats within the Supreme Naval Command which dealt with the problems unique to submarines.

At that time the Navy was also responsible for building its own ships. Dönitz considered that it would be far better if this responsibility could be handed over to industry, thus allowing the Navy to concentrate on fighting the war. So, towards the end of 1942, he approached the Armaments Minister, Dr. Albert Speer, with a view to his ministry taking over U-boat construction. (Speer had already done something similar for the Army.) Speer agreed, and the office for submarine construction at the Supreme Command (U-Bootsamt) was disbanded and replaced by the Shipbuilding Commission, under the leadership of Konter-admiral Karl Topp. This body comprised naval construction experts and industrialists, with an admiral at their head to ensure that they actually built ships that the Navy wanted.

Hitler agreed to this new construction arrangement on 31 March 1943 and, as a result, a new fleet building programme went ahead. It proved most successful, for the industrial representatives, with their knowledge of modern techniques, often cut corners that the Navy alone could not.

The Heinkel 177

The story behind the development of the Heinkel He 177 (Greif) is most interesting and highlights the lack of co-operation between the various branches of the German armed forces. The aero-plane was originally proposed in 1934 as a long-distance bomber. Two prototypes were built: the Dornier Do 19 and the Junkers Ju 89. Neither proved successful and the designs were abandoned until 1938, when they were re-considered under the name of the Heinkel He 177 (Greif). The Navy became very interested in the He 177 because of its suitability to provide long-range reconnaissance support for U-boats, but only a few unsuccessful prototypes were built. Numerous changes to the specifications were required and progress was rather slow. In 1938 the U-boat arm was still in its infancy and was not at that time concerned with air support. The Navy did not push the project, and the idea was dropped.

Dönitz finally asked for the He 177 in 1942. But, instead of producing it, the Luftwaffe informed him that the aircraft would not be available for the U-boat arm. According to Hermann Göring, anything that flew automatically belonged to the Luftwaffe, and the new long-range aeroplane was no exception. It too was considered an exclusive development of the Luftwaffe, who were determined that other interested parties would have to wait their turn. (Relations were so deplorable at one stage that when Raeder asked for urgent air support, he was told that the Navy would get such support when Göring considered the time right!) In the end, research for a very long-range submarine-support aircraft was abandoned in favour of an aeroplane to fill the heavy bomber role, and the few aeroplanes that were built were required by the Air Force for their own bombing projects. So, the weapon that the Navy thought was being kept for a rainy day never materialized.

U-boat policy, September 1942

It has often been stated that the U-boat offensive collapsed suddenly during the summer of 1943. This may be borne out by the statistics if one looks at them quickly, but not by the facts supporting them. What remained of the offensive certainly collapsed during the fateful May of 1943, but it had started to crumble more than a year earlier, a fact realized by the U-boat Command at the time.

In late spring 1942, the new trends in the Atlantic alarmed the U-boat Command sufficiently to prompt a discussion of the changes in the war pattern early that summer. A detailed list of modifications necessary to keep pace with developments was drawn up and laid before Raeder on 28 September 1942. Being so important, it was discussed with Hitler in the Reich's Chancellery, Dönitz outlining the recent trends in the Battle of the Atlantic, and pointing out that the main battle had moved from American waters back into the middle of the ocean, where U-boats were facing much better-protected convoys. The Allies were tending to guard merchant ships with two rings of defence: there was a tight ring of escorts around the convoy, with some warships in the convoy's ranks; and there were also more escorts spread around this net at much greater distances from the core, making it difficult for U-boats to get close-in for their attacks.

Aeroplanes presented one of the biggest problems. The 'air gap' (the area in the middle of the Atlantic that could not be reached by land-based aircraft) was decreasing, and Dönitz predicted it would not be long before it closed completely. He emphasized the importance of aircraft operating in conjunction with U-boats, to reconnoitre and find enemy convoys, and he suggested the new Heinkel 177 be put into production to meet this demand. Dönitz also asked for the performances of U-boats and their armament to be improved. He especially made the following recommendations, with all of which Hitler agreed.

1. To increase the underwater speed by building the new Walter U-boats (see below).
2. To increase the maximum diving depth. (The effectiveness of depth charges and asdic decreases as depth is increased.)
3. To develop new weapons for U-boats.
4. To increase anti-aircraft armament.

New weapons for old U-boats*

During the summer of 1942, it became apparent to the U-boat Command that attacks from both aircraft and small surface warships were preventing some U-boats from getting close enough to convoys. Although very often the warships did not find the submarines, they did prevent the U-boat commanders from pressing home their attacks. Torpedoes had virtually no effect against small surface escorts, which had such shallow draughts that the 'eels' passed harmlessly beneath them. In addition, the escorts travelled too fast for the sub-

*This section deals with the new weapons discussed with Hitler during September 1942, although they were somewhat different to those actually installed less than a year later.

Left: One-man submarines of Type *Molch*. The top view shows one on display at the Deutsches Museum in Munich; it has two torpedoes mounted beneath the hull. (Photo: Author's Collection.) In the lower photograph, the arrangement of the batteries is visible. Type *Molch* was a completely electric submarine, capable of carrying two torpedoes for about 50 nautical miles at a speed of about 4 knots. Just under 400 were completed. (Photo: Imperial War Museum)
Below: A one-man submarine of Type *Marder*. The dome appears to be a post-war addition, since the original would have been an all-glass sphere. Type *Marder* was almost identical to

Type *Neger*: the two can be distinguished by *Neger* having the top and bottom torpedo of the same length. The child in the photograph demonstrates how tiny these midget boats were. (Photo: Author's Collection)

marines to take accurate aim, and they often faced the U-boats head-on, making themselves small, difficult targets.

The German Navy had a weapon to combat this problem, and Dönitz asked for it to be put into mass-production. It was a special torpedo, just like an ordinary G7e, but with a sound-detection head at the front which enabled it to find its way to the target by homing in on propeller noise. However, this Zaunkönig (acoustic torpedo), or T5, did not produce the expected results, although the Naval High Command had high hopes of it (see p. 50).

Torpedoes for use against merchant ships were also modified, to make it possible for U-boats to fire from greater distances without first taking careful aim. These torpedoes travelled in a straight line for a predetermined distance and then zig-zagged. Fired amongst a convoy, there was a good chance of them hitting a ship. Torpedo-firing mechanisms in U-boats were improved by fitting angle deflectors. As a result, it was no longer necessary to point the whole boat at the target, and

torpedoes could be fired at angles of up to ninety degrees to the boat's course.

It is important to emphasize that the German torpedoes still had a minor fault—one that had not been eliminated after the torpedo crisis of 1939/40. Although they detonated, they often failed to sink their targets. The battles of 1943 were plagued by far too many stragglers from the convoys, ships that had either been slowed down or stopped by one U-boat and then had to be sunk by another. This situation was so bad that Dönitz was prompted to note in his diary: "The torpedoes are having less effect than in 1918." Merchant ships produced during the war were built with several watertight compartments to prevent them sinking if the hull were holed. Even so, the torpedoes should have had more effect.

In 1942, 'bees' (German slang for 'aeroplanes') only presented U-boats with a few problems, and it was still possible to avoid conflict. At that time the RAF did not have any long-range aircraft available, so the U-boats were only threatened

when they were close to the coast. The U-boat Command anticipated the closing of the 'air gap' in the Atlantic, and they were planning ahead to meet a situation that would require them to fight off aircraft while attacking convoys. Konter-admiral Werner Lange, Commander-in-Chief of Amtsgruppe U-Bootswesen at OKM/SKL (a department in the Supreme Naval Command dealing with U-boat matters), showed how the conning-towers could be modified to accommodate 15mm machine-guns. 20mm anti-aircraft guns, it was suggested, should be fitted in addition to 37mm and 50mm automatic guns. Hitler showed little interest in the 50mm gun—with which the Luftwaffe had experienced many problems—but Raeder emphasized to the Führer the importance of continuing research. He also reported on the discoveries with the so-called 'N-Stoff', an explosive for igniting heavy oil, which it was hoped would help sink more enemy ships. Several other ideas were discussed at the September meeting. It was suggested that U-boats should be fitted with 10-metre high (33ft.) lookout masts. These were attached to a few U-boats, but they did not become operational on a large scale. It was also thought possible to cover U-boats with a rubber-like skin to absorb radar impulses. Such covering, known as 'Alberich Skin', was used later in 1944/45, but it also had a limited practical use because it was difficult to attach to the outside of the boat.

"Throw the Surface Fleet into the dustbin"

The question of how to employ the surface fleet came to a head shortly after Christmas 1942, when Erich Raeder resigned as Supreme Commander-in-Chief of the Navy, to be replaced by the head of the U-boat arm, Karl Dönitz. The conflict between Raeder and Hitler had entered its final round during those last days of 1942, when part of the North Norway Naval Squadron arrived in the Arctic Seas to intercept convoy JW51B. (This was similar to the famous PQ series, running from Britain to North Russia.) Vizeadmiral Oskar Kummetz moved out to attack with the heavy cruisers *Hipper* and *Lützow* plus six destroyers; but he was forced to approach the operation with virtually one hand tied behind his back, since all commanders had been given strict instructions not to put their ships at risk. This order had been issued shortly after the sinking of the *Bismarck*, whose loss had dealt a stunning blow to German prestige—particularly Hitler's. So, excessive caution, bad weather and good escorts (including the cruisers *Sheffield* and *Jamaica*) were pitched against the German squadron. Shortly after starting the action, Kummetz received a signal by way of a reminder: 'No unnecessary risks'. Then, *Hipper* received a hit in her boiler room, and the destroyer *Eckholdt* was sunk. By this time the light was failing and visibility was bad, making ideal conditions for Allied destroyers to creep in close for a torpedo attack, so Kummetz decided to break off the action, and limped back to Altenfjord.

Meanwhile, over Hitler's headquarters there hung an air of gloom, dispelled for a brief time by the New Year celebrations and by expectations of an impending victory in the Arctic. But Germany had suffered severe setbacks on the Eastern Front: the Army in Russia was in a deplorable state, and the great defeat at Stalingrad was looming large on the horizon. Germany, and Hitler in particular, desperately needed a victory. So, when he received the signal from Kummetz stating 'Am engaging convoy', Hitler literally jumped for joy. A short time later, *U354*, commanded by Kptlt. Karl-Heinz Herbschleb, reported that the battle appeared to have reached its climax: the men in the U-boat could see the fireworks, but they could not give any details of how the battle was progressing. After this, the lines to the north of Norway went dead and nothing more was heard. Despite this ominous occurrence, Hitler bounced around his headquarters like an excited child, telling new-comers they would soon hear some good news, and taking every opportunity to seek out Vizeadmiral Theodor Krancke, the Navy's permanent repre-sentative at the Führer's headquarters, to ask for news. But none came. In the end, Hitler was informed by a BBC announcement that an Allied convoy had successfully beaten off a much stronger German cruiser force in the Arctic Seas. This really activated his adrenalin, and he flew into one of his characteristic rages, threatening to make U-boats out of the whole surface fleet.

To make matters worse, the lines to the north of Norway remained dead; Kummetz could not be contacted by radio, telephone or telex. When Krancke telephoned Raeder, requesting him to come and see Hitler at once, Raeder, guessed what was afoot, waited for news and planned his 'offensive' before setting out. Hitler had cooled

down a little by the time the two men eventually met, but he was not fully composed. Raeder was subjected to a rude and insulting tirade for over an hour, during which he was told that the surface fleet was useless and that the whole capital fleet should be thrown into the dustbin. Instead of losing his temper, however, Raeder played a trump card that he had been contemplating for some time: he asked to be relieved of his post. (The relationship between Hitler and Raeder had started to deteriorate before the start of the war. This situation, plus his dislike of the Führer had led Raeder to contemplate resigning and making way for another person.) Hitler was thrown off

balance by this unexpected broadside, and he immediately changed tack, saying it had not been a personal attack but that the capital ships were no good. Raeder remained adamant and maintained that he could not continue with his duties. He went on to suggest that the whole matter could be solved quietly, without embarrassment to Hitler: the resignation could coincide with the tenth anniver-sary of the NSDAP's (National Socialist Workers' Party) coming to power and it could appear quite natural. This Hitler accepted, but he asked Raeder to consider the matter carefully and to nominate two successors. Raeder suggested Admiral Rolf Carls (Commander-in-Chief of the Naval Group

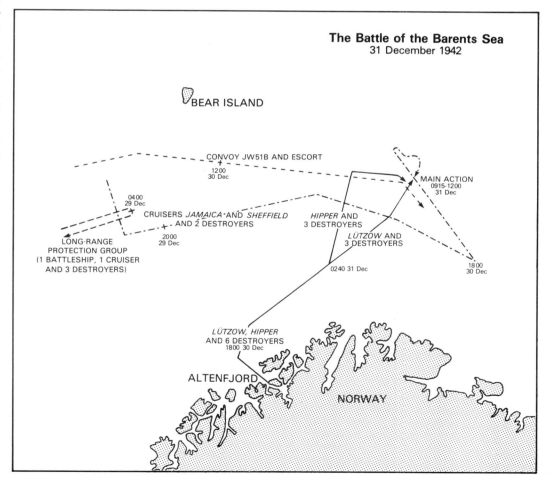

The Battle of the Barents Sea
31 December 1942

BEAR ISLAND

CONVOY JW51B AND ESCORT
1200
30 Dec

MAIN ACTION
0915-1200
31 Dec

0400
29 Dec

CRUISERS *JAMAICA* AND *SHEFFIELD*
AND 2 DESTROYERS

HIPPER AND
3 DESTROYERS

2000
29 Dec

LÜTZOW AND
3 DESTROYERS

LONG-RANGE
PROTECTION GROUP
(1 BATTLESHIP, 1 CRUISER
AND 3 DESTROYERS)

1800
30 Dec

0240 31 Dec

LÜTZOW, HIPPER
AND 6 DESTROYERS
1800 30 Dec

ALTENFJORD

NORWAY

Command North) and Admiral Karl Dönitz. He considered Carls more suitable, because of his experience and, as he would not be 'stepping over' anybody, his appointment would not cause any bad feeling. Hitler might prefer Dönitz, however, if he wished to stress the U-boat war.

Dönitz was called to Hitler's headquarters on 25 January 1943, was officially informed of Raeder's resignation, and was then asked to become his successor. He was requested to take office on 30 January (the tenth anniversary of Hitler's coming to power and the end of the Battle of Stalingrad, which marked one of the great turning points in the Second World War). Dönitz was also told of Hitler's decision to scrap the capital ships in favour of U-boats and, ironically, this important issue was the subject of the first battle between the two men. One would have expected Dönitz to be pleased that Hitler had fully recognized the paramount importance of the U-boat arm, but in fact he took the opposite view. He told Hitler that the surface fleet was tying up vast enemy resources which, once Britain realized the large ships were out of action, would be unleashed against U-boats and German towns. Characteristically, Hitler continued to argue his case against the battleships, saying they were useless, but Dönitz stood firm and, in the end, Hitler acquiesced,

Below: Dönitz greeting the crew of an incoming U-boat, *U30* commanded by Fritz-Julius Lemp. From left to right: Dönitz, Oblt. Fuhrmann (Dönitz's Flag Lieutenant 1941-43), Eberhard Godt (Commander-in-Chief of the U-boat Command) and Lemp (wearing roll-neck sweater). On the right, holding the microphone, is a Petty Officer, who is wearing an AA Gunnery Badge. (Photo: Bundesarchiv, Koblenz)

maintaining nevertheless that it would not be long before Dönitz realized the mistake he was making.

Dönitz as Supreme Commander-in-Chief

Another disagreement between Hitler and the new Grand Admiral occurred when Hitler received news of a German ship being sunk by a British submarine in the eastern Mediterranean. Hitler commented acidly: "The English can do it! We have our submarines sitting all around Gibraltar and they cannot sink a thing!" At this, much to the astonishment of those present, Dönitz retorted: "Our best boats are around Gibraltar, where they are fighting the strongest maritime power in the world. They could also sink ships if they were put into an area totally devoid of submarine-hunters. I have put our best men around Gibraltar and, let me tell you, they are a darn sight better than the English!" Hitler went red in the face at this outburst, but did not reply and, afterwards, Dönitz thought his days as Supreme Commander-in-Chief were numbered. In fact, however, this confrontation marked a turning-point in relations between the two men. Hitler never again lost his temper with Dönitz, and he never again murmured disparaging comments about the Navy —not even after the submarine offensive totally collapsed. The Führer was always correct and polite towards the Grand Admiral. He seemed to appreciate Dönitz's advice and always referred to Dönitz as 'Herr Grossadmiral'. Later, Hitler would often telephone Dönitz's headquarters during air raids to make sure he was safely in his bunker. Hitler also supplied Dönitz with an armoured Mercedes, and requested him not to fly, in case the aircraft were shot down.

The gulf between Hitler and the naval leadership started to close after January 1943, and this has led to several assertions that Dönitz's promotion was a political manoeuvre. His appointment was followed by a certain amount of reorganization that necessitated the sacking of several admirals, and this too has been interpreted as another step towards bringing the Navy in line with party politics. Actually, there was no political motive for Dönitz's appointment. Although in sympathy with the Party, he was never Hitler's puppet, and party politics never permeated the Navy as much as they did the other armed forces. Dönitz remained neutral through-

out any political moves; he did not meddle with Party officials, and neither did he allow them to interfere with the Navy. They tried to infiltrate on several occasions, but got no farther than the Grand Admiral, who presented a solid wall of Prussian principles. Dönitz politely told people he was Supreme Commander and would therefore decide what went on. On one occasion, several naval officials were due to be tried by the People's Court in Berlin for offending Party ideals. Dönitz sent word to have them released, and informed the presiding judge that the Navy's judicial system was quite capable of dealing with breaches of discipline.

It is true that National Socialist Guidance Officers were attached to several ships, as well as naval land units, to spread the gospel of the Party. However, these men had a great deal less power in naval establishments than in the Army or Luftwaffe. Some U-boat commanders even exercised their right of 'instant dismissal' to get rid of such people. (Every man serving in U-boats had the right to leave his boat, without giving a reason, as soon as a replacement could be found. Similarly, a commander could remove any member of his crew. There was no red tape and, usually, such requests were complied with instantly.) But it would be wrong to give the impression of naval justice having been correct at all times. One U-boat commander was recalled from holiday for what his colleagues thought would be a presentation of the Knight's Cross— instead, he was executed. Apparently, he had tuned the ward-room radio to the BBC wavelength. His other misdemeanours included making sour remarks about German leaders and removing a photograph of Adolf Hitler.

The suggestion that the sacking of various admirals in early 1943 was a move to dispose of opposition to the NSDAP in the Navy is somewhat absurd when one considers that several of the retiring admirals were Party sympathisers, while many of those that remained did not support the National Socialists. Neither of the two famous admirals directly under Dönitz, Eberhard Godt and Hans-Georg von Friedeburg, were renowned for their support of the Party.

In order to understand how Dönitz and his generation saw the National Socialists' rise to power, it is necessary to turn back the pages of history to the beginning of this century. Dönitz's

upbringing—like that of his contemporaries— placed little value on individuality, but had instilled in him a deep sense of obedience and service to the State. So, when Dönitz and his contemporaries saw the tremendous strides made by Hitler and the NSDAP to pull Germany from the abyss of depression after the First World War, they could not help but be impressed. The façade of National Socialism was superb. Very few people realized what it disguised, and those who did were quickly and quietly removed from the scene. Many influential visitors to Germany were impressed by what they saw, and returned to their homelands singing the praises of the new order. So, if Hitler was held in such high esteem by foreigners, why should the German people not be proud of their leader and their new national status?

The defeat of the conventional submarine

The war in the Atlantic took a dramatic turn during April and May of 1943. In April, convoy HX231 managed to drive off all attacking U-boats; in May, submarine losses rose to forty-two from only fifteen in the previous month. Losses rocketed to levels the U-boat Command had not thought possible, not even in their worst nightmares. Dönitz recorded in his diary that he was used to disappointments and setbacks, but never in such proportions. On 24 May, he admitted defeat and ordered all U-boats out of the North Atlantic. Boats with little fuel were instructed to return home, and the rest were directed to different areas. The fantastic losses made it quite clear that the conventional submarine was obsolete. But, as the new underwater boats would not be ready for some while, the U-boat Command considered it vital to maintain pressure in the Atlantic by sending in the old boats again, and also by implementing several new ideas straightaway.

1. A scientific branch within the Navy must breach the gap between research and the front-line of the battle, and ensure that the new technology become operational as soon as possible. The development of radar detection apparatus was considered of paramount importance.
2. Anti-aircraft armament must be increased to keep aeroplanes away from submarines, and better protection provided for the men on top of the conning-tower.
3. The acoustic torpedo must be made operational at once.

4. Fast underwater boats must be brought into service as soon as possible.

Improved AA armament

The strengthening of anti-aircraft armament was the easiest to implement of the four points listed above. The large gun in front of the conning-tower was removed, and the existing gun platform behind the tower enlarged to carry two twin 20mm guns. Another platform was also added to the rear of all operational boats—to hold either one quadruple 20mm or a single 37mm AA gun. (There were slight variations in the exact armament; as a result, several interesting and unusual experimental designs can still be seen in photographs.)

The first boat with the modified armament, *U758* (a Type VIIC boat) under command of Kptlt. Helmut Manseck, left Brest on 8 June 1943. A Lysander aircraft attacked early that evening, and the new guns were given their first operational test. The aircraft, not expecting the extra sting, received hits, whereupon it dropped a smoke buoy, jettisoned its bombs and disappeared from view. Shortly afterwards, two more aircraft appeared, and began circling out of range of the boat's guns. Finally, a third aeroplane came on the scene and attacked: it dropped depth-charges, but was hit and crashed into the sea. *U758* kept the other aircraft at a distance of about two miles, but at least eleven of the submarine's crew had been injured, and Manseck decided it was time to 'go down into the cellar'. (This incident taught him that the additional conning tower armour was only sufficient to protect the men from direct hits, for numerous minor injuries had been caused by flying metal.) Despite the injuries, the event was thought quite encouraging and, although the men did not consider the new armament ideal, they felt that the problem could be overcome with more experience and training.

During 1942, the idea of building special submarines as 'submersible AA batteries' had been considered. When Kptlt. Odo Loewe returned to base with his boat, *U256*, badly damaged, and the engineers declared her unfit for further rigorous convoy action (because the pressure hull probably would not withstand deep diving or depth-charging) someone came up with the bright idea of keeping her on the surface as an anti-aircraft submarine in the Bay of Biscay. However, at that time there was no necessity for such craft and, although a suitable deck layout design was completed, nothing else was done. Eventually, it was decided to fit a single 37mm, one quadruple 20mm and two twin 20mm AA guns. It was planned to mount one platform in front of the conning-tower to enable the 'trap' to shoot forwards. (Normally, AA guns mounted on U-boats could only fire backwards or sideways.)

The first boat to sail with these modifications was *U441*, commanded by Kptlt. Götz von Hartmann, which left Brest on 22 May 1943. Next day, their first action against an enemy aeroplane produced mixed fortunes. The gunners only managed to shoot the Sunderland down after it had dropped its depth-charges, and these caused such heavy damage that *U441* was forced to return for repairs. July 1943 found *U441* back in the 'Black Pit of Biscay', where she saw further action on the 11th. Again, her gunners shot down their attacker, but not before it had killed ten crewmen and wounded a further dozen, including the commander. After patching up the men, the medical officer, Dr. Pfaffinger, took control and sailed the boat back to port. The wounded had hardly been removed to hospital before the news spread like wildfire around the base, and numerous people volunteered to take the not-too-badly-damaged boat back to sea.

About another half a dozen boats were converted to aircraft traps, but their limited success merely illustrated the RAF's superiority. Consequently, they were converted back to the ordinary conning-tower design shortly after the anti-aircraft operations started, which helps to explain why there are so few photographs of them.

Operational U-boats crossing the Bay of Biscay also tried a new technique to overcome the aircraft problem. They tried to travel through the most dangerous area, near the coast, in small groups— the idea being that, once enemy aircraft had been spotted, the boats would be brought into a fairly tight formation, and their combined fire used with telling effect. However, the RAF very soon became wary of the boats extra sting and changed their methods of attack. Instead of coming in straightaway, the aircraft would circle out of reach of the anti-aircraft guns, and call for help. Then, either a number of aircraft would attack simultaneously from different directions, or the Royal Navy would appear on the horizon. This increased the odds against the U-boats and they gave up fighting in this way. Instead they returned to an earlier technique of crossing the danger zone in the Bay of Biscay submerged.

Schnorkels

The events of summer 1943 made it clear that U-boats would either have to be removed from the surface completely or give up the battle in the Atlantic. The new electro-submarines were not due to be operational until the summer of the following year, so a stop-gap had to be found. It was decided to fit existing boats with breathing pipes, making it possible for them to run their diesel engines while submerged. Such an idea was not new—indeed, it had been committed to paper long before man had the technology to build submarines, and ventilation masts had also been used by several navies to provide fresh air for the crews of submarines. But it was Commander J. J. Wichers of the Royal Netherlands Navy who developed the first practical air pipe to supply air to the diesel engines as well, and thus he made it possible for submarines to use these engines without breaking the surface. Wichers' idea was only partly exploited, as the Dutch principle could only be used in relatively good conditions. If the seas were rough, the boats still had to come to the surface.

This early Dutch ventilation mast had several advantages that were not unappreciated by submarine crews. When, for example, the Dutch commander, Commodore J. F. van Dulm (who served under the British flag in *021* during the war), was informed of an Admiralty committee's decision to remove *021*'s ventilation mast, he expressed his sorrow. It made life much more comfortable because it could still be raised to draw air into the boat, but at the same time it prevented waves from washing in, and kept the boat's interior much drier.

Some of these Dutch masts were captured when the German forces invaded Holland, but at that time there was no need for such structures, and

they were removed from the boats taken over by the German Navy. In 1942, Ulrich Gabler, together with Engineer Heep, modified the principle to make it possible to use the air mast under all sea conditions, even if the water washed over the top of the duct. Unfortunately, this was most uncomfortable for the crew, because the men could not adjust to the great variations in pressure created. The invention only provided the difference between death from enemy action and an unpleasant and most difficult existence. Schnorkels presented far more problems than they solved, and they certainly did not change the U-boats' role from the defensive back to the offensive.

Constructing and fitting the devices presented no great problem, however, and the work went ahead during the spring of 1944. The Dragoner Group was the first U-boat pack to have all its boats fitted with schnorkels. This pack of five boats was at sea from 20 May 1944 until the end of that month, and their operation proved quite unsuccessful. *U247*, commanded by Oblt.z.S. Gerhard Matschulat, managed to sink the 200-ton trawler *Norneen* on 5 July 1944, but that was hardly the sort of success needed to keep pace with the battle. Not that the U-boat men failed to make the effort; they worked, fought and died harder than ever before. It is really astonishing that so many of them survived those last months, when the odds were weighted so heavily against them.

The torpedo catastrophe

The acoustic torpedo, known as T5 or Zaunkönig (wren), and other special torpedoes used later during the war were basically the same electric Type G7e as made in 1940. The propulsion and detonation systems were similar, but additional equipment was added to the nose.

The T5 had been developed long before the war, but, as the weapon was not required and the Navy wanted to preserve its secrecy, it was not put into general service. It is difficult to pinpoint exactly when the project started, and it may well have roots going back to the First World War, but we do know that working models were available for experiments as early as 1936. This can be determined by an incident involving the torpedo-boat *Möwe*. One of her officers, Freiherr W. Nikolaus von Lyncker, recalled how *Möwe* was passing the firing ranges near Eckernförde, when a

torpedo ran off course, followed the torpedo-boat and ended up in the propeller. A loud clatter alerted all who had not seen the 'eel' approach, and they watched while the apologetic owners of the stray torpedo collected the somewhat battered specimen. After this, the acoustic torpedo appears to have vanished into obscurity and did not reappear until the middle of the war. A special school, under the command of Korvkpt. Otto Köhler, was established in Gotenhafen (Gdynia) during the summer of 1943 to instruct U-boat officers in the operational use of this anti-destroyer weapon. The T5 was introduced exclusively for U-boats, and it was not issued to motor torpedo-boats until the late autumn of 1944. Instruction facilities were later also founded in other parts of Europe, and Köhler commuted with his staff from one end of the Continent to the other, working wherever required.

This acoustic torpedo was no longer a simple device designed to run into a target's propeller. The idea of rendering it useless by the target towing a noise-maker some distance astern was appreciated early in its development, and the T5 had a special programme to avoid such 'foxers'. When it came close to the noise source, an automatic steering control would turn the rudder and make it swim in a circle. The sound-detection head was situated at the end of a small cone-shaped structure, which funnelled noise from about thirty degrees either side of its path and shielded the detector from side noises. Therefore, the torpedo would not respond to the 'foxer' while it was swimming in a small circle. At some point, however, the front would be directed towards the real propeller, and the 'eel' would head for this louder sound source. Again, the automatic steering control would take effect to guide the torpedo around the noise; but this time the ship would be too long to avoid the 'eel's' small circular deviation, and the torpedo would collide with the hull, triggering off a contact pistol or activating a magnetic detonator.

Faults in German torpedoes (page 28) were not fully recognized in 1940, and some of these irregularities kept cropping up later with disastrous results. In fact, these faults—and not the Royal Navy's 'foxers'—were responsible for saving so many British ships. German wartime records show that acoustic torpedoes had but a 50 per cent success rate. Half of the failures were attributed to

recognized mistakes, about 14 per cent to unexplained errors and only about 10 per cent to misfires. But an entirely different picture emerged recently from old British wartime records. Prof. Dr. Jürgen Rohwer has calculated that just over 700 acoustic torpedoes were fired during the war, and only 77 of these were definite hits. His figures boil down to a success rate of just over 16 per cent.

Most of the torpedoes ran erratically and exploded some distance behind the target, making the Allies think the 'foxers' were successful. The U-boat crew, on the other hand, would have regarded the explosion as a sinking because they would have been unable to observe the result; commanders were ordered to dive to sixty metres (about 200 feet) after firing, to prevent the T5 from turning around and homing-in on the noise from the U-boat.

German acoustic torpedoes were also responsible for sinking at least two German U-boats. Both *U377* and *U972* were recorded as 'Lost by unknown cause. No survivors', and the facts surrounding these two sinkings have only recently come to light with the release to the general public of various formerly secret British documents. Each boat sent an SOS call after her last recorded radio contact, stating that she had been torpedoed and was sinking. There is no reference to these signals in the record of losses kept by the U-boat Command, but they were picked up and deciphered by Admiralty Intelligence in London. The Royal Navy knew that the Germans were using new torpedoes, and were keeping an ear cocked for any useful information. When they received the news, the Admiralty made a thorough check of all their operations in the Atlantic and found there had been no Allied torpedo attacks. Both torpedoes must therefore have been fired from German ships.

The witholding of this stunning information from the German wartime media is quite understandable. Yet no one who might have known remembers the calls, and there is no reason for suppressing the details today. Furthermore, no one in Germany, nor anybody in the U-boats, could have known the torpedoes were German. The only significant point at the time was the word 'torpedoed'. Most boats in the Atlantic were sunk either by depth-charges or by gunfire. Obviously it was intended that, should the signal be picked up, people would think the attack had come from the

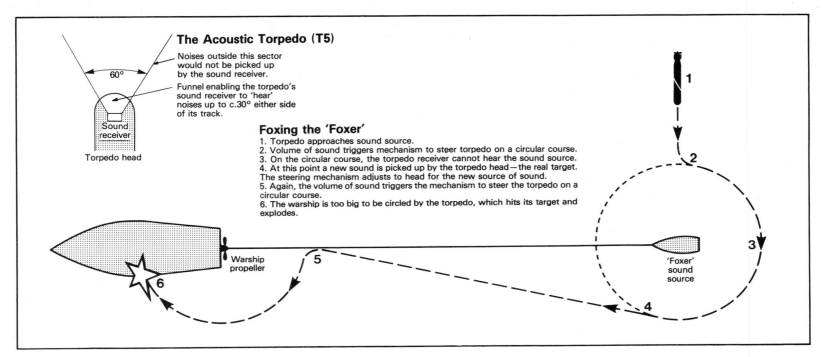

The Acoustic Torpedo (T5)

Noises outside this sector would not be picked up by the sound receiver.

Funnel enabling the torpedo's sound receiver to 'hear' noises up to c.30° either side of its track.

60°

Sound receiver

Torpedo head

Foxing the 'Foxer'
1. Torpedo approaches sound source.
2. Volume of sound triggers mechanism to steer torpedo on a circular course.
3. On the circular course, the torpedo receiver cannot hear the sound source.
4. At this point a new sound is picked up by the torpedo head—the real target. The steering mechanism adjusts to head for the new source of sound.
5. Again, the volume of sound triggers the mechanism to steer the torpedo on a circular course.
6. The warship is too big to be circled by the torpedo, which hits its target and explodes.

Warship propeller

'Foxer' sound source

Allies and no significance would have been attached to it.

The missing SOS calls were discussed with *U377*'s first commander, Kpt.z.S. Otto Köhler, who is a communications expert. He said that such signals were usually very short and were frequently missed by receiving stations. It is highly unlikely that the submarines would have been able to send SOS calls if they had received direct hits, which suggests that faulty German acoustic torpedoes were responsible. However, this point should not be stressed too much, for the Allies also had their share of faulty torpedoes.

Acoustic torpedoes were used for the first time in large-scale combat between 18 and 23 September 1943, when the Leuthen Group of U-boats were operating in the shipping lanes of the eastern Atlantic. Several T5s were fired, but without any success. These boats were also fitted with the new anti-aircraft armament, so it was decided to try a new method of attack: as U-boats were disadvantaged by Allied radar at night, they assembled on the surface in broad daylight and approached a convoy. Their guns were ready to

keep enemy aircraft at bay, and the acoustic torpedoes were ready to deal with any escorts. Despite their forward planning, however, the U-boats were distinctly worsted. On 20 September an Allied aeroplane dropped an acoustic torpedo out of the guns' range and managed to sink *U338*, commanded by Kptlt. Manfred Kinzel.

U-boats were not the only branch of the German Navy with such incredibly misinterpreted torpedo results attributed to them. Motor torpedo-boats (Schnellboote) also failed to sink many of the ships they recorded as sunk. The present-day figures for early 1945 show that in some 350 torpedo-boat operations mines sank 25 ships and damaged 7; torpedoes only sank 6 ships and damaged 1. So, during early 1945, the torpedo-boat arm had far greater success with mines than with their specifically designated weapon. The German records also show that, during a torpedo attack in February/March 1945, a small number of MTBs sank 11 ships and, at roughly the same time, a further 7 ships were sunk by 8 torpedoes fired from 4 MTBs. According to the British records, however, during each operation only 2 ships had

actually been sunk. Such disastrous results were almost certainly due to torpedo failures.

It would appear, then, that the German torpedoes brought into production during the war failed to achieve the expected results, although the Navy did have some noteworthy successes with the Ingolin torpedoes. These revolutionary weapons were put into production just before the end of the war, but none was completed in time to see operational service. Research into the possibilities of a high-performance torpedo that would leave no bubble or oil trail was started at about the same time as the Walter U-boat project. The highly-concentrated hydrogen-peroxide fuel (called 'Ingolin' after Professor Walter's son, Ingo) was mixed with other chemicals in the combustion chamber to drive a variety of power units. One of the simplest forms, Type G7ut, was similar in principle to that used in the early piston engine of Type G7a. It was thought that exhaust gasses would dissolve in sea water before they reached the surface, but an oil mixed with the fuel left a tell-tale wake as it rose to the surface. This problem was eventually overcome and a hundred such

torpedoes were put into production during early 1945. These were probably also fitted with a Zaunkönig type of sound-detection head.

Several different Ingolin torpedo projects were conducted simultaneously, and Korvkpt. Hans-Henrich Giessler was appointed in the summer of 1944 to find out whether any of them could be made for immediate operational use. He found the performances to be most impressive. Goldfisch of Type G5ut reached a speed of forty-five knots for a range of about three and a half kilometres (two miles). The main problem for operational ships was the nature of the fuel, for it would explode if even the smallest particle of impurity found its way into the system. This applied to small dust particles left during the construction of the engine as well as dirt. In submarines, this explosion problem was overcome by storing the fuel on the outside of the pressure hull, where it could mix with sea water and dissolve in the event of an accident. The insides of operational ships, especially U-boats, were not as clean as laboratories, and torpedoes stored there were bound to be a potential danger. Yet the problems were partly overcome and, if the war had lasted longer, the torpedoes might have seen service.

The end of the war

After the fateful month of May 1943, the battle in the Atlantic never regained its momentum. Another battle, this time concentrated in European coastal waters, started during the summer of 1944. Non-German literature tends to give the impression that these were but the death throes of a desperate and badly-beaten navy, vainly trying to make an impact before dying. In fact, it was the German Navy's biggest—and one of its most successful—campaign. It started late in 1944, when, in a spirit similar to that displayed by the British at Dunkirk, the German Navy sent every available seaworthy ship into the Baltic and started the mammoth task of evacuating those in the eastern provinces and ferrying them to the west, out of reach of the advancing Russian Army. The undertaking was the largest evacuation ever, and was a combined operation between the Kriegsmarine and the merchant navy. Between January and 8 May 1945, over two million refugees were transported in some 800 ships. The total number of evacuees was considerably higher, but the exact number may never be determined because of the

chaos at the time. The rescue ships took on as many people as possible, often under heavy attack, and the main concern was to save as many lives as possible.

The evacuation operations started during the autumn of 1944, when Dönitz gave permission for civilian refugees to be carried, together with wounded, aboard naval transports. Some 6,000 members of the Hitler Youth, who had been digging defensive ditches around Memel, Germany's most easterly port, were also evacuated from there during the autumn of 1944, bringing the total to almost 47,000 by the end of the year. The most important evacuations started during January 1945, and the approximate number of refugees transported by sea was as shown in Table 3.

Roughly 20,000 refugees were killed by enemy action during the whole operation; less than 1 per cent of the total. In comparison, 18 per cent of those who attempted to escape overland were lost.

The losses at sea were attributed to three main causes: 1, The rescue transports were over-crowded; 2, Air temperatures dropped down to minus 24°C, which meant that if the ship went down there was no hope of survival in the water; and 3, The transports and hospital ships were easy targets for enemy aircraft and submarines. The largest losses were as shown in Table 4.

One of the conditions of the terms of surrender was that German naval units should hand over their equipment undamaged, and ships should not be scuttled. At the same time, German forces were not permitted to transmit radio messages in code. Dönitz agreed to these conditions and appointed two liaison officers, Fregkpt. Heinrich Liebe and Oblt. z.S. Martin Duppel, to ensure that no ship

was sunk by German soldiers. But, because neither of the two officers would believe this instruction until they had heard it from Dönitz's own lips, most U-boats in German ports were scuttled before the Allies could reach them. On their way to see Dönitz, the two men met the Supreme Commander's adjutant, Walter Lüdde-Neurath, who refused them access, saying Dönitz was too busy to see them. Lüdde-Neurath knew full well that Dönitz would not go against the agreement made with the Allies, and he would order the boats to be preserved. Equally, he knew that Dönitz loathed the idea of giving such an order and he wanted to follow the tradition of the Navy and sink the ships. Lüdde-Neurath handled the issue with great skill, telling the two men that as naval commanders they should know their duty—if he were in their shoes, he would know what to do. Both men understood what he was driving at, and,

Table 3: Refugees transported by sea from Germany's eastern provinces

From Danzig, Gotenhafen and Hela, between January and 8 May, 1945:
  1,047,000 Refugees.
  300,000 Soldiers and wounded.
From Libau, between January and 8 May, 1945:
  75,000 Wounded.
  25,000 Soldiers.
From Königsberg and Pillau, between 25 January and 25 April, 1945:
  451,000 Refugees.
  141,000 Soldiers and wounded.
From Kolberg, during mid-March 1945:
  70,000 Refugees.
  7,500 Soldiers and wounded.
2,116,500 Total.

Table 4: Principal losses in seaborne evacuations from Germany's eastern provinces

Date (1945)	Name of ship:	Size (GRT):	Number saved:	Number killed:
30/31 Jan.	Wilhelm Gustloff	25,484	900	4,000 to 6,000
9/10 Feb.	General v. Steuben	14,660	300	3,000
17 Feb.	Eifel	1,429	?	680
12 March	Andross	3,000	2,000	550
9 April	Albert Jensen	5,500	Not loaded	
10 April	Neuwerk	803	?	800
11 April	Moltkefels	7,862		
11 April	Posen	1,062	3,500	1,000
13 April	Karlsruhe	897	150	800
16/17 April	Goya	5,230	100 ?	6,000
25 April	Emily Sauber	2,475	2,000	50

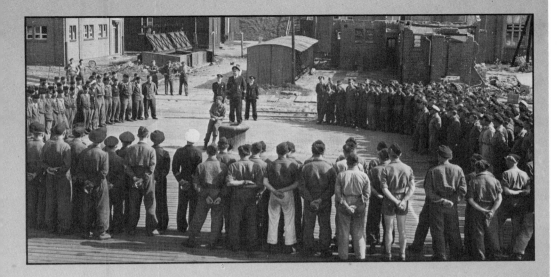

as the radio could not be used, the vital code word 'Regenbogen' ('scuttle all ships') was passed by telephone and word of mouth to many German ports.

The Navy did not come to an abrupt end in May 1945, but disbanded slowly. At first, the men carried on as before, (although they were not permitted to wear swastikas on their uniforms). Some German officers, fearing a rebellion from the younger faction, took to wearing pistols. Later, the men were screened in prisoner-of-war camps, and the hard-line National Socialists and war criminals were weeded out. The vast majority of Germans in Western hands were soon released to start rebuilding their shattered homeland.

Numerous ships not scuttled were distributed among the Allied navies, and the vast majority of the U-boats were deliberately sunk in the Atlantic by the Royal Navy in 1945/46 (Operation 'Deadlight'). Only a limited number of small ships, suitable for minesweeping, remained in German hands.

All German armed forces were disbanded during May 1945 after the arrest of the Dönitz government. However, an active branch of the Navy was refounded on 1 August 1945 in the form of the German Minesweeping Administration, which, using ex-Kriegsmarine personnel, was to help clear mines from European waters. Ironically, under the Geneva Convention these men were technically prisoners-of-war, and could not be employed for tasks that would put their lives at risk, but in Germany they had the status of 'free men' under the control of Allied Forces.

The German Minesweeping Administration operated with two commands—one based in Kiel serving the Baltic, the other based in Cuxhaven for the North Sea—and later with six. At its peak, there were just under 28,000 men and over 20 flotillas of approximately 400 floating units. They were eventually disbanded in 1948 and replaced by another minesweeping unit of a more civilian character. This in turn was dissolved in June 1951, and the ships passed over to other existing organizations. Interestingly enough, however, at least two Kriegsmarine flotillas were never put out of action: 13th and 16th Räumbootsflottille (13th and 16th Motor Minesweeper Flotillas). They continued to serve under the Minesweeping Administration and were later incorporated in the new Federal Navy.

The Organization of the Kriegsmarine

THE NAVY IN 1922

The reorganization programme begun after the First World War was not completed until a year after the new Reichsmarine flag was introduced in April 1921 (p. 6), and the first Navy List was not published until 5 March 1922. Published annually, until 1937 this List gave details of all units; the 1938 edition only had a list of personnel. During the war years, it is doubtful whether the exact details of naval organization were committed to paper, or, at least, as a bound volume.

In 1922, the Navy was divided into two operational sections covering the Baltic and the North Sea areas. There were also several additional educational units and some inspectorates. The structure of the Navy in 1922 was as follows.

Supreme Naval Command (Marineleitung)

Chef der Marineleitung (Chief of the Navy): Admiral Paul Behncke.

Under the Emperor, the Supreme Naval Command was known as the Admiralität (Admiralty); it was later called Oberkommando der Marine (OKM).

Naval Command Baltic

Commander: Ernst Freiherr von Gagern.
Headquarters: Kiel.
Naval Forces Baltic. Battleship: *Hannover*. Cruisers: *Berlin, Medusa, Thetis*. Survey ship: *Panther*. Smaller ships: 1st Flotilla, 5th Half Flotilla.
Land Forces Baltic. Coastal Defence Departments I, III and IV. Communication Departments with training establishment. Schiffsstammdivision der Ostsee (Training Division for New Recruits).

Naval Command North Sea

Commander: Hans Zenker. Headquarters: Wilhelmshaven.
Naval Forces North Sea. Battleship: *Braunsch-*

weig. Cruisers: *Arcona, Hamburg.* Smaller ships: 2nd Flotilla, 11th Half Flotilla.
Land Forces North Sea. Coastal Defence Departments II, IV and VI. Schiffsstammdivision der Nordsee (Training Division for New Recruits).

Other Main Units
Artillery Inspectorate.
Torpedo and Mine Inspectorate.
Naval Schools: Flensburg (Mürwik) and Kiel (Wyk).
Naval Archive.
Naval Shipyards: Wilhelmshaven and Kiel.
Main Naval Depots with Command Posts: Cuxhaven, Emden, Kiel, Pillau, Swinemünde, Wilhelmshaven.
Ports with smaller naval offices: Bremen, Hamburg, Königsberg, Lübeck, Stettin.

THE FLEET IN 1932
With the appearance of several new ships during the 1920s, the naval administration adapted to meet the additional demands put upon it. As a result, coastal sections—the Naval Commands for the Baltic and North Sea—were enlarged, and the Fleet itself underwent several changes. The following is a rough outline of its organization during October 1932—a few months before Hitler was appointed Chancellor. Ships not listed here were either temporarily out of commission or were under the command of other establishments.

The Fleet Command (Flottenkommando)
Flottenchef (Fleet Commander): Walter Gladisch.
Stabschef (Chief of Staff): Hermann Boehm.

Battleships (Linienschiffe)
Befehlshaber der Linienschiffe or B.d.L. (Commander-in-Chief Battleships): Kpt.z.S. and Kommodore Max Bastian.
Hessen: Kpt.z.S. Friedrich Götting.
Schlesien: Kpt.z.S. Wilhelm Canaris.
Schleswig-Holstein: Kpt.z.S. Rolf Carls.
Meteor (survey ship): Korvkpt. Friedrich-Wilhelm Kurze.

Reconnaissance Forces (Aufklärungsstreitkräfte)
Befehlshaber der Aufklärungsstreitkräfte or B.d.A. (Commander-in-Chief Reconnaissance Forces): Konteradmiral Carl Kolbe.

Cruisers:
Emden: Fregkpt. Werner Grassmann.
Königsberg: Fregkpt. Otto von Schrader.
Leipzig: Kpt.z.S. Hans-Herbert Strobwasser.
1st Torpedo-Boat Flotilla: Korvkpt. Kurt Fricke.
1st Torpedo-Boat Half Flotilla: Kptlt. Hans Bütow.
G7: Kptlt. Hans Geisse.
G8: Oblt.z.S. Kurt Johannessen.
G10: Oblt.z.S. Eberhard Godt.
G11: Oblt.z.S. Hans Henigst.
2nd Torpedo-Boat Half Flotilla: Korvkpt. Wilhelm Meisel.
T151: Oblt.z.S. Georg Waue.
T153: Oblt.z.S. Heinrich Bassenge.
T156: Kptlt. Heinz-Dietrich von Conrady.
T158: Kptlt. Claus Trampedach.
2nd Torpedo-Boat Flotilla: Fregkpt. Hermann Mootz.
3rd Torpedo-Boat Half Flotilla: Korvkpt. Leopold Bürkner.
Iltis: Kptlt. Hans Gloeckner.
Jaguar: Kptlt. Gottfried Pönitz.
Tiger: Oblt.z.S. Herbert Friedrichs.
Wolf: Kptlt. Hans Michahelles.
3rd Torpedo-Boat Half Flotilla (Training): Kptlt. Hellmuth Heye.
Albatros: Oblt.z.S. Alfred Schemmel.
Falke: Oblt.z.S. Ernst Thienemann.
Kondor: Oblt.z.S. Heinz Bonatz.
Möwe: Oblt.z.S. Hermann Jordan.
1st Minesweeper Half Flotilla: Kptlt. Friedrich Ruge.
M66: Oblt.z.S. Alfred Wolf.
M98: Kptlt. Heinrich Bramesfeld.
M109: Oblt.z.S. (?) Kobel.
M111: Oblt.z.S. Jürgen Wattenberg.
M126: Kptlt. Johannes Isenlar.
M129: Kptlt. Axel von Blessingh.
M132: Oblt.z.S. Kurt Thoma.
M146: Kptlt. Max Freymadl.
1st Motor Torpedo-Boat Half Flotilla: Kptlt. Erich Bey.
S2: Oblt.z.S. Hans Eckermann.
S3: Oblt.z.S. Hans-Rudolf Rösing.
S4: Oblt.z.S. Manfred Fuhrke.*
S5: Oblt.z.S. Karl Stockmann.
Nordsee (tender): Oblt.z.S. Hello Zimmermann.

*Fuhrke was killed in an air crash while flying from Spain to Germany in 1938 and, therefore, is not mentioned in wartime records.

THE FLEET IN 1935
In 1935, two years after Hitler's appointment as Chancellor, new defence laws were passed. These included the repudiation of the Treaty of Versailles and the re-introduction of national conscription. In addition, some previously banned branches of the Navy were re-established, thus opening the way for the Third Reich to embark upon its objective of rapid military development.

The Fleet Command (Flottenkommando)
Flottenchef (Fleet Commander): Vizeadmiral Richard Foerster.
Stabschef (Chief of Staff): Kpt.z.S. Otto Schniewind.
Flagship: *Admiral Scheer.*
Main port for flagship: Kiel.
Fleet tender: *Hela.*

Battleships and Pocket Battleships (Linienschiffe)
Befehlshaber der Linienschiffe or B.d.L. (Commander-in-Chief Battleships): Konteradmiral Rolf Carls.
Flagship: *Deutschland.* Main port: Wilhelmshaven.
Admiral Graf Spee: Kpt.z.S. Conrad Patzig. Main base: Wilhelmshaven. Still training; to be commissioned during January 1936 and will then become flagship for Fleet Commander.
Admiral Scheer: Kpt.z.S. Wilhelm Marschall. Main base: Kiel.
Deutschland: Kpt.z.S. Paul Fanger. Main base: Wilhelmshaven.
Schleswig-Holstein: Kpt.z.S. Günther Krause. Main base: Wilhelmshaven.

Reconnaissance Forces (Aufklärungsstreitkräfte)
Befehlshaber der Aufklärungsstreitkräfte or B.d.A. (Commander-in-Chief for Reconnaissance Forces): Konteradmiral Hermann Boehm.
Flagship: *Königsberg,* later *Leipzig,* later *Nürnberg.* Main port: Kiel.

Cruisers:
Köln: Fregkpt. Otto Backenköhler. Main base: Wilhelmshaven.
Königsberg: Fregkpt. Oswald Paul. Main base: Kiel.

Leipzig: Fregkpt. Otto Schenk. Main base:
Wilhelmshaven. (Still undergoing trials).
Nürnberg: Kpt.z.S. Hubert Schmundt. Main
base: Kiel. (To be commissioned during
November 1935.)

Torpedo-boats:
Führer der Torpedoboote or F.d.T. (Flag
Officer for Torpedo-Boats): Fregkpt. Oskar
Kummetz.
Flag Officer's boat: *Leopard*: Kptlt. Hans von
Davidson. Base: Swinemünde.
Tender: *Jagd*. (No commissioned officer in
command during October 1935.)
1st Torpedo-Boat Flotilla: Korvkpt. Carl Gutjahr.
Base: Swinemünde.
G7: Kptlt. Franz Frerichs.
G8: Kptlt. Moritz Schmidt (Flagship).
G10: Kptlt. Gerhardt Böhmig.
G11: Kptlt. Theodor Detmers.
2nd Torpedo-Boat Flotilla (Training): Korvkpt.
Kurt Weyher
Base: Swinemünde.
Albatros: Kptlt. Hubert Freiherr von
Wangenheim.
Leopard:

Luchs: Kptlt. Richard Rothe-Roth.
Seeadler: Kptlt. Georg Langheld.
3rd Torpedo-Boat Flotilla (Training): Korvkpt.
Günther Gumprich.
Base: Wilhelmshaven.
Iltis: Kptlt. Arthur Wenninger.
Jaguar: Kptlt. Karl Smidt.
Tiger: Kptlt. Hugo Förster.
Wolf: Kptlt. Hans Erdmenger.
4th Torpedo-Boat Flotilla: Korvkpt. Hans
Henning.
Base: Wilhelmshaven.
Falke: Kptlt. Alwin Albrecht.
Greif: Kptlt. Manfred Fuhrke.
Kondor: Kptlt. Conrad Engelhardt.
Möwe: Kptlt. Hansjürgen Reinicke.

Motor Torpedo-Boats:
1st Motor Torpedo-Boat Flotilla: Korvkpt. Paul
Schubert.
Base: Kiel.
Tender: *Tsingtau*: Kptlt. Anton Ruhland.
S7: Kptlt. Kurt Sturm.
S8: Kptlt. Eberhard von Bogen.*

*Eberhard von Bogen was killed in a sailing-boat accident in 1936.

S9: Kptlt. Rudolf Petersen.
S10: Oblt.z.S. Hans-Henning von Salisch.
S11: Kptlt. Fro Harmsen.
S12: Oblt.z.S. Günther Hosemann.

Minesweepers and Escorts: Kpt.z.S. Kurt Ramien.
Base: Kiel.
Commander's boat: *T196*: Oblt.z.S. Hagen
Küster.
1st Minesweeper Flotilla: Korvkpt. Ernst-Felix
Krüder.
Base: Pillau.
M75: Kptlt. Karl Neitzel.
M89: Oblt.z.S. Archibald MacLean.
M111: Kptlt. Heinz-Ehler Beucke.
M132: Kptlt. Gerhard von Kamptz.
M146: Kptlt. Walter Rauff.
M151: Kptlt. Hans Sönnichsen.
1st Escort Flotilla (Training): Korvkpt. Siegfried
Weiss.
Base: Kiel.
M133 (*FI*): Kptlt. Siegfried Flister.
M117 (*F2*): Kptlt. Bernhard Busse.
M104 (*F5*): Kptlt. Hans John.
T157 (*F6*): Kptlt. Alfred Schumann.
F9: Kptlt. Paul Morgenstern.

F10: Kptlt. Hermann Knuth.
2nd Escort Flotilla (Training): Korvkpt. Ernst Lucht.
  Base: Kiel.
M89 (*F3*): Kptlt. Rudolf Lell.
M50 (*F4*): Kptlt. Werner Musenberg.
F7: Oblt.z.S. Hans-Werner Neumann.
F8: Kptlt. Peter Reichmann.
1st Motor Minesweeper Flotilla: Kptlt. Hugo Pahl.
  Base: Kiel.
  Tender: *Zieten*: Oblt.z.S. Hans Stubbendorff.
R11, R12, R13, R14, R18, R19. (These boats were probably not commanded by commissioned officers; so their names would not have been recorded in the Navy Lists.)

Submarine Flotilla Weddigen: Kpt.z.S. Karl Dönitz.
  Base: Kiel.
  Escort ship: *T23*: Kptlt. Heinz Fischer.
  Tender: *Saar*: Korvkpt. Rudolf Wiegner.
U7: Kptlt. Kurt Freiwald.
U8: Kptlt. Walter or Harald Grosse.
U9: Kptlt. Hans-Günther Looff.
U10: Oblt.z.S. Heinz Scheringer.
U11: Kptlt. Hans-Rudolf Rösing.

U12: Oblt.z.S. Werner von Schmidt.
(*U1 - U6* were attached to the Submarine School.)

Major ships not under command of the Fleet Commander

The list below gives the ship's name, year launched and main port. Wilhelmshaven came under command of the North Sea Naval Station and Kiel came under the Baltic Station.

Arkona (*M115*)	1918	Kiel
Bremse	1931	Kiel
Brummer	1935	Wilhelmshaven
Delphin (*M108*)	1919	—
Drache	1908	Kiel
Elbe	1931	Wilhelmshaven
Emden	1925	Training ship
Frauenlob (*M134*)	1919	Wilhelmshaven
Fuchs	1919	Kiel
Gorch Fock	1933	Kiel
Grille	1934	Kiel
Hannover	1905	Wilhelmshaven (?)
Hela	1919	Kiel
Karlsruhe	1927	Training ship
Meteor	1915	Wilhelmshaven
Nautilus (*M81*)	?	Kiel
Nire	1914	Kiel
Nordsee	1914	Kiel
Peilboot II	1911	Wilhelmshaven
Peilboot V	1912	Wilhelmshaven
Pelikan (*M28*)	1917	Kiel
Schlesien	1906	Training ship
Taucher	1934	Kiel
T23	1912	Kiel
T151	1907	Pillau
T153	1907	Kiel
T156	1907	Kiel
T157	1907	Kiel
T158	1907	Kiel

Naval bases

Main Naval Bases with deep water anchorage: Kiel, Wilhelmshaven.
Other Naval Bases: Berlin, Bremen,* Borkum, Cuxhaven, Eckernförde,* Emden, Flensburg (Mürwik), Grauerort near Stade,* Hamburg,* List on island of Sylt,* Malente, Neumünster,* Norderney, Pillau, Stettin,* Stopmühle,* Stralsund, Swinemünde, Wangerooge, Wesermünde (Bremerhaven).

*This town only had one or two small offices.

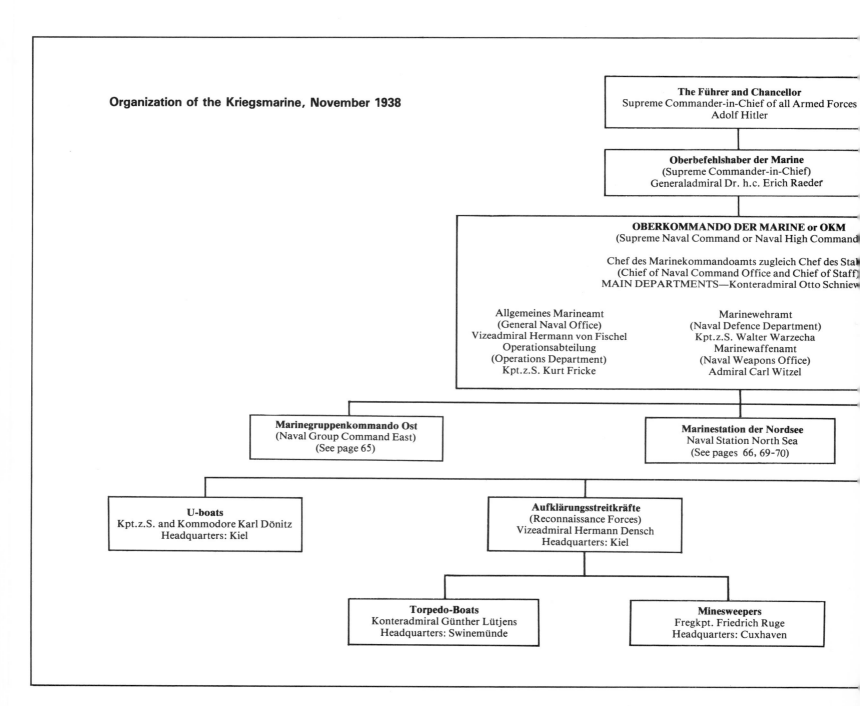

Organization of the Kriegsmarine, November 1938

The Führer and Chancellor
Supreme Commander-in-Chief of all Armed Forces
Adolf Hitler

Oberbefehlshaber der Marine
(Supreme Commander-in-Chief)
Generaladmiral Dr. h.c. Erich Raeder

OBERKOMMANDO DER MARINE or OKM
(Supreme Naval Command or Naval High Command)

Chef des Marinekommandoamts zugleich Chef des Stab
(Chief of Naval Command Office and Chief of Staff)
MAIN DEPARTMENTS—Konteradmiral Otto Schniew

Allgemeines Marineamt
(General Naval Office)
Vizeadmiral Hermann von Fischel
Operationsabteilung
(Operations Department)
Kpt.z.S. Kurt Fricke

Marinewehramt
(Naval Defence Department)
Kpt.z.S. Walter Warzecha
Marinewaffenamt
(Naval Weapons Office)
Admiral Carl Witzel

Marinegruppenkommando Ost
(Naval Group Command East)
(See page 65)

Marinestation der Nordsee
Naval Station North Sea
(See pages 66, 69-70)

U-boats
Kpt.z.S. and Kommodore Karl Dönitz
Headquarters: Kiel

Aufklärungsstreitkräfte
(Reconnaissance Forces)
Vizeadmiral Hermann Densch
Headquarters: Kiel

Torpedo-Boats
Konteradmiral Günther Lütjens
Headquarters: Swinemünde

Minesweepers
Fregkpt. Friedrich Ruge
Headquarters: Cuxhaven

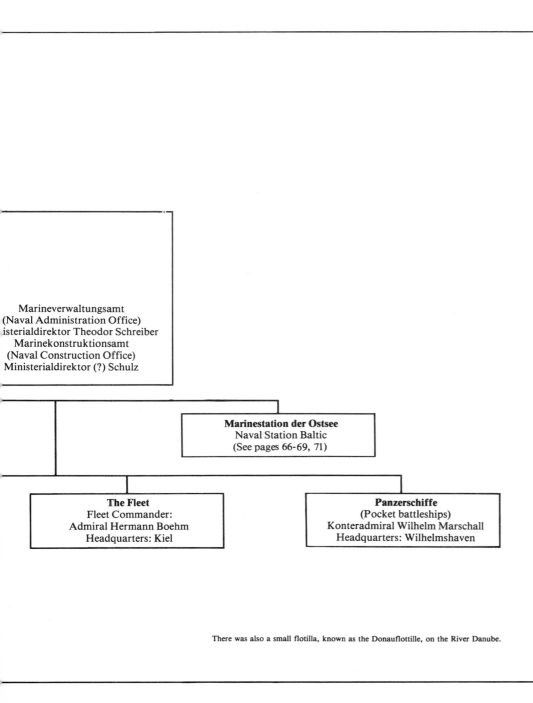

Marineverwaltungsamt
(Naval Administration Office)
...isterialdirektor Theodor Schreiber
Marinekonstruktionsamt
(Naval Construction Office)
Ministerialdirektor (?) Schulz

Marinestation der Ostsee
Naval Station Baltic
(See pages 66-69, 71)

The Fleet
Fleet Commander:
Admiral Hermann Boehm
Headquarters: Kiel

Panzerschiffe
(Pocket battleships)
Konteradmiral Wilhelm Marschall
Headquarters: Wilhelmshaven

There was also a small flotilla, known as the Donauflottille, on the River Danube.

ORGANIZATION STRUCTURE IN 1938

Hitler appointed himself Supreme Commander-in-Chief of the German armed forces on 4 February 1938 and, during that year, all men in the Navy took an oath swearing obedience to him. Technically, this gave Hitler direct command, but in reality there was little interference from him or the NSDAP. The Navy clung fiercely to the traditions it had forged under the Emperor, and all the Führer's orders were filtered through the Naval High Command (which, on occasion, saw fit to refuse his instructions). Although Erich Raeder did not like Hitler, on balance he probably followed the Führer's wishes more closely than did his successor, Karl Dönitz. Dönitz was one of the few with the courage and character to voice his opinions, even if they contradicted those of the Führer.

THE FLEET AT THE START OF THE WAR

Ships not mentioned in this section were either temporarily out of service, in dock or still undergoing trials.

Battleships, Pocket Battleships and Cruisers

The following list gives the commander* of each ship and its location at the beginning of the war.

Admiral Graf Spee: KS Hans Langsdorff. Left Wilhelmshaven on 21 August to operate in the South Atlantic.

Admiral Scheer: KS Hans-Heinrich Wurmbach. Lying at anchor in the Schillig Roads, outside Wilhelmshaven.

Deutschland: KS Paul Wenneker. North Atlantic.

Emden: KS Werner Lange. At anchor off Wilhelmshaven.

Köln: KS Theodor Burchardi. The Baltic.

Königsberg: KS Kurt Caesar Hoffmann. She was in the Baltic on the last day of August, patrolling off Poland. From there she sailed via the Kiel Canal into the North Sea.

Leipzig: KS Heinz Nordmann. With *Admiral Graf Spee* off the coast of Mexico.

Nürnberg: KS Otto Klüber. The Baltic.

Schlesien: KS Kurt Utke. The Baltic.

Schleswig-Holstein: KS Gustav Kleikamp. In the Baltic off Danzig. She fired the first shots of the war at sea.

*KS = Kapitän zur See.

Right: Close-up of destroyer *Z15, Erich Steinbrinck*, after the war. The 'dustbins' with chimneys, standing on the deck, were portable smoke-making canisters; trolleys, for moving torpedoes, are also visible. The little wheels on the mast are aerials for a special early-warning radar to detect approaching aircraft. (Photo: Imperial War Museum)

U-boats

The following list gives the boats that were in commission on 1 September 1939, the commander,* type (A = Atlantic, C = Coastal) and operational status (O = Operational, T = Training boat, Tr = Operational/on trials) of each boat.

U1: KL Jürgen Deecke		C/T
U2: KL Helmuth Rosenbaum		C/T
U3: KL Joachim Schepke		C/T
U4: KL Harro von Klot-Heydenfeldt		C/T
U5: KL Günter Kutschmann		C/T
U6: KL Joachim Matz		C/T
U7: OL Otto Salmann		C/T
U8: KL Georg Peters		C/T
U9: KL Ludwig Mathes or Max Schulte		C/O
U10: KL Wilhelm Schulz		C/T
U11: KL Victor Schütze		C/T
U12: KL Dietrich von der Ropp		C/O
U13: KL Karl Daublebsky von Eichhain		C/O
U14: KL Horst Wellner		C/O
U15: KL Peter Frahm		C/O
U16: KL Hannes Weingaertner		C/O
U17: KL Heinz von Reiche		C/O
U18: KL Max Hermann Bauer		C/O
U19: KL Hans Meckel		C/O
U20: KL Karl-Heinz Moehle		C/O
U21: KL Fritz Frauenheim		C/O
U22: KL Werner Winter		C/O
U23: KL Otto Kretschmer		C/O
U24: KL Udo Behrens		C/O
U25: OL Georg-Heinz Michel		A/?
U26: FK Oskar Schomburg		A/O
U27: KL Johannes Franz		A/O
U28: KL Günter Kuhnke		A/O
U29: KL Otto Schuhart		A/O
U30: KL Fritz-Julius Lemp		A/O
U31: KL Johannes Habekost		A/O
U32: OL Hans Jenisch		A/O
U33: KL Hans-Wilhelm von Dresky		A/O
U34: KL Wilhelm Rollmann		A/O
U35: KL Werner Lott		A/O
U36: KL Wilhelm Fröhlich		A/Tr?
U37: KL Heinrich Schuch		A/O
U38: KL Heinrich Liebe		A/O
U39: KL Gerhard Glattes		A/O
U40: KL Werner von Schmidt		A/O
U41: KL Gustav-Adolf Mugler		A/O
U42: KL Rolf Dau		A/Tr
U43: KL Wilhelm Ambrosius		A/Tr

*Rank abbreviations: OL = Oberleutnant zur See, KL = Kapitänleutnant, FK = Fregattenkapitän, KK = Korvettenkapitän.

U44: Commissioned on 4 Nov 1939		
U45: KL Alexander Gelhaar		A/O
U46: KL Herbert Sohler		A/O
U47: KL Günther Prien		A/O
U48: KL Herbert Schultze		A/O
U49: KL Curt von Gossler		A/Tr
U50: Commissioned on 12 Dec 1939		
U51: KL Dietrich Knorr		A/Tr
U52: KL Wolfgang Barten		A/O
U53: KL Ernst-Günther Heinicke		A/Tr
U54: Commissioned on 23 Sept 1939		
U55: Commissioned on 21 Nov 1939		
U56: KL Wilhelm Zahn		C/O
U57: KL Claus Korth		C/O
U58: KL Herbert Kuppisch		C/O
U59: KL Harald Jürst		C/O
U60: KL Georg Schewe		C/Tr
U61: KL Jürgen Oesten		C/Tr

Destroyers

Destroyers' numbers were prefixed by the letter 'Z', which stood for Zerstörer (destroyer). In addition to a number, some of them were also given a name. (Details will be found on page 91.)

Z1: KK Fritz Bassenge (Flagship for Commander-in-Chief Torpedo-Boats).
Z2: KK Max-Eckart Wolff.
Z3: KK Claus Trampedach.
Z4: KK Moritz Schmidt.
Z5: KK Hans Zimmer (Flagship, 2nd Flotilla).
Z6: KK Gerhardt Böhmig.
Z7: KK Theodor Detmers.
Z8: KK Fritz Berger.
Z9: KK Gottfried Pönitz.
Z10: KK Karl-Jesko von Puttkamer.
Z11: KK Kurt Rechel.
Z12: KK Karl Smidt.
Z13: FK Alfred Schulze-Hinrichs.
Z14: FK Rudolf von Pufendorf.
Z15: KK Rolf Johannesson.
Z16: KK Alfred Schemmel.
Z17: KK Erich Holtorf.
Z18: KK Herbert Friedrichs.
Z19: KK Friedrich Kothe.
Z20: KK Theodor Bechtolsheim Freiherr von Mauchenheim.
Z21: KK Hans Erdmenger. (Ship still undergoing trials at the start of the war.)

Torpedo-Boats

Albatros: KL Herbert Schultze.
Falke: KL Günther Hessler.
Greif: KL Wilhelm Verlohr.
Iltis: KL Heinz Schuur.
Jaguar: KL Franz Kohlauf.
Kondor: KL Hans Wilcke.
Leopard: KL Karl Kassbaum.
Luchs: KL Eckart Prölss.
Möwe: KL Konrad Edler von Rennenkampff.
Seeadler: KL Werner Hartenstein.
Tiger: KL Helmut Neuss. (Boat sunk after a collision on 25 August 1939.)
Wolf: KL Lutz Gerstung.

Motor Torpedo-Boats

These numbers were prefixed by the letter 'S'. The following were operational at the start of the war:
S6, S7, S8, S9, S10, S11, S12, S13, S14, S15, S16, S17, S18, S19, S20, S21, S22.

Minesweepers

These boat numbers were prefixed by the letter 'M': M1, M2, M3, M4, M5, M6, M7, M8, M9, M10, M11, M12, M13, M14, M15, M16, M17, M18. M19, M20, M21, M22.

THE SUPREME NAVAL COMMAND (Oberkommando der Marine, or OKM)

The Supreme Naval Command comprised the Supreme Commander-in-Chief's staff and the main departments mentioned in the diagram on pages 60-61. This organization became somewhat complicated as the war progressed: the armaments section alone mushroomed to nine main departments and over fifty sub-departments. (For detailed information on these and other departments, the reader should consult *Die deutsche Kriegsmarine, 1939-1945,* Volume I, by W. Lohmann and H. H. Hildebrand.) There was one major change during the reorganization of October/November 1939: the General Naval Office (Allgemeines Marineamt) was disbanded and replaced by the Seekriegsleitung or SKL (Chief of Naval War Staff). This was not a completely new innovation, for the title had first appeared during the 1930s when it was used synonymously with OKM.

The Supreme Naval Command's headquarters were in Berlin—at Tirpitzufer (now called Reichpietschufer) next to the Landwehr Canal—until November 1943 when the building was bombed. Then the staff were moved to new quarters in

Below: This bunker in Kiel shows the type of construction used for naval command bunkers. Very few received any noteworthy damage, although they were plastered with bombs; indeed some of them were so strongly-built that it was impracticable to demolish them after the war. (Photo: Imperial War Museum)

Below: The Naval School in Mürwik near Flensburg, last head-quarters of the Navy's Supreme Command and also of the last government of the Third Reich (the so-called Dönitz Government). The guard consisted mainly of ex-U-boat men, commanded by Korvkpt. Peter Cremer. They wore infantry uniforms, as seen in this photograph, with U-boat badges. (Photo: Imperial War Museum)

Eberswalde, code-named 'Bismarck'. A small core of men remained in the city, where alternative accommodation was under construction, but this was never occupied by the Navy. In addition to 'Bismarck', two other quarters were erected, but only one of them was used. Code-named 'Koralle' it was situated in the small, isolated village of Bernau, about nineteen miles north-east of the Reich's Chancellery. It was there that Dönitz moved with his staff in the summer of 1943.

In 1944 it became clear that the Supreme Naval Command would have to move out of reach of the advancing Russian Army and vacate its offices in the Berlin region. Dönitz decided to split the High Command and, early in 1945, the core of the staff from 'Bismarck' were ordered to move west. Dönitz considered it to be his duty, as Supreme Commander-in-Chief, to remain near Hitler's headquarters in order to keep in touch with the rapidly moving front. He did this by commuting between 'Koralle' and Hitler's command bunker.

Dönitz and his Naval War Staff evacuated the thick concrete bunkers at 'Koralle' during early April 1945, and took up residence in the command train 'Auerhahn'. Unfortunately, this proved to be a case of 'out of the frying pan and into the fire'. Shortly after their arrival, a shunting operation put paid to all electrical power; then, to cap it all, enemy aircraft were reported overhead and the emergency lights went out too! When this happened, Dönitz acted on a suggestion from his adjutant and ordered everybody back to 'Koralle'.

Although Berlin's defences deteriorated rapidly under the new Russian bombardment begun on 16 April, the decision to move from 'Koralle' was not made until the 19th. Even so, it came as a surprise to Dönitz's adjutant, Walter Lüdde-Neurath, for he had just gone to bed that night when the telephone rang and he was told to be ready to move within the hour. It was not a moment too soon. Just half an hour after Dönitz's armoured Mercedes, staff cars, vans and the important mobile radio transmitter (which could reach most ships at sea via the huge fixed radio station 'Goliath') rolled out of the compound, the first of the Russian troops arrived. The German Naval War Staff remained at Dönitz's flat in the heart of Berlin for a few days before finally moving west to Plön in Schleswig-Holstein. Meanwhile, other branches of the Naval High Command had been staying at Varel, near Wilhelmshaven, since

February 1945, and now they too moved north of the Elbe to occupy a small camp near Eutin in Schleswig-Holstein.

Time was fast running out. The situation in Plön became quite hectic after Lüdde-Neurath telephoned the Dräger Works in Lübeck—which was about half an hour's drive from Plön—only to be told that there were enemy tanks driving past. He lost no time in collecting the Grand Admiral and beating a hasty retreat to Flensburg, where the German Naval War Staff remained until disbanded by the Allies.

NAVAL GROUP COMMMANDS
The pre-war administration pattern changed on 18

August 1939, when the previously planned 'Three Front War Programme' came into effect as an emergency measure to cover possible conflict in the Baltic, North Sea and the Atlantic. These three areas were to be controlled by Naval Group Command East, Naval Group Command West and by the Naval War Staff (SKL). Naval Group Command East had been in existence since November 1938—the date of its foundation in Kiel—with the aim of defending the Baltic. (See diagram, p. 60.) A similar department for the west was then founded in Sengwarden, near Wilhelmshaven, during August 1939. At first, it was only concerned with the defence of the German Bight and the North Sea, but later it also took control of

Norwegian waters. Eventually its headquarters were moved to France, where the Command restricted its operations to French Atlantic waters. The German Bight, the North Sea, Norwegian waters and other parts previously controlled by the Naval Group Command East were taken over by a new unit called Naval Group Command North. A further division was created during 1941 to cover the waters of northern Norway. This was called Admiral Polar Seas (Admiral Nordmeer), and its headquarters were in Kirkenes, aboard the depot ship *Tanga*. During May 1942 the staff moved aboard the yacht *Grille* moored at Narvik, where they remained until the Command was disbanded in June 1944.

NAVAL COMMANDS BALTIC AND NORTH SEA

After the First world War these two Commands were called Stationskommando Ostee and Stationskommando Nordsee (Station Command Baltic and Station Command North Sea). Later, they were known as Marinestation der Ostsee or Nordsee (Naval Station for Baltic or North Sea). Both Commands were upgraded to Marineoberkommando and their commanding officers promoted from Commanders-in-Chief to Supreme Commanders-in-Chief during February 1943. The two Commands operated as separate, autonomous divisions under their own leaders (see diagram on p. 60) and were responsible for coastal defence, the training of new recruits and other general training. (In this book they will be dealt with as one unit, because it will save duplicating information and should be easier to understand.)

Naval Command Baltic and Operation 'Barbarossa'

As soon as the office of Naval Commander-in-Chief 'C' was created in May 1941, the staff were positioned in Memel to await the start of the attack on Russia. Several naval forces moved from there to support the Army, and a few were engaged in battles of their own—especially during the storming of Libau. In November 1941, the post was disbanded and all existing forces were placed under the command of Naval Commander-in-Chief 'D'—a position that had also been established in May. From then on C-in-C 'D' was responsible for the entire coastal defences of the far-eastern Baltic. (For a list of the forces under

his command, see 'Coastal Commander East Baltic' on p. 71.) Later, in May 1944, he was given the title Commanding Admiral East Baltic.

Originally, the forces under Naval Commander-in-Chief 'C' were known as Marinestosstruppabteilung (Naval Assault Detachment). Two special units were later founded and known by their commanders' names—Special Command Bigler and Special Command Gläser. Although the important forces under Naval Commander-in-Chief 'D' have been listed, there were also several other AA and artillery divisions.

It is difficult, if not impossible, to provide direct translations of certain German proper nouns. On the other hand, keeping some of the original German names would only help confuse readers who do not understand German. The following translations may lend a guiding hand.*
Training Regiment: Schiffsstammregiment
Training Detachment: Schiffsstammabteilung
NCO Training Detachment: Marinelehrabteilung
Naval Reserve Detachment: Marineersatzabteilung
Naval Artillery Regiment: Marineartillerieregiment
Naval Artillery Detachment (Art. Det.): Marineartillerieabteilung
Naval AA Regiment: Marineflakregiment
Naval AA Detachment (AA Det.): Marineflakabteilung
Naval Artillery Reserve: Marineersatzartillerie
Port Protection Flotilla: Hafenschutzflottille

Training New Recruits

Before the end of the First World War, new recruits were trained by Naval Inspectorates (Marine Inspektion). These were allotted the suffixes 'I' for the Baltic and 'II' for the North Sea. Both Inspectorates were disbanded after the war and replaced by two new departments: Schiffsstammdivision der Ostsee and Nordsee. They, too, were later replaced by Schiffsstammregiment der Ostsee and Nordsee, each of which were sub-divided into Schiffsstammabteilung. In

this book they have been translated as meaning 'Training Regiment' and 'Training Detachment'.

Training Regiments (Schiffsstammregiment):
The following list gives the Command (B = Baltic, N = North Sea) and main base for each regiment.
1. B; Stralsund. Disbanded, January 1944.
2. N; Wesermünde. Disbanded, November 1939.
3. B; Libau (Liepaja). Founded during January 1943 and moved to Epinal in April 1943.
4. N; Groningen. Moved to Steenwijk, October 1943.
5. B; Pillau. Only operational from January 1944 until February 1945.
6. N; Belfont. Only operational from December 1943 until September 1944.

Training Detachments (Schiffsstammabteilung):
The following list gives the Command (B = Baltic, N = North Sea) and main base for each.
1. B; Kiel. Renamed 1st Naval Reserve Detachment, January 1944 (see also 7th Detachment).
2. N; Wilhelmshaven. Moved to Norden in April 1941; renamed 8th Naval Reserve Detachment during January 1944.
3. B; Kiel. Moved to Eckernförde, then to Waren near Müritz; it was renamed 9th Naval Reserve Detachment.
4. N; Wilhelmshaven. Renamed 4th Naval Reserve Detachment during 1944.
5. B; Eckernförde. Moved to Libau and later to Epinal.
6. N; Wilhelmshaven. Moved to Gotenhafen; renamed 16th Training Detachment during January 1940. Moved to Steenwijk and Wazep in Holland during April 1941.
7. B; Stralsund. Renamed 1st Training Detachment during January 1944 and moved to Epinal. Later moved to Fort Schiesseck near Bitsch.
8. N; Leer. Renamed 28th Naval Reserve Detachment, October 1944.
9. B; Stralsund. Renamed 3rd NCO Training Detachment, January 1944.
10. N; Wesermünde. Renamed 4th NCO Training Detachment, January 1944.
11. B; Stralsund. Renamed 3rd Training Detachment, January 1944.
12. N; Brake. Later renamed 6th NCO Training Detachment.
13. B; Sassnitz. Moved to Libau, then to Pillau and later to Epinal.

*Anyone finding these German names difficult might be pleased to know that I have not included the school called Marinenachrichtenhelferinnenausbildungsabteilung! (See Glossary.)

German names are used in the singular throughout this section, even where they should be in the plural. As plurals in German are not simply formed by adding an 's' and as, usually, the names in documents or on badges would have been in the singular, I hope this style will simplify matters for non-German readers.

Below: Passing out parade at the Schiffsstammdivision der Nordsee in Wilhelmshaven during the summer of 1933. Graduates in naval uniform can be seen towards the inside of the rectangular formation swearing their oath of allegiance. Newer recruits still wearing naval infantry uniform are seen towards the back, with their instructors. (Photo: Author's Collection)

14. N; Glückstadt. Moved to Breda in Holland, September 1940.

15. B; Beverloo. Moved from near Beverloo to Copenhagen during January 1944 and was renamed 5th NCO Training Detachment.

16. N; Bergen-op-Zoom. Moved to Gotenhafen,

June 1940. It was originally known as 6th Training Detachment.

17. B; Memel. Moved in 1944.

18. N; Buxtehude. Moved from Buxtehude near Hamburg to Husum, May 1943; went to Belfont in December of that year. The Detachment was

handed over to the Army during September 1944.

19. B; Near Diedenhofen. Founded in July 1942. Later moved to Beverloo and afterwards to Hansted in Denmark.

20. N; Near Arnhem. Founded during July 1941 in Norden; moved to near Arnhem shortly afterwards. Later, the Detachment was also at Harkamm.

21. B; Leba. Moved to Copenhagen in 1944.

22. N; Beverloo. Later moved to Almelo in Holland.

23. B; Deutsch Krone. Known as the 3rd Naval Artillery Reserve Detachment before January 1944.

24. N; Groningen. Known as the 6th Naval Artillery Reserve Detachment before September 1943.

25. B; Pillau. Known as the 5th Naval Artillery Reserve Detachment before January 1944.

26. N; Helchteren. Originally founded in Wazep.

27. B; Ollerup (Denmark). Known as the 7th Naval Artillery Reserve Detachment before January 1944.

28. N; Sennheim. Only operational from October 1943 until October 1944. It was a special training unit for non-German naval volunteers.

29. Not operational.

30. N; Wittmund.

31. B; Windau. Moved to Windau during August 1942. It was disbanded during December 1944.

32. N; Stralsund. Renamed 2nd Training Detachment during January 1944. This was probably disbanded, because it was refounded as 22nd Naval Reserve Detachment during October 1944.

NCO Training Detachments

These units were first called Marineunteroffizier-abteilung, until January 1944 when they were renamed Marinelehrabteilung. Both were concerned with the training of non-commissioned officers. There were two regiments: Number 1 was in Eckernförde under the Baltic Command, and Number 2 was in Wesermünde under the North Sea Command. These two regiments were divided into seven detachments; the following list gives the command of each unit (B = Baltic, N = North Sea) and its main base.

1. B; Kiel. Moved to Glücksburg, January 1944.

2. N; Wesermünde. Moved to Glückstadt, September 1940.

3. B; Stralsund. Moved to Aarhus in Denmark,

July 1944.

4. N; Lehe near Wesermünde. Founded, January 1944.

5. B; Copenhagen. Earlier, it was also known as the 15th Training Detachment.

6. N; Varel. Founded in January 1944 by renaming the 12th Training Detachment. The unit was disbanded in October 1944.

7. B; Lütjenholm. Moved to Hirtenstall, September 1944. Later the Detachment moved to Norddorf on the island of Amrum; some members moved to Büsum and Sülzenholm.

Naval Reserve Units

Naval Reserve Regiments (Marineersatzregiment):

1. Baltic Command, with headquarters in Kiel. This regiment dealt with personnel for special missions.

2. North Sea Command, with headquarters in Wilhelmshaven. Founded during January 1944. The following detachments were operational: 2, 4, 6, 8, 10, 12, 28, 42.

3. Baltic Command, with headquarters in Neustrelitz. This regiment was for armament specialists and technical personnel.

4. North Sea Command, with headquarters in Cuxhaven.

Naval Reserve Detachments (Marineersatz-abteilung):

The following list gives the command of each detachment (B = Baltic, N = North Sea) and its base.

1. B; Kiel. Founded in January 1944 by changing the name of the 1st Training Detachment.

2. N; Wilhelmshaven. Founded in September 1944.

3. B; Neustrelitz. Founded during September 1944, it later moved to Schlochau.

4. N; Wilhelmshaven. Founded in 1944 by changing the name of the 4th Training Detachment.

5. B; Westerland. On the island of Sylt. Founded in September 1943.

6. N; Hörnum. On the island of Sylt. Founded in January 1944.

7. B; Schwesing. Founded in January 1944.

8. N; Norden. Founded in January 1944 by changing the name of the 2nd Training Detachment.

9. B; Waren. Probably also at Müritz. Founded in January 1944 by changing the name of the 3rd Training Detachment.

10. N; Near Godenstedt. Founded in January 1944 by changing the name of 2nd Naval Artillery Reserve Detachment.

11. B; Deutsch-Eylau (Ilawa). Founded in January 1944 by changing the name of the 11th Naval Artillery Reserve Detachment.

12. N; Cuxhaven. Founded in January 1944 by changing the name of the 4th Naval Artillery Reserve Detachment.

13. B; Sassnitz. Founded in January 1944 by changing the name of Marinestammkompanie. Also had bases in Neustrelitz and Bornholm.

14. N; Wilhelmshaven.

15. B; Swinemünde. Founded in January 1944.

16. N; Only operational for one month during 1944.

17. B; Flatow (Zlotow). Operational for one year from January 1944.

18. N; Leer. Founded in October 1944 by changing the name of the 2nd NCO Training Detachment.

19. B; Neustrelitz. Founded in January 1944 by changing the name of Ausbildungsstammkompanie Neustrelitz (Training Company Neustrelitz).

20. Probably not operational.

21. B; Memel.

22. N; Wyk/Föhr. Founded in December 1944 by changing the name of the 32nd Training Detachment.

23. B; Pilsen (?). Founded in June 1944.

24. N; Probably not operational.

25. B; Neustrelitz. Founded in May 1944.

26. N; Probably not operational.

27. B; Esbjerg. Founded in March 1945.

28. N; Leer. Founded in October 1944 by changing the name of the 8th Training Detachment.

29. B; Not operational.

30. N; Not operational.

31. B; Kiel. Founded in September 1944.

32. N; Hamburg. Founded in September 1944.

33. B; Stettin. Only operational for one month during 1944.

34. N; Bremen. Founded in November 1944.

35. B; Gotenhafen (Gdynia). Operational between November 1944 and March 1945. The name was then changed to 37th Naval Reserve Detachment.

36. N; Bremen. Founded in September 1944.

37. B; Königsberg. Founded in August 1944; moved to several other locations later.

38, 39, 40, 41. Not operational.

42. N; (?). Founded in December 1944.

Coastal Defence, Naval Command North Sea

Two Fortress Commanders had been responsible for coastal defence of the North Sea coast before the war: the East Fresian Area had its headquarters in Wilhelmshaven and the North Fresian Area was in Cuxhaven. But when war broke out the term Fortress Commander (Festungskommandant) was replaced by Coastal Commander (Küstenbefehlshaber). The two areas continued to function separately until they were amalgamated in February 1941, and a new post of Coastal Commander German Bight (Küstenbefehlshaber Deutsche Bucht) was created. Headquarters of the amalgamated section remained in Wilhelmshaven for some time, but the offices were later moved to Cuxhaven. The office of Coastal Commander German Bight existed until September 1944, when there was a drastic reorganization of Germany's coastal defences.

The following is an outline of the main units directly controlled by the Coastal Commander between September 1939 and September 1944. This is followed by an outline of the reorganized administration.

Section Borkum Island:
Borkum is a small island of about thirteen and a half square miles at the mouth of the Ems.
Port Protection Flotilla.
Naval Art. Det. 116.
Naval AA Det. 216.

Section Emden:
The five northerly Dutch provinces came under the jurisdiction of this section during May 1940.
6th Naval AA Regt. Founded in Emden during March 1942, the following detachments were operational.
Naval AA Det. 236; Emden.
Naval AA Det. 246; Harlingen.
Naval AA Det. 256; Delfzijl. (Founded, March 1942.)
Naval AA Det. 266; Westerhusen. (Founded, March 1942.)
Naval AA Det. 276; Kanalpolder. (Founded, December 1943.)

6th Naval Art. Res. Founded in Emden during August 1943. Also at Assen and Groningen. It was renamed 24th Naval Training Detachment during September 1943.

10th Naval Art. Res. Operational in Norden for a few weeks during January 1940.

8th Naval Motor Transport Det. Founded in Emden during March 1942.

Section Norderney:
Norderney is a small island, about eight and a half square miles, north of Emden.
Naval Art. Det. 126. Operational from October 1939 until July 1940.
Naval AA Det. 226. Operational from October 1939.

Section Wangerooge:
Wangerooge is an island of about five and three quarter square miles. This section also had small units on adjoining islands.
Naval Art. Det. 112. Operational from October 1939 until June 1940.
Naval Art. Det. 132.
Naval AA Det. 232.
2nd Naval Training Det. for light AA guns.

Section Wilhelmshaven:
Port Protection Flotilla.
2nd Naval AA Regt. Wilhelmshaven. Renamed 2nd Naval AA Brigade (2 Marineflakbrigade) in May 1942. The following detachments were operational.
Naval AA Det. 212; Wilhelmshaven.
Naval AA Det. 222; Wilhelmshaven. Also the floating AA battery *Medusa*. (*Medusa* was an old pre-First World War cruiser.)
Naval AA Det. 232; Wilhelmshaven.
Naval AA Det. 252; Heidmühle.
Naval AA Det. 262; Wilhelmshaven.
Naval AA Det. 272; Tossens.
Naval AA Det. 282; Wilhelmshaven. Founded during the spring of 1940. The floating AA battery *Niobe* belonged to this detachment. (*Niobe* was a Royal Netherlands Navy cruiser.)
2nd Naval Art. Res.
2nd Naval Motor Transport Det.

Section Wesermünde:
Situated at the mouth of the River Weser, Wesermünde is now renamed Bremerhaven.
Naval AA Det. 244.
Naval AA Det. 264.

Section Heligoland:
Naval AA Det. 242.
Naval Art. Det. 122.

Section Cuxhaven:
Port Protection Flotilla.
Naval AA Det. 214.
Naval 4th Art. Res.

Section Brunsbüttel:
Brunsbüttel or Brunsbüttelkoog is a small town at the mouth of the River Elbe, where the Kiel Canal terminates. It is famous for the huge locks that control the canal's water level.
14th Naval AA Regt. The following detachments were operational.
Naval AA Det. 254; Sandhayn and later Friedrichshof.
Naval AA Det. 274; Brunsbüttel.
Naval AA Det. 294; Near Stade.
Naval AA Det. 224. Founded in Wilhelmsburg; moved to France during May 1943.

Section Sylt:
Sylt is an island in the North Sea near the Danish border. It is connected to the German mainland by a dam which carries a railway line.
8th Naval AA Reg. Westerland. Disbanded during February 1942.
Naval AA Det. 204; Westerland. Moved to Esbjerg during April 1940.
Naval AA Det. 234; Westerland.
Naval AA Det. 264; Hörnum plus other locations. Disbanded during April 1943, after which the battery came under control of Naval AA Det. 234.
Naval Art. Det. 134; Vogelkoje and other locations.

Admiral German Bight
There were drastic changes in coastal defence during September 1944. The Coastal Commander for the German Bight was renamed Commanding Admiral German Bight and the area was divided into three Sea Defence Regions, each subdivided as follows.

Sea Defence Region East Friesland:
Headquarters at Tidefeld near Norden.
Sections Borkum, Emden, Norderney, Wangerooge and Wilhelmshaven.

Sea Defence Region Elbe-Weser:
Headquarters at Ottendorf, near Cuxhaven.
Sections Cuxhaven, Brunsbüttel, Wesermünde and Heligoland.

Sea Defence Region North Friesland:
Headquarters at Husum.
Sections Friedrichstadt and Sylt.

Sea Defence Sections and their bases were as listed below.

Section Borkum:
Port Protection Flotilla.
Naval AA Det. 216.
Naval Art. Det. 116.
Naval Island Bttn. 350.

Section Emden:
6th Naval AA Regt. with Naval AA Det. 236; Emden.
Naval AA Det. 246; Harlingen.
Naval AA Det. 256; Delfzijl.
Naval AA Det. 266; Westerhusen.
Naval AA Det. 276; Kanalpolder.
Naval Art. Det. 126; Leer.
Naval Fortress Bttns: 363, 366, 367, 368.
Naval Island Bttn. 353. Founded in January 1945 on the island of Amrum and moved to Emden before the end of the war.

Section Norderney:
Naval AA Det. 226.
Naval Island Bttn. 355; Juist.

Section Wangerooge:
Naval Art. Det. 631.
Naval Island Bttn. Based on the islands of Wangerooge and Langeoog.
(The Naval AA Training establishment in this section was disbanded during November 1944.)

Section Wilhelmshaven:
Port Protection Flotilla.
Naval AA Dets. 212, 222, 232, 272, 282; all based in the town.
Naval AA Det. 252; Heidmühle.
Three Naval Fortress Bttns.: 363, 364 and 365.

Section Cuxhaven:
Port Protection Flotilla.
Naval Art. Det. 114. Founded in September 1944.

Naval AA Det. 214.
Naval Fortress Bttns. 359 and 360.

Section Brunsbüttel:
14th Naval AA Regt. with
Naval AA Det. 224; Wilhelmsburg.
Naval AA Det. 254; Friedrichshof.
Naval AA Det. 274; Zweidorf.
Naval AA Det. 294; Near Stade.
Naval Fortress Bttn. 358.

Section Wesermünde:
Naval AA Det. 244.
Naval AA Det. 264.
Naval Fortress Bttn. 362; Nordenham.
Naval Art. Det. 122 was also allocated, but
probably not operational.

Section Heligoland:
Naval AA Det. 242.
Naval Art. Det. 122.
Naval Island Bttn. 349 was also allocated, but
probably not operational.

Section Friedrichstadt:
Naval Art. Det. 124.
Naval Fortress Bttn. 357; Tönning.

Section Sylt:
Naval AA Det. 234; Westerland.
Naval Art. Det. 134. Founded in September
1944.
Naval Island Bttns. 351, 352 and 353.

Coastal Defence, Naval Command Baltic
The Baltic was divided into three autonomous
defence zones: West Baltic, Pommern Coast and
East Baltic. Each was headed by a Coastal
Commander who was responsible for the
following forces.

Coastal Commander West Baltic:
This post was later called Commander of Sea
Defences for Schleswig-Holstein and
Mecklenburg.
Naval Art. Det. 121; Laboe. Operational from
August 1939 until April 1940.
1st Naval AA Regt. (Renamed 1st Naval AA
Brigade during May 1942.)
The following detachments were operational:
Naval AA Det. 211; Eckernförde.
Naval AA Det. 221; Kiel later also at Dehnhöft.
Naval AA Det. 231; Kiel. Moved to Brest

(France) during July 1944.
Naval AA Det. 241; Kiel.
Naval AA Det. 243; Rendsburg. Disbanded
early on in the war and later refounded.
Naval AA Det. 251; Kiel.
Naval AA Det. 261; Kiel.
Naval AA Det. 271; Kiel.
Naval AA Det. 281. Founded in March 1942.
1st Naval Motor Transport Det.
5th Naval Motor Transport Det. Founded
during the summer of 1942.
There were also several other major naval units
in Kiel.

Coastal Commander Pommern:
The following units were based at Swinemünde,
unless otherwise stated.
3rd Naval AA Regt. with.
Naval AA Det. 233.
Naval AA Det. 711.
Naval AA Det. 713.
(The last two were founded shortly before the
end of the war.)
Light Naval Art. Det. 536; Wolin. Founded
during March 1945.
Light Naval Art. Det. 537. Founded during
January 1945.
Naval Art. Det. 123.
3rd Naval Art. Res. Det.
3rd Naval Motor Transport Detachment.
There were also several other naval units based
in Swinemünde.

Coastal Commander East Baltic:

Section Gotenhafen:
9th Naval AA Regt. (Founded during September
1942) with
Naval AA Det. 219; Gotenhafen. Founded
during February 1940.
Naval AA Det. 229; Gotenhafen and also at
Danzig (Gdansk). Later renamed Naval AA Det.
814 and moved to Denmark.
Naval AA Det. 259; Gotenhafen. Founded
during December 1942.
Naval AA Det. 818; Hela. Moved to Lorient
(France) during 1943.
Naval Art. Det. 119; Hela (Hel). Founded
during February 1940.
Naval Art. Det. 629; Gotenhafen. Founded
during January 1944.
11th Naval Art. Res. Det.; Deutsch-Eylau.

Founded during August 1942, it was renamed
Naval Art. Det. 11 during April 1944.

Section Pillau:
Naval AA Det. 215. Operational from
September 1939 until January 1940. Refounded
during February 1941.
Naval AA Det. 225. Operational from
September 1939 until January 1940. Refounded
during June 1941, it was later disbanded, then
refounded during August 1944.
Naval Art. Det. 115. Operational from the start
of the war until January 1940. Refounded
during May 1940; it was renamed Naval Art.
Det. 5 during September 1942.
Naval Art. Det. 535. Founded during July 1944.

Section Memel:
Naval AA Det. 217. Operational from
September 1939 until October 1939. Refounded
during March 1941 and then disbanded. It was
refounded again in Zevern near Bremen, from
where the Detachment moved to Memel.
Naval Art. Det. 117. Renamed 7th Naval Art.
Res. Det. and moved to Libau.

The following posts were created towards the end
of the war:

Sea Defence Zone Estland:
Naval AA Dets. 239 and 711.
Naval Art. Dets. 530 and 532.

Sea Defence Zone Baltic Islands:
Naval AA Det. 239.
Naval Art. Dets. 531 and 532.

Sea Defence Zone Lettland:
10th Naval Art. Regt. with Art. Dets. 530, 532
and 534.
Naval AA Div. 712.
9th Naval Motor Transport Det.; based mainly
in Libau.

Sea Defence Zone East Prussia:
Naval Art. Det. 533.
Naval AA Dets. 215 and 225; all based at Pillau.

Sea Defence Zone West Prussia:
Naval Art. Det. 629.
9th Naval AA Regt. with Naval AA Dets. 219,
249, 259 and 818. These were mainly based at
Gotenhafen.

Sea Defence Zone Memel:
Naval AA Dets. 217 and 218.

German Naval Bases in the Netherlands and Baltic

Ports outside Germany with:
□ Port Protection Flotilla, Port Commander
and Naval Fitting Out Base
▲ Port Protection Flotilla and Port Commander
⊕ Port Commander for the most part of the war
⊖ Port Commander for only a short period of the war

WINDAU
(VENTSPILS)

RIGA

LIBAU (LIEPAJA)

MEMEL (KLAIPEDA)

River Neman

SINGOR

OPENHAGEN

BORNHOLM

LEBA

PILLAU (BALTIYSK)
HELA (HEL)

KONIGSBERG
(KALININGRAD)

GULF OF DANZIG

SASSNITZ

GOTENHAFEN (GDYNIA)
ZOPPORT (SOPOT)
DANZIG (GDANSK)

River
Weichsel
(Wisla)

ELBING

RUGEN ISLAND

STRALSUND

KOLBERG (KOLOBRZEG)

SWINEMUNDE
(SWINOUJSCIE)   WOLIN

DEUTSCH EYLAU (ILAWA)

WAREN

STETTIN (SZCZECIN)

FLATAW (ZLOTOW)
DEUTSCHE KRONE (WALCZ)

NEUSTRELITZ

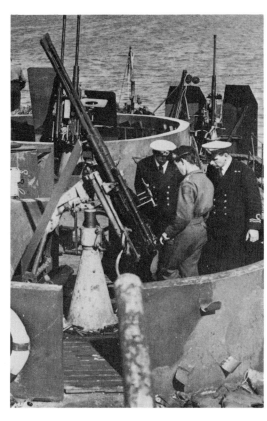

Above: An artillery barge especially fitted out as an anti-aircraft battery being examined by British personnel after the war. 88mm and 105mm guns were also fitted to these barges. The guns appear to be 20mm twins, with a single on the far right. The deck armour appears to be metal, but concrete was sometimes put underneath. (Photo: Author's Collection)
Right: Naval coastal artillery in action—for the benefit of the photographer; the men would usually be wearing more practical clothing than what looks like their best uniforms. (Photo: Bundesarchiv, Koblenz)

NAVAL COMMAND POSTS OUTSIDE GERMANY

Denmark

Naval Anti-Aircraft Detachments (Marineflak-abteilung):
The following list gives the location and command section of each detachment.

204. Esbjerg (South Jutland). Moved from Sylt in April 1940.
716. Frederikshavn (North Jutland). Founded in November 1944.
717. Århus (South Jutland). Founded in October 1944.
814. Hansted (North Jutland). Moved from Gotenhafen, where it was known as Detachment 229.

Naval Artillery Detachments (Marineartillerie-abteilung)
The following list gives the location and command section of each detachment.

118. Hansted (North Jutland). Founded in 1941.
508. Copenhagen (South Jutland). Founded during April 1940 as Artillery Detachment Seeland and renamed in July 1940.
509. Frederikshavn and Lökken (North Jutland). Founded in May 1940 by renaming Detachment 309.
518. Fanö (South Jutland). Founded in September 1944.
522. Copenhagen (Danish Islands). Founded in October 1944.
523. Grenå (South Jutland). Founded in October 1944.
524. Århus (South Jutland). Founded in January 1945 when Detachment 523 was split.
525. Fünen (Danish Islands). Founded in January 1945.
814. Hansted (North Jutland). Moved from Gotenhafen, where it was known as Detachment 229.

Naval Artillery Arsenals
Copenhagen: Established during June 1940.
Thisted: Established during September 1941.

Right: Minesweepers on their way from Wilhelmshaven to Heligoland shortly after the end of the war. The gun on the bows is a quadruple 20mm anti-aircraft gun.

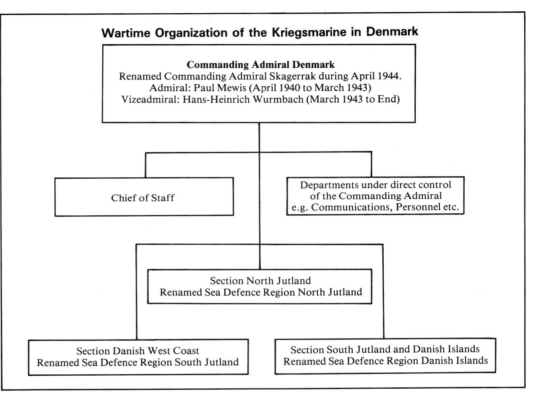

Wartime Organization of the Kriegsmarine in Denmark

Commanding Admiral Denmark
Renamed Commanding Admiral Skagerrak during April 1944.
Admiral: Paul Mewis (April 1940 to March 1943)
Vizeadmiral: Hans-Heinrich Wurmbach (March 1943 to End)

Chief of Staff

Departments under direct control of the Commanding Admiral e.g. Communications, Personnel etc.

Section North Jutland
Renamed Sea Defence Region North Jutland

Section Danish West Coast
Renamed Sea Defence Region South Jutland

Section South Jutland and Danish Islands
Renamed Sea Defence Region Danish Islands

Norway

Naval Artillery Detachments (Marineartillerie-abteilung):
The following list gives the location of each detachment.
501. Horten. Founded in March 1940.
502. Kristiansand Süd.
503. Near Stavanger. Founded in April 1940.
504. Near Horten. Founded in Bergen, April 1940.
505. Molde. Founded in June 1940.
506. Trondheim. Founded in May 1940.
507. Husöen. Founded in August 1940.
510. Bodo. Founded in August 1940.
511. Harstad. Founded in Narvik, July 1940.
512. Tromso. Operational for one year from October 1940.
513. Vardö. Founded in September 1940.
514. Lofoten. Founded in Narvik, March 1942.
516. Lodingen.

Naval AA Detachments (Marineflakabteilung):
The following list gives the location of each detachment.
701. Trondheim. Founded in June 1941.
702. Trondheim. Founded in June 1940.
706. Narvik. Founded in June 1941.
709. Harstad. Founded in November 1941.
710. Narvik. Founded in Gotenhafen during October 1941, the detachment moved to Narvik in January 1942 and later, in April 1943, to Altenfjord. The anti-aircraft cruiser *Nymphe* was operated by this unit. (She was the ex-Norwegian ship *Tordenskjold*, launched in 1897.)
714. Kristiansand Süd. Founded in November 1944.
715. Trondheim. Founded in February 1945.
801. Bergen. Founded in June 1940 as Detachment 301, it was renamed during the same month.
802. Bergen. Founded in June 1940, this unit amalgamated with Detachment 801 during January 1944.
822. Bergen. Founded in November 1944.

Wartime Organization of the Kriegsmarine in Norway

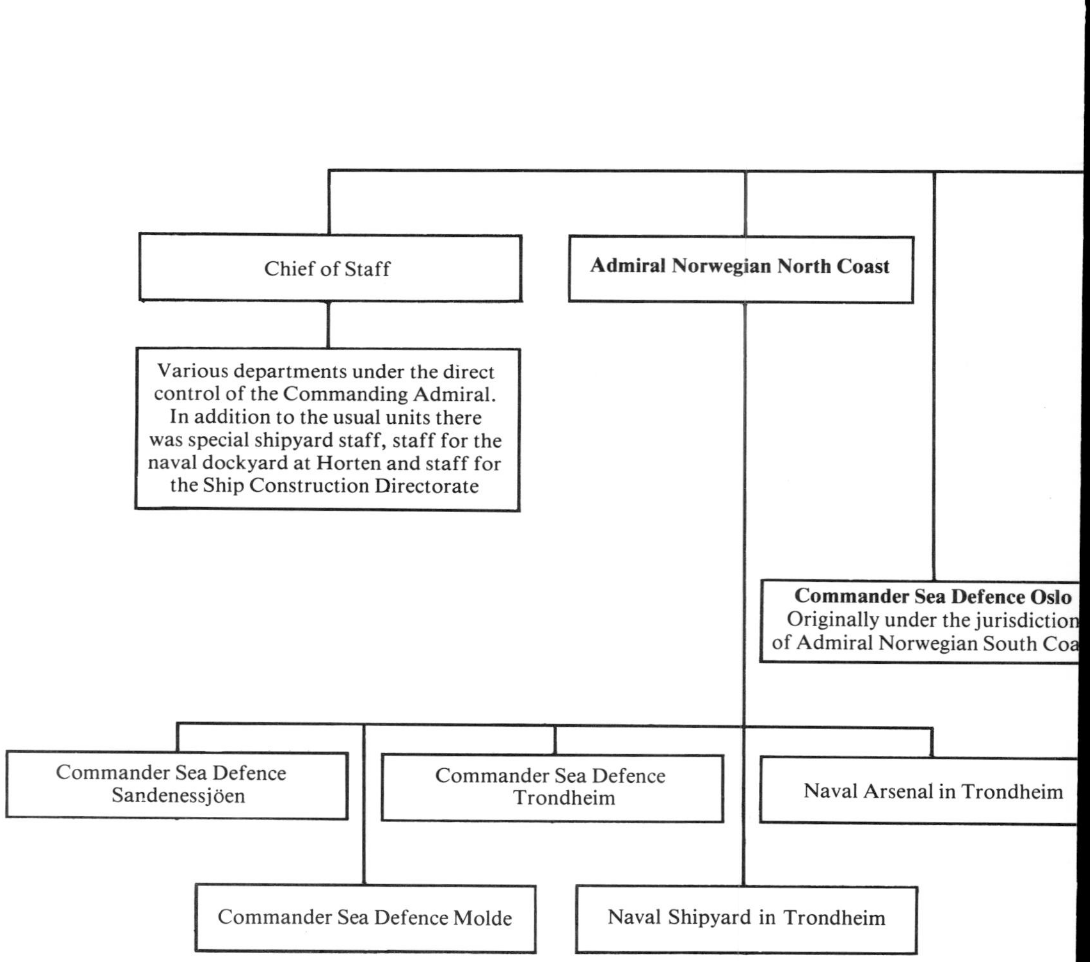

Chief of Staff

Admiral Norwegian North Coast

Various departments under the direct control of the Commanding Admiral. In addition to the usual units there was special shipyard staff, staff for the naval dockyard at Horten and staff for the Ship Construction Directorate

Commander Sea Defence Oslo
Originally under the jurisdiction of Admiral Norwegian South Coast

Commander Sea Defence Sandenessjöen

Commander Sea Defence Trondheim

Naval Arsenal in Trondheim

Commander Sea Defence Molde

Naval Shipyard in Trondheim

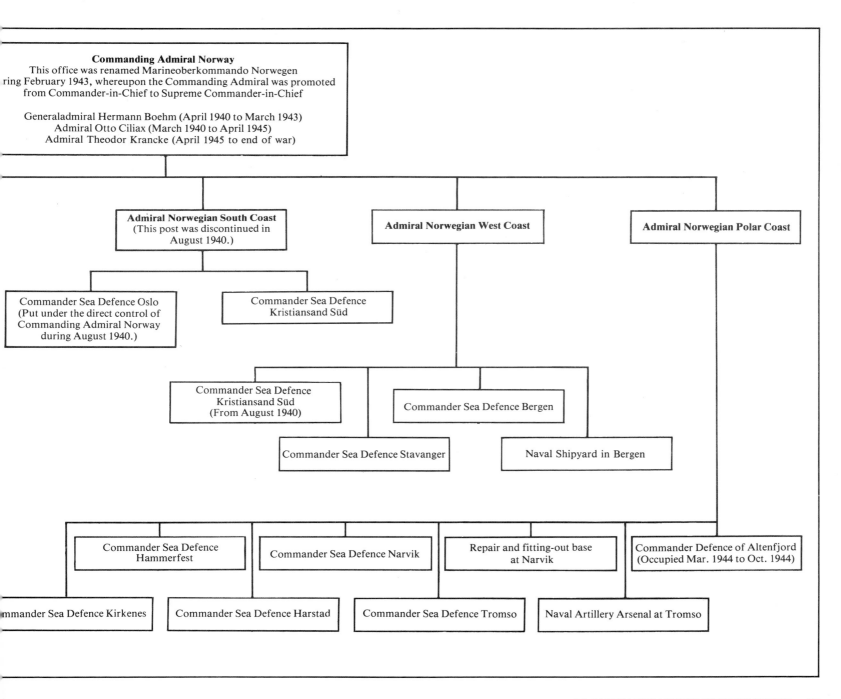

Commanding Admiral Norway
This office was renamed Marineoberkommando Norwegen
[du]ring February 1943, whereupon the Commanding Admiral was promoted
from Commander-in-Chief to Supreme Commander-in-Chief

Generaladmiral Hermann Boehm (April 1940 to March 1943)
Admiral Otto Ciliax (March 1940 to April 1945)
Admiral Theodor Krancke (April 1945 to end of war)

Admiral Norwegian South Coast
(This post was discontinued in
August 1940.)

Admiral Norwegian West Coast

Admiral Norwegian Polar Coast

Commander Sea Defence Oslo
(Put under the direct control of
Commanding Admiral Norway
during August 1940.)

Commander Sea Defence
Kristiansand Süd

Commander Sea Defence
Kristiansand Süd
(From August 1940)

Commander Sea Defence Bergen

Commander Sea Defence Stavanger

Naval Shipyard in Bergen

Commander Sea Defence
Hammerfest

Commander Sea Defence Narvik

Repair and fitting-out base
at Narvik

Commander Defence of Altenfjord
(Occupied Mar. 1944 to Oct. 1944)

[Co]mmander Sea Defence Kirkenes

Commander Sea Defence Harstad

Commander Sea Defence Tromso

Naval Artillery Arsenal at Tromso

Left: The battleship *Tirpitz*, the Lonely Queen of the North, lying behind anti-submarine nets in Altenfjord. (Photo: Imperial War Museum)

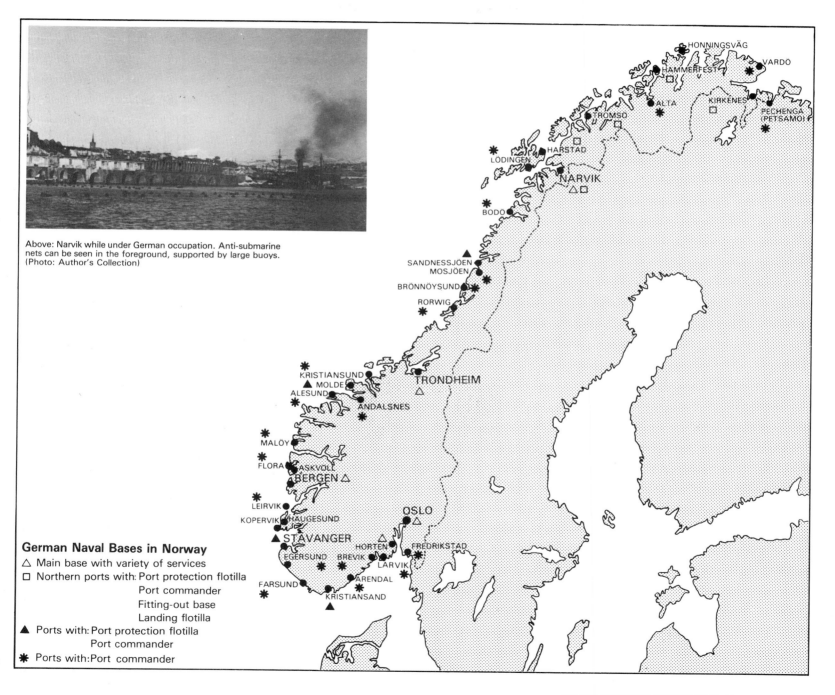

Above: Narvik while under German occupation. Anti-submarine nets can be seen in the foreground, supported by large buoys. (Photo: Author's Collection)

HONNINGSVÄG

VARDÖ

HAMMERFEST

ALTA

KIRKENES

PECHENGA (PETSAMO)

TROMSÖ

HARSTAD

LÖDINGEN

NARVIK

BODO

SANDNESSJÖEN

MOSJÖEN

BRÖNNÖYSUND

RORWIG

KRISTIANSUND

MOLDE

TRONDHEIM

ALESUND

ANDALSNES

MALÖY

FLORA ASKVOLL

BERGEN

LEIRVIK

KOPERVIK HAUGESUND

OSLO

STAVANGER

HORTEN

FREDRIKSTAD

EGERSUND

BREVIK

LARVIK

FARSUND

ARENDAL

KRISTIANSAND

German Naval Bases in Norway

△ Main base with variety of services

☐ Northern ports with: Port protection flotilla
　　　　　　　　　　　Port commander
　　　　　　　　　　　Fitting-out base
　　　　　　　　　　　Landing flotilla

▲ Ports with: Port protection flotilla
　　　　　　　　Port commander

✳ Ports with: Port commander

Below: Naval anti-aircraft gunners in action in France, probably Lorient, during 1942. The gun is a 37mm, similar to those installed on ships. The man standing on the left would slot the magazines into the gun; the man in the foreground is operating a Zeiss optical rangefinder. (Photo: Bundesarchiv, Koblenz)

Netherlands

Naval Artillery Detachments (Marineartillerie-abteilung):
The following list gives the location of each detachment.

201. Den Helder and, later, Wijk aan Zee.
202. Vlissingen (Flushing) and, later, Domburg.
203. Ijmuiden.
204. Ostende.
205. Hook of Holland.
206. Blankenberge.
607. Den Helder.

Naval AA Detachments (Marineflakabteilung):
The following list gives the location of each detachment.

246. Harlingen.
703. Vlissingen (Flushing).
808. Den Helder.
810. Vlissingen (Flushing).
813. Hook of Holland.
816. Ijmuiden.

Small Floating Units
Small flotillas in Holland came under the command of the Flag Officer for Motor-Boat Divisions (Führer der Motorbootsverbände, or F.d.Mot.), whose office was founded during January 1941 and disbanded again in March 1945. The Flag Officer's headquarters were first in Den Haag and later in Dordrecht. The following flotillas were operational.

Port Protection Flotilla North Holland. Founded, June 1941. At first based in Ijmuiden, the flotilla moved to Den Helder.

Port Protection Flotilla South Holland. Founded during June 1940 as Port Protection Flotilla Holland. It was later renamed. Main bases were at Vlissingen and the Hook of Holland.

River Clearing Flotilla. Founded during December 1940. The boats were passed on to the Rhine Flotilla when this command was disbanded in March 1945.

Rhine Flotilla. Founded in January 1940.

Danube Flotilla. Moved to Holland during January 1941 and returned to the Danube during April of that year.

Maas Flotilla. Founded during April 1941. When the unit was finally disbanded its boats were passed on to the Rhine Flotilla.

Waal Ferry Flotilla. Founded in autumn 1944, it was mainly used as an army support unit.

Boom Defence Flotilla North Sea Holland. (Netzsperrflottille). Main headquarters probably in Utrecht.

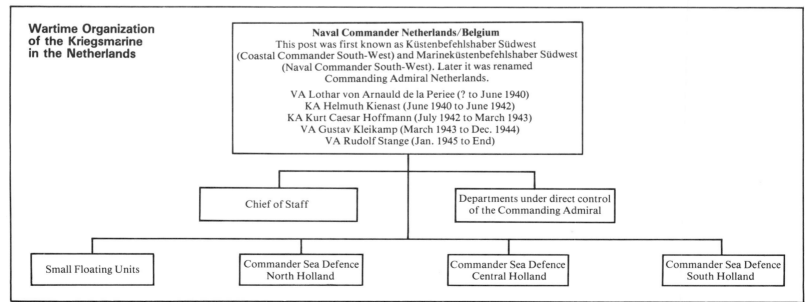

Wartime Organization of the Kriegsmarine in the Netherlands

Naval Commander Netherlands/Belgium
This post was first known as Küstenbefehlshaber Südwest (Coastal Commander South-West) and Marineküstenbefehlshaber Südwest (Naval Commander South-West). Later it was renamed Commanding Admiral Netherlands.

VA Lothar von Arnauld de la Periee (? to June 1940)
KA Helmuth Kienast (June 1940 to June 1942)
KA Kurt Caesar Hoffmann (July 1942 to March 1943)
VA Gustav Kleikamp (March 1943 to Dec. 1944)
VA Rudolf Stange (Jan. 1945 to End)

- Chief of Staff
- Departments under direct control of the Commanding Admiral

- Small Floating Units
- Commander Sea Defence North Holland
- Commander Sea Defence Central Holland
- Commander Sea Defence South Holland

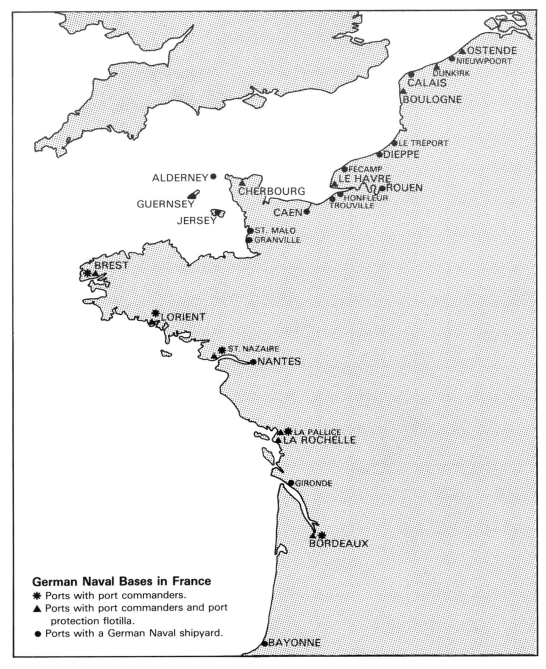

German Naval Bases in France

✳ Ports with port commanders.
▲ Ports with port commanders and port protection flotilla.
● Ports with a German Naval shipyard.

France

The German naval network in France was vast and its organization somewhat complicated. Details can be found in Volume II of *Die deutsche Kriegsmarine, 1939-1945,* by W. Lohmann and H. H. Hildebrand.

Naval Artillery Detachments (Marineartillerie-abteilung):
The following list gives the location of each detachment.

204. Ostende.
240. Wimeraux.
242. (?).
244. Calais.
260. Cherbourg.
262. Brest.
264. Lorient.
266. Le Havre.
280. Lorient and St. Nazaire.
282. Vendée.
284. Rouen.
286. Bayonne.
610. Sète.
611. Marseilles.
612. Toulon.
618. Gironde.
682. Toulon.
683. (?).
684. Noirmoutier.
685. (?).
686. (?).
687. Ile d'Oléron.
688. Probably Toulon.
812. Ile d'Oléron.
819. Toulon.

Naval AA Detachments (Marineflakabteilung):
703. St. Nazaire.
704. Lorient.
705. St. Nazaire.
803. Brest.
804. Brest.
805. Brest.
806. Lorient.
807. Lorient.
809. Nantes.
817. Lorient.
818. Lorient.
819. St. Nazaire.
820. St. Nazaire.

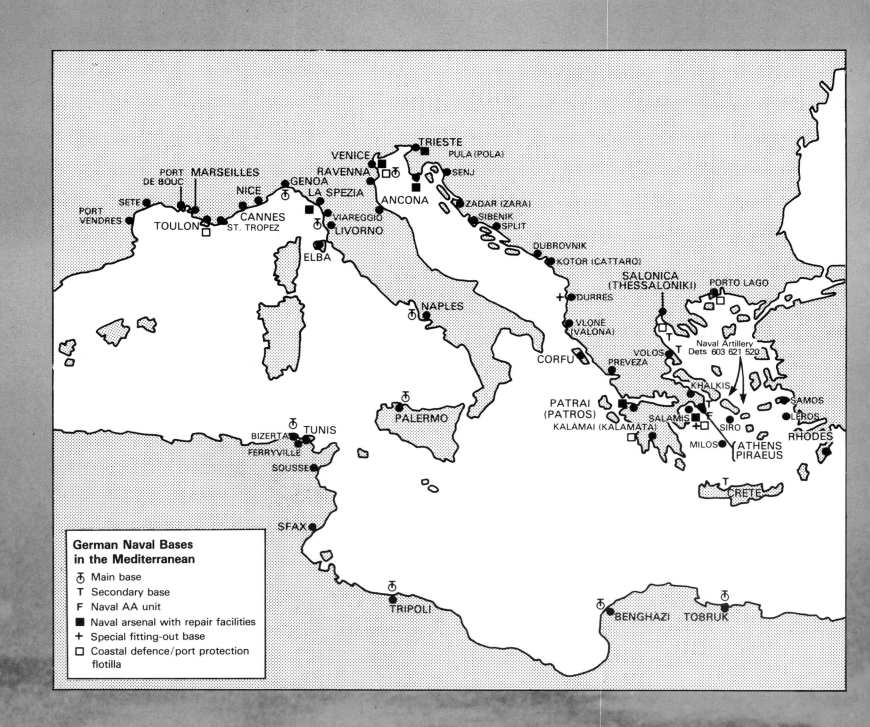

TRIESTE
PULA (POLA)
VENICE
RAVENNA
PORT MARSEILLES
DE BOUC
SENJ
GENOA
NICE LA SPEZIA
SETE ANCONA
PORT VENDRES TOULON CANNES VIAREGGIO ZADAR (ZARA)
ST. TROPEZ LIVORNO SIBENIK
SPLIT
ELBA
DUBROVNIK
KOTOR (CATTARO)
SALONICA
(THESSALONIKI) PORTO LAGO
NAPLES DURRES
VLONE
(VALONA)
CORFU VOLOS
PREVEZA
Naval Artillery
Dets 603 621 520
KHALKIS
PALERMO SAMOS
PATRAI LEROS
(PATROS) SALAMIS SIRO
KALAMAI (KALAMATA)
TUNIS MILOS ATHENS RHODES
BIZERTA PIRAEUS
FERRYVILLE
SOUSSE
CRETE

SFAX

**German Naval Bases
in the Mediterranean**

⚓ Main base
T Secondary base
F Naval AA unit
■ Naval arsenal with repair facilities
+ Special fitting-out base
□ Coastal defence/port protection
  flotilla

TRIPOLI
BENGHAZI TOBRUK

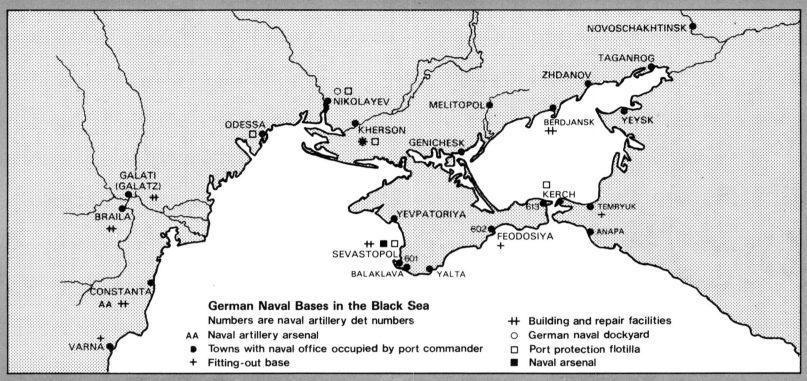

Below: One of the early motor torpedo-boats following in the wake of another at speed. Some of these boats managed to do just under 40 knots, which is 46 mph or 74 kmph. (Photo: Bundesarchiv, Koblenz)

German Naval Bases in the Black Sea
Numbers are naval artillery det numbers

AA   Naval artillery arsenal

⬤   Towns with naval office occupied by port commander

+   Fitting-out base

╫   Building and repair facilities

○   German naval dockyard

☐   Port protection flotilla

■   Naval arsenal

Operation 'Weserübung': The German Invasion of Norway and Denmark 9 April 1940

Group 1 Kpt.z.S. and Kommodore Friedrich Bonte
Z2 KK Max-Eckart Wolff
Z9 FK Gottfried Pönitz
Z11 KK Kurt Rechel
Z12 KK Karl Smidt
Z13 KK Alfred Schulze-Hinrichs
Z17 KK Erich Holtorf
Z18 KK Herbert Friedrichs
Z19 KK Friedrich Kothe
Z21 KK Hans Erdmenger (Group Commander's flagship)
Z22 KK Friedrich Böhme
Group 1 loaded Army troops in Wesermünde and then sailed to the Schillig Roads, off Wilhelmshaven, to join Group 2 and their escorts.

Group 2 Kpt.z.S. Hellmuth Heye
Admiral Hipper KS Hellmuth Heye
Z5 KK Hans Zimmer
Z6 KK Gerhardt Böhmig
Z8 KK Georg Langheld
Z16 KK Alfred Schemmel
Group 2 left Cuxhaven and sailed to the Schillig Roads to join Group 1 and their escorts.

Escorts for Group 1 and 2:
Gneisenau Kpt.z.S. Harald Netzbandt
Scharnhorst Kpt.z.S. Kurt Caesar Hoffmann

Group 3 Konteradm. Hubert Schmundt
A: 1st Motor Torpedo-Boat Flotilla KL Heinz Birnbacher
S19, S21, S22, S23, S24.
B: Karl Peters (tender) KL Otto Hinzke
Wolf (torpedo-boat) OL Broder Peters
Leopard (torpedo-boat) KL Hans Trummer
C: Königsberg (cruiser) KS Heinrich Rufus
Köln (cruiser) KS Ernst Kratzenberg
Bremse (artillery training ship) FK Jak Förschner

Group 4 Kpt.z.S. Friedrich Rieve
A: Karlsruhe (cruiser) KS Friedrich Rieve
Seeadler (torpedo-boat) KL Franz Kohlauf
Luchs (torpedo-boat) KL Karl Kassbaum
2nd Motor Torpedo-Boat Flotilla KK Rudolf Petersen
S7, S8, S17, S30, S31, S32, S33.
Tsingtau (tender) KS Karl Klinger
B: Greif (torpedo-boat) KL Wilhelm Freiherr von Lyncker

Group 5 Konteradm. Oskar Kummetz
Kpt.z.S. August Thiele (after sinking of Blücher)
E: Lützow (heavy cruiser) KS August Thiele
F: Blücher (heavy cruiser) KS Heinrich Woldag
Emden (light cruiser) KS Werner Lange
Möwe (torpedo-boat) KL Helmut Neuss
Kondor (torpedo-boat) KL Hans Wilcke
Albatros (torpedo-boat) KL Siegfried Strelow
1st Motor Minesweeper Flotilla KL Gustav Forstmann
R17, R18, R19, R20, R21, R22, R23, R24.

Group 6 Korvkpt. Kurt Thoma
M2, M9, M13.

Group 7 Kpt.z.S. Gustav Kleikamp
Schleswig-Holstein (battleship) KS Gustav Kleikamp
Claus von Bevern
Nautilus (experimental craft)
Pelikan
Six armed fishing boats FK Oskar Dannenberg M.D.
Two transport freighters

Group 8 Korvkpt. Wilhelm Schroeder
Hansestadt Danzig (minelayer) KK Wilhelm Schroeder
Stettin (icebreaker)

Group 9 Kpt.z.S. Helmuth Leissner
Otto Braun (ex-M129)
Arkona (ex-M115) (experimental craft)
M157
V102
V103
R6
R7
U-J 107
Monsun
Passat (naval tugs)
Rugard (freighter) (Group Commander's flagship)

Group 10 Kpt.z.S. and Kommodore Friedrich von Kamptz
2nd Motor Minesweeper Flotilla KK Gerhard Ruge
R25, R26, R27, R28, R29, R30, R31, R32.
Königin Luise (ex-F6)
M4, M20, M84, M102, M1201, M1202, M1203, M1204, M1205, M1206, M1207, M1208.

Group 11 Kpt.z.S. Walter Berger
M89, M110, M111, M134, M136, M61, R33, R34, R35, R36, R37, R38, R39, R40.
Von der Groeben (depot ship)

Mines laid during the night of 8/9 April by the following minelayers:
Roland KK Karl Kutzleben
Königin Luise KL Kurt Foerster
Cobra KK Karl Brill
Preussen KK Karl Freiherr von Recke
M6, M10, M11, M12

U-boat Group 1
U25 KK Victor Schütze
U46 KL Herbert Sohler
U51 KL Dietrich Knorr
U64 KL Wilhelm Schulz
U65 KL Hans-Gerrit von Stockhausen

U-boat Group 2
U30 KL Fritz-Julius Lemp
U34 KL Wilhelm Rollmann

U-boat Group 3
U9 OL Wolfgang Lüth
U14 OL Herbert Wohlfahrt
U56 OL Otto Harms
U60 KL Peter Schewe
U62 OL Hans Michalowski

U-boat Group 4
U1 KL Jürgen Deecke
U4 OL Hans-Peter Hinsch

U-boat Group 5
U37 KK Werner Hartmann
U38 KL Heinrich Liebe
U47 KL Günther Prien
U48 KL Herbert Schultze
U49 KL Curt von Gossler
U50 KL Max Bauer
U52 KL Otto Salmann
U21 KL Wolf Stiebler Ran aground on 27.3.40 and interned in Kristiansand Süd.

U-boat Group 6
U13 OL Max Schulte
U57 KL Claus Korth
U58 KL Herbert Kuppisch
U59 KL Harald Jürst

U-boat Group 8
U2 KL Helmuth Rosenbaum
U3 KL Gerd Schreiber
U5 KL Wilhelm Lehmann-Willenbrock
U6 OL Adalbert Schnee

U-boat Group 9
U7 OL Günther Reeder
U10 KL Joachim Preuss
U19 KL Joachim Schepke

Not attached to a group:
U17 KL Udo Behrens
U23 KL Heinz Beduhn
U24 KL Udo Heilmann
U61 OL Jürgen Oesten

U-boat Transporters
U26 KK Heinz Scheringer (?)
U29 KL Otto Schuhart
U32 OL Hans Jenisch
U43 KL Wilhelm Ambrosius
U101 KL Fritz Frauenheim
UA KL Hans Cohausz

Support and Transport Ships to Narvik area
F Alster
F Bärenfels
F Ravenfels
T Kattegat
T Jan Wellem

Support and Transport Ships to Trondheim area
F Levante
F Main
F Moonsund
F Sao Paolo

Support and Transport Ships to Bergen area
T Belt
F Curityba
F Marie Leonhardt
F Rio de Janeiro

Support and Transport Ships to Stavanger-Egersund area
T Dollart
F Mendoza
F Roda
F Tijuca
F Tübingen

Support and Transport Ships to Kristiansand-Arendal area
F August Leonhardt
F Kreta
F Westsee
F Wiegand

Support and Transport Ships to Oslo area
T Euroland
T Senator
F Antares
F Espana
F Friedenau
F Hamm
F Hanau
F Ionia
F Itauri
F Kellerwald
F Muansa
F Neidenfels
F Rosario
F Scharhörn
F Tucuman
F Wandsbek
F Wolfram

NARVIK

Below: Naval infantry wearing the field grey uniform during a display at an 'open day' some time before the start of the war. (Photo: Author's Collection)

Below: Tugs in the port of Hamburg. (Photo: Imperial War Museum)

Bottom of page: Barges, like this one, were purpose-built from 1941 onwards. They were originally intended as landing craft, and the plans were later modified to enable several different designs to be constructed. This one was obviously a transport ferry. They also saw service as minelayers, auxiliary minesweepers, tankers and later carried anti-aircraft guns or even heavier artillery. The barges may look clumsy, but they were most successful and were employed in almost every coastal water where the German armed forces were fighting. (Photo: Bundesarchiv, Koblenz)

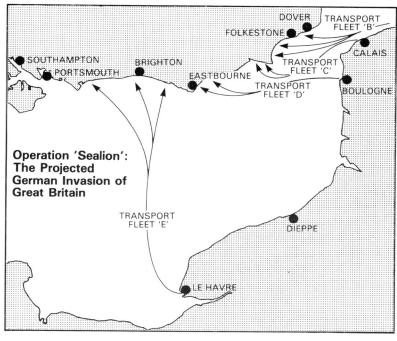

Operation 'Sealion': The Projected German Invasion of Great Britain

KEY TO TRANSPORT FLEETS FOR OPERATION 'SEALION'

Transport Fleet 'B'
Commander: Vizeadm. Hermann von Fischel
Departure base: Dunkirk
  3rd Minesweeper Flotilla
  11th Motor Minesweeper Flotilla
  3rd Coastal Defence Flotilla
  75 barges
Departure base: Ostende
  3rd Motor Minesweeper Flotilla
  2nd Coastal Defence Flotilla
  25 barges
Departure base: Ostende
  16th Minesweeper Flotilla
  8 steamers
  15 barges
  15 motor-boats
Departure base: Rotterdam
  4th Minesweeper Flotilla
  50 steamers
  100 barges

Transport Fleet 'C'
Commander: Kpt.z.S. Gustav Kleikamp
Departure base: Calais
  1st Minesweeper Flotilla
  32nd Minesweeper Flotilla
  4th Motor Minesweeper Flotilla
  7th Coastal Defence Flotilla
  100 barges
Departure base: Antwerp

  15th Minesweeper Flotilla
  50-60 steamers
  Approximately 100 barges
  14 motor-boats.

Transport Fleet 'D'
Commander: Kpt.z.S. Werner Lindenau
Departure base: Boulogne
  2nd Minesweeper Flotilla
  18th Minesweeper Flotilla
  2nd Motor Minesweeper Flotilla
  15th, 16th and 18th Coastal Defence Flotillas
  160 barges, to be towed four abreast in rows

Transport Fleet 'E'
Commander: Kpt.z.S. Ernst Scheurlen
Convoy 4
Commander: Kpt.z.S. Ulrich Brocksien
Departure base: Le Havre
  12th Minesweeper Flotilla
  25 steamers
  50 barges
  25 tugs
Convoy 5
Commander: Kpt.z.S. Ulrich Brocksien
Departure base: Le Havre
  14th Minesweeper Flotilla
  25 steamers
  50 barges
Additional Forces
  1st Motor Minesweeper Flotilla
  4th, 13th and 20th Coastal Defence Flotillas
  200 motor-boats
  100 sailing boats with engines.

The German Fleet: Organization

The Fleet was divided as follows.

1. Flottenstreitkräfte	The High Seas Fleet
Schlachtschiffe und Kreuzer	Battleships and cruisers
Zerstörer	Destroyers
Torpedoboote	Torpedo-boats
Schnellboote (S-Boote)	Motor torpedo-boats, MTBs, E-boats
Hilfskreuzer	Auxiliary cruisers, etc
Flottentrossschiffe	Fleet supply ships
Schulschiffe	Fleet training ships

2. Sicherungsstreitkräfte	Security Forces
Flottillen:	Flotillas:
Minensuchboote	Minesweepers
Räumboote	Motor minesweepers
Sperrbrecher	Auxiliary minesweepers
Vorpostenboote	Patrol boats, Coastal defence boats
Sicherungsboote	Picket boats, Coastal defence boats
Unterseebootsjäger	Submarine-hunters
Geleitboote	Escorts
Hafenschutzboote	Port protection boats, Harbour defence boats
Küstenschutzboote	Coastal defence boats

3. Unterseeboote (Uboote)	Submarines (U-boats)

In the English language, the word 'U-boat' is used specifically when referring to a German submarine, whereas in German it embraces all submarines, whatever their country of origin. Originally spelt either 'U-Boot' or 'U-boot', the recognized German spelling is now 'Uboot'.

THE HIGH SEAS FLEET (Flottenstreitkräfte)

The Fleet Command

The Fleet Commanders were as follows.
Adm. Hermann Boehm: Nov. 1938 to Oct. 1939.
Adm. Wilhelm Marschall: Oct. 1939 to July 1940.
Adm. Günther Lütjens: July 1940 to May 1941; Lütjens and his entire staff went down with the battleship *Bismarck* on 27 May 1941.
Genadm. Otto Schniewind: June 1941 to July 1944.
Vizeadm. Wilhelm Meendsen-Bohlken: July 1944 to end of war.
The office of 'Chief of the High Seas Fleet' was discontinued shortly after the First World War, and the few remaining ships were placed under the control of naval commanders within the Baltic

and North Sea Naval Stations. A Supreme Commander-in-Chief of Seagoing Forces (Oberbefehlshaber der Seestreitkräfte) was appointed during 1923. Two years later, this rather long-winded title was condensed to Flottenchef (Fleet Commander).

Gneisenau was succeeded as flagship by *Bismarck* until her sinking, when it was planned to use her sister-ship *Tirpitz*. However, although she did fly the Fleet Commander's flag for a brief period, it was not long before a combination of circumstances made it impracticable. Her replacement was the tender *Hela*, which was used in this capacity for most of the remaining war years.

Before the Second World War, battleships and heavy cruisers came under the direct control of the Supreme Naval Command until summer 1939, when the Naval Group Commands were given operational control. At this time, light cruisers were commanded by the Commander-in-Chief Reconnaissance Forces (Befehlshaber der Aufklärungsstreitkräfte, or B.d.A.), who was also responsible for destroyers, torpedo-boats and minesweepers. But this arrangement only lasted until the autumn of 1939, when further changes were implemented. The post of Commander-in-Chief Cruisers (Befehlshaber der Kreuzer, or B.d.K.) was created, and all cruisers were placed under his command. Disbanded again during October 1941, the position was renamed Admiral Northern Seas (Admiral Nordmeer). Destroyers and minesweepers were also given their own commands.

The post of Commander-in-Chief Battleships (Befehlshaber der Schlachtschiffe, or B.d.S.) was not created until June 1941, after the sinking of *Bismarck*, and the first to hold this office was Vizeadmiral Otto Ciliax. Later, during May 1942, he was made Commander-in-Chief Naval Forces in Norway, and his old job was taken over by Vizeadmiral Oskar Kummetz, who was given the new title Commander-in-Chief Cruisers (Befehlshaber der Kreuzer, or B.d.K.). The designation was later changed again by replacing the word 'Kreuzer' with 'Kampfgruppe' (Task Force), but the initials 'B.d.K.' remained the same. (This Command was also known as 1st Task Force and North Norway Naval Squadron.) Kummetz was absent for some periods, at which times Erich Bey held command. In February 1944, both men were replaced by Kpt.z.S. Rolf Johannesson, and Konteradmiral Rudolf Peters was commander of the Task Force from June 1944 until the post was disbanded in October 1944.

Table 5: Operational Dates for Major German Warships

Name:	Built:	Commissioned:	End of Operational life:
Battleships:			
Bismarck	Hamburg	24 Aug. 1940	27 May 1941
Gneisenau	Kiel	21 May 1938	26 Feb. 1942
Scharnhorst	Wilhelmshaven	7 Jan. 1939	26 Dec. 1943
Tirpitz	Wilhelmshaven	25 Feb. 1941	12 Nov. 1944
Pocket Battleships:			
Admiral Graf Spee	Wilhelmshaven	6 Jan. 1936	17 Dec. 1939
Admiral Hipper	Hamburg	29 April 1939	3 May 1945
Admiral Scheer	Wilhelmshaven	12 Nov. 1934	10 April 1945
Heavy Cruisers:			
Blücher	Kiel	20 Sept. 1939	9 April 1940
Deutschland	Kiel	1 April 1933	4 May 1945
Prinz Eugen	Kiel	1 Aug. 1940	Summer 1946
Light Cruisers:			
Emden	Wilhelmshaven	15 Oct. 1925	26 April 1945
Karlsruhe	Kiel	6 Nov. 1929	9 April 1940
Köln	Wilhelmshaven	15 Jan. 1930	31 March 1945
Königsberg	Wilhelmshaven	17 April 1929	10 April 1940
Leipzig	Wilhelmshaven	8 Oct. 1931	16 Dec. 1946
Nürnberg	Kiel	2 Nov. 1935	6 Jan. 1946*
Training Ships (Old Battleships):			
Schlesien	Danzig	5 May 1908	4 May 1945
Schleswig-Holstein	Kiel	6 July 1908	20 Dec. 1944

Warships not commissioned in the Kriegsmarine:
Graf Zeppelin aircraft carrier.
Lützow heavy cruiser; sold to Russia.
Seydlitz heavy cruiser; see p. 23.

*Renamed *Admiral Makarov* and commissioned in the Russian Navy.

Destroyers

The post of Führer der Zerstörer or F.d.Z. (Flag Officer/Commander for Destroyers) was held by the following officers.

Kommodore Friedrich Bonte: Nov. 1939 to April 1940.
Kpt.z.S. Alfred Schemmel: April 1940 to May 1940.
Konteradm. Erich Bey: May 1940 to Dec. 1943.
Kpt.z.S. Max-Eckart Wolff: Dec. 1943 to Feb. 1944.
Vizeadm. Leo Kreisch: Feb. 1944 to End.

Before the war, destroyers came under the jurisdiction of the Flag Officer for Torpedo-Boats, whose immediate superior was Commander-in-Chief Reconnaissance Forces. By September 1939, there were some twenty separate and completely autonomous destroyer groups. However, this state of affairs did not last long, for in November 1939 there was a drastic reorganization. Destroyers were formed into flotillas of six boats and given their own Flag Officer, who was responsible to the Fleet Commander. Many destroyers did not operate under his direct command because they were partly at the disposal of various task force commanders. There were major changes in the destroyer arm after the heavy losses incurred in the Norwegian Campaign of April 1940 (for details, see below).

Some destroyers were better known by an official traditional name, instead of their number. These names and their corresponding numbers are shown below.

Z1 Leberecht Maass.
Z2 Georg Thiele.
Z3 Max Schultz.
Z4 Richard Beitzen.
Z5 Paul Jacobi.
Z6 Theodor Riedel.
Z7 Hermann Schoemann.
Z8 Bruno Heinemann.
Z9 Wolfgang Zenker.
Z10 Hans Lody.
Z11 Bernd von Arnim.
Z12 Erich Giese.
Z13 Erich Koellner.
Z14 Friedrich Ihn.
Z15 Erich Steinbrinck.
Z16 Friedrich Eckoldt.
Z17 Diether von Roeder
Z18 Hans Lüdemann.
Z19 Hermann Kühne.
Z20 Karl Galster.
Z21 Wilhelm Heidkamp.
Z22 Anton Schmitt.

Destroyer Flotillas

1st Destroyer Flotilla: Founded during the autumn of 1938 with the amalgamation of the 1st and 3rd Destroyer Divisions, this unit was disbanded in April 1940. The remaining boats were passed on to the 5th Flotilla.
Commanders: KS Wilhelm Meisel (Oct. 1938 to Oct. 1939); FK Fritz Berger (Oct. 1939 to end).
Ships: *Z2, Z3, Z4, Z14, Z15, Z16.*

2nd Destroyer Flotilla: Founded during the autumn of 1938 when the 2nd Destroyer Division was renamed, the unit was disbanded in May 1940. The remaining ships went to the 6th Flotilla.
Commanders: KS Friedrich Bonte (Oct. 1938 to Oct. 1939); KK Rudolf von Pufendorf (Oct. 1939 to end).
Ships: *Z1, Z5, Z6, Z7, Z8.*

3rd Destroyer Flotilla: This unit was founded in December 1939 by renaming the 5th Destroyer Division. It was disbanded four months later. The only remaining destroyer (*Z20*) was passed on to the 6th Flotilla.
Commander: FK Hans-Joachim Gadow (Dec. 39 to end).
Ships: *Z17, Z18, Z19, Z20, Z22.*

4th Destroyer Flotilla: The unit was founded during April 1939 by amalgamating the 6th and 8th Destroyer Divisions. It was disbanded again in April 1940, and its only remaining destroyer (*Z10*) was passed on to the 6th Flotilla. The 4th was refounded in October 1942.
Commanders: FK Erich Bey (until April 1940); KK Georg Langheld (Oct. 1942 to April 1943); KS Rolf Johannesson (April 1943 to Dec. 1944); KS Hubert Freiherr von Wangenheim (Dec. 1944 to end of war).
Ships: (until 1940) *Z9, Z10, Z11, Z12, Z13*; (after 1942) *Z31, Z32, Z33, Z34, Z37, Z38, Z39.*

5th Destroyer Flotilla: This unit was founded during May 1940 with boats from the 1st Flotilla.
Commanders: FK Alfred Schemmel (May 1940 to Aug. 1940); KS Fritz Berger (Aug. 1940 to July 1942); KS Alfred Schemmel (July 1942 to Dec. 1942); KS Max-Eckart Wolff (Feb. 1943 to

Below: Like their predecessors, the newer torpedo-boats launched from 1926 onwards resembled small destroyers. *Möwe* is next to the quay and *Kondor* is moored alongside; *Falke* and possibly *Greif* are astern of them. (Photo: Druppel)

Feb. 1944); KS Theodor Freiherr von Mauchenheim genannt[1] Bechtolsheim (Feb. 1944 to April 1944); KS Georg Langheld (April 1944 to end of war).

Ships: *Z4, Z14, Z15, Z16, ZH1.*

6th Destroyer Flotilla: The unit was founded during May 1940 with destroyers from the 2nd, 3rd and 4th Flotillas.

Commanders: KS Erich Bey[2] (May 1940 to Nov. 1940); KS Alfred Schulze (Nov. 1940 to April 1943); KS Friedrich Kothe (April 1943 to Dec. 1944); KS Heinz Peters (Jan. 1944(?) to end of war).

Ships: *Z5, Z6, Z7, Z8, Z10, Z20, Z35, Z36, Z43.*

7th Destroyer Flotilla: Probably not operational.

8th Destroyer Flotilla: Also known as Flotilla Narvik, the unit was founded during December 1940. It was disbanded during August 1944, and refounded in November 1944.

Commanders: KS Gottfried Pönitz (Dec. 1940 to March 1943); KS Hans Erdmenger (March 1943

1 'Known as'.
2 He was also Flag Officer for the destroyer arm at that time.

to Dec. 1943); FK Georg Langheld (Jan. 1944 to April 1944); KS Theodor Freiherr von Mauchenheim genannt Bechtolsheim (April 1944 to June 1944); FK Georg Ritter und edler Herr von Berger (June 1944 to Aug. 1944); KS Heinrich Gerlach (Nov. 1944 to end of war).

Ships: *Z23, Z24, Z25, Z26, Z27, Z28, Z29, Z30.*

Torpedo-boats

In German parlance, a torpedo-boat is a ship roughly resembling a small destroyer, but the main armament of which is torpedoes. (The very small, fast, motor torpedo-boats, called Schnellboote, are dealt with in the next section.)

Until the autumn of 1939, when an administrative change altered things, the Flag Officer for Torpedo-Boats had also been responsible for destroyers and motor torpedo-boats. When the office was finally disbanded in April 1942, the remaining torpedo-boats were placed under the control of the Flag Officer for Destroyers. At the same time, a new post of Flag Officer for Motor Torpedo-Boats (Führer der Schnellboote, or

F.d.S.) was created. However, the Flag Officer for Torpedo-Boats was only partly responsible for their operational control, because—as with destroyers—many boats were at the disposal of various task force commanders.

The post of Führer der Torpedoboote, or F.d.T. (Flag Officer for Torpedo-Boats) was held by the following officers.

Konteradm. Günther Lütjens: Oct. 1937 to Oct. 1939.

Kpt.z.S. Friedrich Bonte: Oct. 1939 to Nov. 1939.

Kpt.z.S. Hans Bütow: Nov. 1939 to April 1942.

Torpedo-Boat Flotillas

1st Torpedo-Boat Flotilla: Operational from October 1939 until August 1941.

T1, T2, T3, T4, T9, T10.

2nd Torpedo-Boat Flotilla: Founded October 1939.

T5, T6, T7, T8, T11, T12.

From August 1941 also: *T2, T3, T4, T9, T10.*

T1 joined the flotilla during late 1942.

3rd Torpedo-Boat Flotilla: Founded in April 1941.

T13, T14, T15, T16, T17, T18, T19, T20, T21.
4th Torpedo-Boat Flotilla: Operational from February 1943 until April 1944.
T22, T24, T25, T26, T27.
T28 and *T29* were later transferred from the 6th Flotilla.
T24 and *T25* joined the 5th Flotilla during April 1944.
5th Torpedo-Boat Flotilla: *T34, T35, T36, T22, T23, T24, T25, T28, T29 Albatros, Falke, Greif, Iltis, Jaguar, Kondor, Seeadler, Tiger.*
6th Torpedo-Boat Flotilla: Disbanded in February 1941.
Iltis, Jaguar, Leopard, Luchs, Seeadler, Wolf.
Refounded during November 1943 and operational until August 1944.
T28, T29, T30, T31, T32, T33.
7th Torpedo-Boat Flotilla: Operational from June 1940 until December 1940.
Leopard, Löwe, Panther, Tiger.
8th Torpedo-Boat Flotilla: Not operational.
9th Torpedo-Boat Flotilla: Operational from September 1943 until October 1944.

TA14,* TA15, TA16, TA17, TA18, TA19.
Refounded during February 1945.
TA40, TA41, TA42, TA43, TA44, TA45.
10th Torpedo-Boat Flotilla: Founded during January 1944.
TA23, TA24, TA27, TA28, TA29, TA30, TA31, TA32, TA33.

Motor Torpedo-Boats (Schnellboote)

The post of Flag Officer for MTBs (Führer der Schnellboote or F.d.S.) was created during April 1942, when the office of Flag Officer for Torpedo-Boats was discontinued. The new position was held by Kpt.z.S. and Kommodore Rudolf Petersen throughout the remaining war years.

The 1st MTB Division was founded in July 1943 to operate in the Mediterranean with 3rd, 7th, 21st, 22nd and 24th flotillas. Motor torpedo-boats in other areas were not formed into divisions and they operated as autonomous flotillas. The following flotillas were operational:

* 'TA' denoted that the boat had been acquired from a foreign navy.

1st, 2nd, 3rd, 4th, 5th, 6th, 7th, 8th, 9th, 10th, 11th, 21st, 22nd, 24th.

MTB Escort Ships:
Adolf Lüderitz (June 1940 to end).
Buea (May 1944 to end).
Carl Peters (Jan. 1940 to end).
Gustav Nachtigal (May and June 1944).
Hermann von Wissmann (Dec. 1943 to end).
Romania (March 1942 to Oct. 1943).
Tanga (Jan. 1939 to end).
Tsingtau (Sept. 1934 to end).

Auxiliary Cruisers

Auxiliary cruisers were originally known as Handelsschutzkreuzer or HSK (Trade Protection Cruisers). Later, they were called Hilfskreuzer or HK (Auxiliary Cruiser). During the war the initials HSK were also taken to mean Handelsstörkreuzer (Cruiser for Harassing Merchant Ships). These ships were first identified by using numbers from 1 to 8, prefixed by the letters HSK. Later, they were given a two-digit

administration number, which was prefixed by the word Schiff (ship). They were also given a traditional name, usually by their first commanders: *HSK2*, Schiff 16, for example, was also known as *Atlantis*. The British Admiralty chose to identify the German auxiliary cruisers by allotting a letter to each. The following list gives the names and commanders of each ship, plus its name before conversion to auxiliary cruiser and its name after its career as such.

Atlantis (*HSK2*, Schiff 16, Raider C): KS Bernhard Rogge (Dec. 1939 to Nov. 1941). Before the war it was the merchant ship *Goldenfels*.

Coronel (HSK —, Schiff 14, Raider K): FK Rudolf Betzendahl (to April 1942); KS Ernst Thienemann (April 1942 to Feb. 1943); KK Rudolf Lück (Sept. 1943 to end). Ex-*Togo*; later became merchant ship *Svalbard*.

Hansa (HSK —, Schiff 5, Raider —): KS Hans Henigst (April 1943 to Aug. 1943); KS Fritz Schwoerer (Feb. 1944 to end). Ex-*Meersburg*, ex-*Glengarry*; later became merchant ship *Empire Humber*, then *Glengarry* again.

Komet (*HSK7*, Schiff 45, Raider B): KA Robert Eyssen (Dec. 1939 to Feb. 1942); KS Ulrich Brocksien (Feb. 1942 to Oct. 1942). Ex-*Ems*.

Kormoran (*HSK8*, Schiff 41, Raider G): FK Theodor Detmers (June 1940 to Nov. 1941). Ex-*Steiermark*.

Michel (*HSK9*, Schiff 28, Raider H): KS Hellmuth von Ruckteschell (Sept. 1941 to March 1943); KS Günther Gumprich (May 1943 to Oct. 1943). Ex-*Bielsko*.

Orion (*HSK1*, Schiff 36, Raider A): FK Kurt Weyher (Dec. 1939 to Sept. 1941); KK Gerhard Meyer (Oct. 1942 to Oct. 1944); KK Wilhelm Kiesewetter (to Dec. 1944); KS Joachim Asmus (Dec. 1944 to May 1945). Ex-*Kurmark*; became artillery training ship *Hektor* in January 1944.

Pinguin (*HSK5*, Schiff 33, Raider F): KS Ernst-Felix Krüder (Sept. 1939 to May 1941). Ex-*Kandelfels*.

Stier (*HSK6*, Schiff 23, Raider J): KS Horst Gerlach (April 1940 to Sept. 1942). Ex-*Cairo*.

Thor (*HSK4*, Schiff 10, Raider E): KS Otto Kähler (March 1940 to July 1941); KS Günther Gumprich (to Nov. 1942). Ex-*Santa Cruz*.

Widder (*HSK3*, Schiff 21, Raider D): KK Hellmuth von Ruckteschell (May 1940 to Nov. 1940). Ex-*Neumark*; later became merchant ship *Ulysses*, then *Fechenheim*.

Naval Supply Ships

The ships listed below were built as naval supply ships, and they were used for that purpose between the dates indicated. During the war, more than a hundred other ships were also employed as supply vessels.

Dithmarschen (July 1938 to end of war). Used after the war under the names *Southmark* (GB) and *Conecuh* (USA).

Ermland (Aug. 1940 to Aug. 1944).

Nordmark (Dec. 1938 to end of war). Earlier known as *Westerwald*; after the war became HMS *Bulawayo*.

Uckermark (Nov. 1938 to Nov. 1942). Earlier known as *Altmark*.

Franken (March 1943 to April 1945).

SECURITY FORCES (Sicherungs-streitkräfte)

After the First World War, all security duties at sea came under the control of the Flag Officer for Minesweepers. During the 1930s, there was a tendency to divide these activities into two groups, which resulted in the overall administration being taken over by the 2nd Admirals of the Baltic and North Sea Naval Stations. But, at the start of the Second World War, the Flag Officer for Mine-sweepers, Kpt.z.S. Friedrich Ruge, was back holding the reins again. At that time, only a war against Poland was envisaged, so Ruge moved into the Baltic with his flagship (*T196*). A similar post—filled by Konteradmiral Hans Stohwasser—was then created in the North Sea region.

During the war, coasts under German control were put under the jurisdiction of eleven different Security Divisions (Sicherungsdivision), with the exception of Norway, which had a security force called Küstensicherungsverband (Coastal Security Unit).

Minesweeper Flotillas (Minensuchflottillen)

The numbers of the boats were prefixed by the letter 'M' meaning Minensuchboot (Mine-sweeper). Flotilla numbers 33, 35, 37, 39, 41, 43, 45, 47-51, 53, 55 and 57-69 were never operational.

1st Minesweeper Flotilla: Operational from 1924 until the summer of 1946.
M1, M3, M4, M5, M7, M8, M14, M15, M17, M18, M20, M36, M37, M132, M155, M203, M204, M255, M256.

2nd Minesweeper Flotilla: Operational from 1936 until the summer of 1944.
M2, M6, M9, M10, M11, M12, M13, M21, M25, M38, M152, M153, M156.
The flotilla was refounded during February 1945, and was kept operational until November 1947:
M606, M607, M608, M611, M805, M806.

3rd Minesweeper Flotilla: Operational from April 1940 until summer 1945.
M15, M16, M17, M18, M19, M22, M29, M30, M151 and Flakjäger 25 and 26.

4th Minesweeper Flotilla: Operational from the start of the war until spring 1945.
M61, M89, M136, M510, M511, M534, M582, M584.
Later also:
M1, M2, M36, M81, M101, M132, M151, M203, M204, M255.

5th Minesweeper Flotilla: Operational from late 1940 until October 1947.
M4, M23, M31, M35, M81, M154, M201, M202, M205, M251, M252, M253.

6th Minesweeper Flotilla: Operational from the start of the war until January 1942.
M4, M23, M31, M35, M81, M154, M201, M202, M205, M251, M252, M253.
Refounded during May 1942, and kept operational until August 1944:
M38, M39, M82, M83, M102, M135, M155, M156, M206, M256, M265, M267.

7th Minesweeper Flotilla: Operational from the start of the war until March 1940.
M75, M84, M102, M122, M126 and *Oxhöft* and *Westerplatte*.
The 7th Flotilla was refounded in September 1942, and kept operational until November 1947:
M23, M32, M33, M82, M102, M103, M104, M201, F4, F5, F7.

8th Minesweeper Flotilla: Operational from early 1941 until 1945.
M24, M26, M27, M28, M32, M34, M152, M254, M256, M265, M277, M292, M329, M370.

9th Minesweeper Flotilla: Operational between March 1943 and summer 1947.
M272, M273, M274, M276, M306, M326, M346, M348, M364, M365.

10th Minesweeper Flotilla: Operational from April 1943 until September 1944.
M263, M264, M275, M307, M347, M366, M367, M385, M408, M428, M438.

11th Minesweeper Flotilla: Operational with

Below: Minesweeper *M18* in Norway. Minesweepers were frequently used for a variety of other duties and, on the whole, these small ships saw much more action than the larger units. (Photo: Author's Collection)

twelve large fishing boats from the start of the war until August 1942. The flotilla was refounded during August 1943, and remained operational until February 1945 with:
M291, M327, M329, M348, M368, M386, M264, M307, M347.

12th Minesweeper Flotilla: Operational with about eight fishing boats from the start of the war until late 1942. The flotilla was later refounded, and remained operational until November 1947 with:
M601, M602, M603, M604, M605, M612, M801, M803, M804.

13th Minesweeper Flotilla: Operational with about eight fishing boats from the start of the war until December 1942.

14th Minesweeper Flotilla: Operational from the start of the war until August 1941. The flotilla was composed of converted drifters.

15th Minesweeper Flotilla: Operational with about eight fishing boats from the start of the war until early 1943.

16th Minesweeper Flotilla: Operational with several fishing boats from October 1939 until January 1943.

17th Minesweeper Flotilla: Operational with several fishing boats from September 1939 until November 1942.

18th Minesweeper Flotilla: Operational with several fishing boats from September 1939 until November 1942.

19th Minesweeper Flotilla: Operational with several fishing boats from September 1939 until October 1943.

20th Minesweeper Flotilla: Founded during May 1945 to clear mines from the Baltic. It was not operational during the war.

21st Minesweeper Flotilla: Operational from January 1942 until shortly before the end of the war.
M261, M305, M323, M324, M327, M341, M342, M343, M362, M383, M526, M545.

22nd Minesweeper Flotilla: Operational from September 1941 until early 1948.
M301, M302, M303, M321, M322, M361, M368, M381, M382, M436.

23rd Minesweeper Flotilla: Operational from August 1942 until 1947.
M324, M401, M411, M421, M423, M441, M443, M467, M468.

24th Minesweeper Flotilla: Operational from November 1942 until the end of the war.

M343, M402, M412, M422, M432, M442, M452, M475, M483.

25th Minesweeper Flotilla: Operational from December 1942 until the end of 1947.
M278, M294, M295, M328, M330, M341, M342, M403, M413, M423, M433, M443, M451, M453, M459, M460.

26th Minesweeper Flotilla: Operational from January 1943 until August 1944.
M404, M424, M434, M444, M454, M476, M486, M495.

27th Minesweeper Flotilla: Operational from January 1943 until 1946.
M261, M323, M327, M329, M369, M405, M414, M425, M434, M455, M461, M469, M484.

28th Minesweeper Flotilla: Operational from December 1942 until August 1944.
M262, M271, M304, M325, M344, M345, M363, M384, M463.

29th Minesweeper Flotilla: Operational from October 1943 until June 1945.
M265, M267, M293, M301, M386, M403, M406, M415, M426, M436, M445, M455, M462, M470.

30th Minesweeper Flotilla: Operational until shortly after the end of the war.
M266, M291, M348, M407, M416, M427, M437, M446, M456, M489, M496.

31st Minesweeper Flotilla: Operational with several Dutch fishing boats and some German R-boats from September 1940 until the end of 1947.

32nd Minesweeper Flotilla: Operational from June 1940 until shortly after the end of the war. This flotilla was equipped with Dutch fishing boats and a few German R-boats.

34th Minesweeper Flotilla: Founded during the summer of 1940; the flotilla comprised several Dutch fishing boats.

36th Minesweeper Flotilla: Operational from July 1940 until after the end of the war. It mainly comprised captured fishing boats.

38th Minesweeper Flotilla: Operational from summer 1940 until after the end of the war. This flotilla mainly comprised captured fishing boats.

40th Minesweeper Flotilla: Operational from June 1940 until the autumn of 1944. It was made up mainly of French fishing boats. Possibly refounded during 1945.

42nd Minesweeper Flotilla: Operational from July 1940 until autumn of 1944. It mainly comprised French fishing boats.

44th Minesweeper Flotilla: Operational with several French fishing boats from November 1940 until autumn 1944.

46th Minesweeper Flotilla: Operational with a variety of fishing vessels from December 1941 until after the end of the war.

52nd Minesweeper Flotilla: Operational in Norwegian waters from early 1941 until October 1944. M1, M2, M534 and several Norwegian vessels.

54th Minesweeper Flotilla: Probably first operational in early 1941 until about 1944. It was composed of Norwegian vessels.

56th Minesweeper Flotilla: Operational with several Norwegian fishing boats from June 1940 until the end of the war.

70th Minesweeper Flotilla: Operational in the Mediterranean from summer 1943. The name was changed to 13th Sicherungsflottille in October 1944.

First World War Minesweepers

Some of the First World War minesweepers were given a traditional name and most were re-numbered.

Original number:	New number:
M28 Pelikan	M528
M50 Brommy	M550
M60 Hecht	M560
M61	
M66 Störtebeker	M566
M72	M572
M75	M575
M81 Nautilus	M581
M82 Jagd	M581
M84	M584
M85	
M89	M589
M98	M598
M102	M502
M104	M504
M107 von der Groben	M507
M108 Delphin	M508
M109 Sundewall	M509
M110	M510
M111	M511
M113 Acheron	M513
M115 Arkonda	M515
M117	M517
M122	M522
M126 Alders	M526
M129 Otto Braun	M529
M130 Fuchs	M530
M132	
M133 Wacht	M533
M134 Frauenlob	M534
M135 Gazelle	M535
M136 Havel	
M138 Nettelbeck	M538
M145	M545
M146 von der Lippe	M546
M157	M557

Motor Minesweepers (Räumboote)

Flotilla numbers 18-20, 22-24 and 26-29 were never operational.

1st Flotilla: Operational in the Baltic and North Sea until early 1948.

2nd Flotilla: This flotilla operated mainly in the North Sea until August 1944 when it was disbanded. Operational again during early 1945.

3rd Flotilla: Operational first in the eastern Baltic and later in Holland. From there the flotilla moved to France. Eventually the boats were taken overland to the Black Sea, where they operated until the summer of 1944.

4th Flotilla: Operational in the North Sea at the start of the war. Some boats went as far as Holland and Belgium. In 1944 they were taken to Norway, where they continued to work until the summer of 1945.

5th Flotilla: Operational in the Baltic and Norwegian waters from August 1939 until the end of 1945.

6th Flotilla: Operational for a few months of 1941 in the Mediterranean area. Refounded during the summer of that year, from when it probably remained in commission until the spring of 1945.

7th Flotilla: Operational from October 1940 until November 1946. Based at first in Holland and later in Norway. It may also have served in Denmark.

8th Flotilla: Based in the North Sea from early 1942 it then moved westwards to France and, towards the end of the war, to Denmark. Disbanded in late 1947.

9th Flotilla: Operated mainly from Rotterdam in Dutch waters. Probably founded in 1942 and disbanded in 1947.

10th Flotilla: Operational from March 1942 until August 1944 in the North Sea region and in French waters.

11th Flotilla: Operational in the Baltic and probably Danish waters from before the war until October 1940.

12th Flotilla: Founded in Brugge (Belgium) during May 1942 and operational until early 1945. Based at first in the English Channel area and later in the Mediterranean.

13th Flotilla: Founded towards the end of 1943, its purpose was to clear mines from the German Bight. The flotilla continued to work in the North Sea and in the Baltic after the war. It was amalgamated into the Federal Armed Forces in 1957 and is still operational.

14th Flotilla: Operational from late 1943 until the summer of 1946, first in the German Bight and later in the Baltic. The flotilla worked in Danish waters and was eventually handed over to the Royal Danish Navy.

15th Flotilla: This flotilla operated in the Baltic and some of the boats went into Norwegian waters. Probably disbanded during the summer of 1945.

16th Flotilla: Based in Norway and later in Holland from October 1944 until the end of 1947.

17th Flotilla: Operational from July 1944 until the end of 1947 in the Baltic and later in Dutch waters.

21st Flotilla: Operational from the summer of 1943 until the end of 1945 in Norway and later in Russia.

25th Flotilla: Not operational during the war. The flotilla was founded during the summer of 1945 and operated until the end of that year in Danish waters.

30th Flotilla: Operational in the Black Sea for one year from summer 1943, probably with small Dutch boats.

Auxiliary Minesweepers (Sperrbrecher)

Flotilla number 7 was never operational.

1st Flotilla: Operational in the Baltic and North Sea from the start of the war until the summer of 1946.

2nd Flotilla: Founded towards the end of 1939 by amalgamating several auxiliary minesweeper groups. It was disbanded again during the summer of 1944. The flotilla operated in French waters and in the Baltic.

3rd Flotilla: Founded during late 1940 by amalgamating several groups. It then operated in the Baltic until 1946.

4th Flotilla: Operational in the English Channel from summer 1940 until summer 1943.

5th Flotilla: Founded during the autumn of 1941, it was renamed 8th Flotilla before the end of the year.

6th Flotilla: Founded during July 1941 by splitting the 2nd Auxiliary Minesweeper Flotilla. It was then operational in France until September 1941.

8th Flotilla: Founded towards the end of 1941 to operate in Dutch waters and in the North Sea.

Coastal Defence Boats

Patrol Boats (Vorpostenboote):
The following flotillas were operational during the periods indicated; numbers 5, 21-50, 52, 54, 56, 58, 60 and 62 were never operational.

1st Flotilla: Oct. 1939 to Oct. 1940.

2nd Flotilla: Sept. 1939 to Dec. 1944.

3rd Flotilla: Probably operational for most of the war.

4th Flotilla: Sept. 1939 to Sept. 1944.

6th Flotilla: From early 1944 until about the end of the war.

7th Flotilla: From about the start of the war until Sept. 1944.

8th Flotilla: Operational for most of the war.

9th Flotilla: Operational for most of the war.

10th Flotilla: Operational from the start of the war until October 1943 when it was renamed 10 Sicherungsflottille (10th Security Flotilla).

11th Flotilla: Operational for most of the war.

12th Flotilla: Operational until the end of 1947.

13th Flotilla: Operational for most of the war.

14th Flotilla: Founded during Feb. 1943.

15th Flotilla: Operational for most of the war.

16th Flotilla: Founded in summer 1940.

17th Flotilla: Founded in summer 1940.

18th Flotilla: Operational from autumn 1940.

19th Flotilla: Operational from summer 1940 until autumn 1943.

20th Flotilla: Operational from July 1940.

51st Flotilla: Operational from early 1941.

53rd Flotilla: Operational from early 1941.

55th Flotilla: Operational from early 1941.

57th Flotilla: Operational from summer 1943.

59th Flotilla: Founded in 1940, but it may not have started operations until the following year.

61st Flotilla: Operational from November 1940.

63rd Flotilla: Operational from summer 1944.

64th Flotilla: Operational from summer 1944.

65th Flotilla: Operational from May 1944.

66th Flotilla: Operational from May 1944.

67th Flotilla: Operational from July 1944.

68th Flotilla: Operational from May 1944.

Picket Boats (Sicherungsboote):
The following flotillas were operational during the periods indicated.

1st Flotilla: Founded in the Baltic during October by renaming the 'Coastal Protection Flotilla: Western Baltic'.

2nd Flotilla: Operational in the central Baltic region towards the end of the war.

3rd Flotilla: Operational in the Danzig (Gdansk) area towards the end of the war.

4th Flotilla: Operational in southern Danish waters of the Baltic towards the end of the war.

5th Flotilla: Operational in the Great Belt towards the end of the war.

6th Flotilla: Operational in French Mediterranean waters during the middle war years. Either the boats were moved to the Baltic in 1945 or the flotilla was refounded there with new boats.

7th Flotilla: Probably not operational.

8th Flotilla: Founded during October 1943 and operational in the waters around Copenhagen.

9th Flotilla: Founded during October 1943 and operational in the Kattegatt.

10th Flotilla: This flotilla was originally called 10th Patrol Boat Flotilla. It was renamed during October 1943 and operated in the Kattegatt.

11th Flotilla: Operational in the Adriatic from the end of 1943 until early 1944.

12th Flotilla: Operational in the Great Belt from early 1944 until the end of the war.

13th Flotilla: Founded in the Mediterranean during early 1944.

14th Flotilla: Founded in the eastern Baltic during the summer of 1944.

15th Flotilla: Founded during the summer of 1944 and operated in the waters around Esbjerg.

16th Flotilla: Also founded during the summer of 1944 and also operated in the waters around Esbjerg.

Submarine-Hunters (Unterseebootsjäger)

Submarine-hunters had the numbers of their boats prefixed by the letters 'UJ'. Many other boats, especially minesweepers, were also engaged in hunting submarines. The following flotillas were

Below: An R-boat has come out of Lorient in France to escort a Type IX U-boat through the coastal minefield. The photograph was taken during August 1940, and shows the war flag of the German Navy in the foreground. R-boats or Räumboote (motor minesweeping) were used for a wide variety of duties including minesweeping, minelaying and convoy escort work. (Photo: Bundesarchiv, Koblenz)

operational; numbers 4-10, 13 and 18-20 were never operational; numbers 15 and 16 probably not operational.

1st Flotilla: Operational in the Black Sea from the summer of 1943 for one year. The flotilla was later refounded in the Baltic.

2nd Flotilla: Operational in the Adriatic Sea for the last nine months of 1944.

3rd Flotilla: Founded in the Black Sea region during the summer of 1944, but only operational for a few months. Later, the flotilla was refounded in the Baltic and remained operational until the end of the war.

11th Flotilla: Operational for most of the war, at first in the Baltic and later in Norwegian waters. Some boats went far north and worked along the northern coast of Norway.

12th Flotilla: Operational for most of the war. This was either a large flotilla with boats operating in different areas or the group moved around. Boats from this flotilla worked in the North Sea, in the approaches to the Baltic, along the French Atlantic coast, in the English Channel and along the northern coast of Norway.

14th Flotilla: This flotilla was originally founded as the 13th U-boat Hunting Group, and was renamed during 1940. It was operational in France and Norway.

17th Flotilla: Operational in the Baltic and in Norwegian waters for most of the years of the war.

21st Flotilla: Operational in the Mediterranean from early 1942 until early 1944.

22nd Flotilla: Operational in the Mediterranean from the end of 1942 until shortly before the end of the war.

23rd Flotilla: Operational in the Black Sea for a few months during the summer of 1944.

Escorts (Geleitboote)

Numbers 6-29 were never operational.

1st Flotilla: Also known as the 9th Torpedo-Boat Flotilla. Operational in the Adriatic towards the end of the war.

2nd Flotilla: Founded during March 1944. It was operational in the Adriatic Sea.

3rd Flotilla: Operational in the Mediterranean during the middle war years.

4th Flotilla: Operational in the Mediterranean for a few months in 1943.

5th Flotilla: Operational in the Baltic during the last months of the war.

30th Flotilla: Operational in the Black Sea towards the end of 1943 and early 1944.

31st Flotilla: Operational in the Black Sea for part of the war.

THE U-BOAT ARM (Unterseeboote)

The U-boat arm evolved from one small operational flotilla in 1935 to what has been described as the fourth branch of the armed forces (i.e., Navy, Army, Air Force and U-boats); as a result, its administration became very intricate. The following outline concentrates on the aspects that relate directly to a study of the war in the Atlantic.

Headquarters Staff before the war

Since many of the men mentioned in this section are more famous as U-boat commanders than as staff officers, the boats they commanded have been indicated after their names. The dates show when they were appointed.

Führer der Unterseeboote or F.d.U. (Flag Officer for Submarines): Kpt.z.S. and Kommodore Karl Dönitz.*

Staff Officer for U-boats: Kpt.z.S. Hans-Georg von Friedeburg (July 1939).

Naval Staff Officers:

1st Officer: KK Eberhard Godt (*U25*) Jan. 1938.

2nd Officer: KL Hans-Gerrit von Stockhausen (*U13* and *U65*) Oct. 1938.

3rd Officer: KL Hans Cohausz (*U30* and *UA*) Jan. 1936.

Chief Engineer: FK Otto Thedsen (Served during First World War) Jan. 1936.

Medical Officer: Dr. Gerold Lübben, Oct. 1938.

The pre-war administration pattern was changed on 18 August 1939, when the Supreme Naval

*Dönitz held the office of Flotilla Commander until January 1936, when the post was upgraded to Flag Officer.

Command ordered the immediate implementation of the 'Three Front War Programme' (details of which can be found on p. 65).

Dönitz was chosen for the post of Flag Officer for Submarines with the Naval War Staff, and was made responsible for both the war in the Atlantic and any other area where U-boats played a major role. His first step was to move his headquarters to Swinemünde, for at that stage only war against Poland was on the cards. Western waters were controlled by U-boat Flag Officer West from his headquarters at Wilhelmshaven. This position was held by Korvkpt. Hans Ibbeken (*U27* and *U178*).

Even before the war had begun, it was clear to Dönitz that no great submarine battles would be fought in the Baltic. So, on 1 September he moved his headquarters to Wilhelmshaven, where he held the position of Flag Officer U-Boats for all three theatres of war. At the same time the new post of Flag Officer East was created to help complete mopping-up operations in the Baltic. Fregkpt. Oskar Schomburg held this office until 19 September 1939, when operations in the Baltic

came to a standstill and all resources were poured into the West.

Before the war, Dönitz had aimed to build a powerful and flexible submarine arm. In order to do this, he concentrated on putting flotillas in as many key positions as possible, rather than attempting to construct any system of effective fighting groups (which would have meant a few, large flotillas). Usually, he had training boats and fighting units in the same areas, and while at sea they were often controlled through the same channels. But when war broke out this entire concept was radically altered: training boats were removed from the enemy's reach, and the cumbersome flotilla structure was streamlined. The reorganization machinery ground into action in September 1939, and in the following month a temporary plan was introduced. Changes continued until Christmas, after which the established plan remained in effect until the end of the war. There were several alterations and expansions, but on the whole the administration pattern remained the same.

The U-boat arm was split into two main departments: Operations and Organization. (At that time, Dönitz was not responsible for U-boat construction, which was organized by a department under the Supreme Naval Command, called the U-bootsamt.)

The Operations Department, later called 'U-Boat Command' (U-bootsführung) was responsible for virtually all operational boats. Its commander was Eberhard Godt, who later held the title of Commander-in-Chief U-Boats (Operations) (B.d.U.-Ops). Other aspects, such as training, weapons, supplies and personnel, were dealt with by the Organization Department headed by Hans-Georg von Friedeburg. No sooner had the war begun than he was despatched into the Baltic with Dönitz's flagship, *Erwin Wassner*, to find suitably safe venues for setting up shop.

Dönitz, with the title of Flag Officer U-boats, was promoted to the rank of Rear Admiral in October 1939. At the same time, he was given the new title 'Commander-in-Chief U-boats'. Also appointed were three Flag Officers to be responsible for the important operation areas of West (for the Atlantic), Norway and Arctic. A fourth, Central, was added later. None of these Flag Officers had operational control of U-boats —only, occasionally, those that were in their immediate coastal waters—but were basically responsible for their organization. While at sea, the U-boats were usually controlled directly by the Operations Department; but, once they entered coastal waters, they came under the jurisdiction of the flotilla commander, who was responsible for 'domestic' details like replenishment and repairs.

Operations Department later called U-Boat Command (U-bootsführung)
Commander-in-Chief Operations:
KA Eberhard Godt, Oct. 1939 to end of war.
1st Staff Officers:
KL Victor Oehrn (*U14* and *U37*) Oct. 1939 to May 1940.
KK Werner Hartmann (*U26, U37* and *U198*) May 1940 to Nov. 1940.
KK Victor Oehrn Nov. 1940 to Nov. 1941.
FK Günther Hessler (*U107*) Nov. 1941 to end.
KL Adalbert Schnee (*U6, U60, U201, U2511*) Nov. 1942 to July 1944.
KL Heinrich Schroeteler (*U667, U1023*) July 1944 to Dec. 1944.

KK Ernst Hechler (*U870*) April 1944 to end of war.

2nd Staff Officers:

KK Hans-Günther Looff (*U9, U122*) Oct. 1939 to April 1940.

KL Karl Daublebsky von Eichain (*U13*) April 1940 to Feb. 1943.

KL Peter Cremer (*U152, U333, U2519*) Feb. 1943 to April 1943.

KK Alfred Hoschatt (*U378*) April 1943 to end of war.

3rd Staff Officers:

KL Herbert Kuppisch (*U58, U94, U516, U849*) Sept. 1941 to June 1942.

KL Johann Mohr (*U124*) June 1942 to end of war.

4th Staff Officers:

KL Hans-Gerrit von Stockhausen (*U13, U65*) Oct. 1939 to Nov. 1939.

KK Hans Meckel (*U3, U19*) Nov. 1939 to June 1944.

KL Hermann Rasch (*U106*) June 1944 to Oct. 1944.

KK Waldemar Mehl (*U62, U72, U371*) Oct. 1944 to end of war.

5th Staff Officer:

KL Werner Winter (*U22, U103*) until June 1941.

6th Staff Officers:

KL Herbert Kuppisch (*U58, U94, U516, U849*) June 1942 to Dec. 1942.

KK Herbert Schultze (*U2, U48*) Dec. 1942 to March 1944.

KK Hans Witt (*U161, U129, U3524*) March 1944 to Sept. 1944.

KL Kurt Leide (*U415*) Sept. 1944 to end of war.

Engineering Officers:

KL (Ing.) Hans Looschen.

KK (Ing.) Karl Scheel.

KL (Ing.) Gerd Suhren.

KL (Ing.) Karl-Heinz Wiebe.

There were also several other posts, such as legal advisers and medical officers.

Organization Department

Commander-in-Chief Organization: Hans-Georg von Friedeburg.

Chiefs of Staff:

FK Heinz Beucke (*U173*) to May 1943.

KA Ernst Kratzenberg June 1943 to just before end of war.

KS Kurt Dobratz (*U1232*) During last few months of war.

Weapons Unit:

Torpedoes*

KK Klaus Ewerth (*U1, U35, U36, U26, U850*).

FK Heinrich Schuch (*U37, U38, U105, U154*).

Artillery and Navigation:

KK Hans Pauckstadt (*U193*).

KK Claus Korth (*U57, U93*).

KK Wilhelm Zahn (*U56, U69*).

KL Helmut Möhlmann (*U143, U571*).

KL Siegfried Lüdden (*U188*).

Communications Unit:

KL Kurt Grundke.

KL Wilhelm Grundmann.

Technical Division:

KA (Ing.) Otto Thedsen.

Personnel Department:

KK Harald Jeppener-Haltenhoff (*U17, U24*).

KK Wilhelm Müller-Arnecke (*U19*).

KL Wilhelm Franken (*U565*).

Administration Office:

FK Dr. Walter Bucholz.

FK Carl Wuttke.

KK Heinz Mursch.

Locations of Headquarters of Supreme Commander-in-Chief U-Boats

Before the war: Mainly in Kiel.

August 1939, for a short period: Swinemünde.

1 Sept. 1939 to Nov. 1939: Wilhelmshaven Naval Station.

Nov. 1939 to Sept. 1940: Sengwarden near Wilhelmshaven.

Sept. 1940 to Nov. 1940: Boulevard Suchet in Paris.

Nov. 1940 to March 1942: Kernevel near Lorient.

March 1942 to March 1943: Avenue Marechal in Paris.

March 1943 to Dec. 1943: Steinplatz in Berlin-Charlottenburg.

Dec. 1943 to early 1945: Staff quarters at Bernau near Berlin (code-name 'Koralle').

The Naval Command Staff was split in February 1945. Part of the staff was moved to Sengwarden near Wilhelmshaven while the other half remained

*This unit was responsible for the submarines' torpedoes and had no connection with the department of the Supreme Command, which was partly responsible for the torpedo crisis mentioned on p. 28.

at 'Koralle'. Eventually, the staff met again at Plön and from there moved to Flensburg-Mürwik.

U-Boat Flotillas

Flotilla numbers 15, 16, 17 and 28 were never operational.

1st Flotilla (Flotilla Weddigen): Kiel, later Brest.

2nd Flotilla (Flotilla Salzwedel): Wilhelmshaven, later Lorient.

3rd Flotilla (Flotilla Lohs): Kiel, later La Pallice and La Rochelle.

4th Flotilla (Training): Stettin (Baltic).

5th Flotilla (Flotilla Emsmann): Kiel.

6th Flotilla (Flotilla Hundius): Wilhelmshaven, then Danzig and later St. Nazaire.

7th Flotilla (Flotilla Wegener): Kiel, then St. Nazaire and later Norway.

8th Flotilla (Training): Königsberg and later Danzig.

9th Flotilla: Brest.

10th Flotilla: Lorient.

11th Flotilla: Bergen.

12th Flotilla: Bordeaux.

13th Flotilla: Trondheim.

14th Flotilla: Narvik.

18th Flotilla: Only operational for the first three months of 1945.

19th Flotilla (Training): Pillau and Kiel.

20th Flotilla (Training): Probably Pillau.

21st Flotilla (Training): Pillau.

22nd Flotilla (Training): Gotenhafen.

23rd Flotilla (Training): Danzig.

24th Flotilla (Training): Danzig, Memel, Trondheim and back to Memel. Later also at Gotenhafen and Eckernförde.

25th Flotilla (Training): Danzig, Trondheim, Memel, Libau, Gotenhafen and Travemünde.

26th Flotilla (Training): Pillau and later Warnemünde.

27th Flotilla (Training): Probably never operational. There was only one boat attached to this flotilla.

29th Flotilla: La Spezia, Toulon, Pola (Pula), Marseilles and Salamis.

30th Flotilla: Constanta (Black Sea).

31st Flotilla (Training): Hamburg, Wilhelmshaven and Wesermünde.

32nd Flotilla (Training): Königsberg and, towards the end of the war, Hamburg.

33rd Flotilla: Flensburg, with some boats in the Far East (Japan).

The German Fleet: Ships

BATTLESHIPS

Bismarck

Bismarck, the Fleet Commander's flagship, left Gotenhafen in East Prussia early in May 1941. Her commander, Kpt.z.S. Ernst Lindemann, had orders to break out into the Atlantic with the heavy cruiser *Prinz Eugen*. Both ships were to remain together until they had passed through the Denmark Strait—the waters between Iceland and Greenland—after which they would be free to go their separate ways. However, they were spotted by British forces and the subsequent action against HMS *Hood* and HMS *Prince of Wales* reached its height when shells from *Bismarck* pierced *Hood's* magazine, causing her to blow up and sink instantly.

The next two days saw the now famous events that led to the sinking of the *Bismarck*. Although she managed to escape from the guns of the Royal Navy, her crew thought they were still being pursued and so they radioed a report to Germany. This was her undoing, because the report was picked up by the British Navy, who then continued the hunt in earnest. *Bismarck* was located again by light aircraft from the carriers *Victorious* and *Ark Royal*. An aerial torpedo first damaged *Bismarck's* steering gear and propeller shafts, and then she came under fire from the British battleships *King George V* and *Rodney*. Damage was too severe for *Bismarck* to continue and, after expending all her ammunition, she was eventually scuttled. Sinking was accelerated by a torpedo from the cruiser HMS *Dorsetshire*.

Tirpitz

This famous battleship's most valuable contribution to the war effort was her mere existence. Although she was only used for minor tasks and never took part in any real action, her potential posed such a threat that Britain injected terrific resources into effecting her destruction. In fact, the daring attacks on *Tirpitz* are far more interesting than her few aggressive sorties. *Tirpitz* was not fitted out for action until October 1941, and she underwent trials until the end of that year. Eventually, on 16 January 1942, she left Wilhelmshaven for Norwegian waters as flagship to Vizeadmiral Otto Ciliax (Commander-in-Chief Battleships). *Tirpitz* called at Trondheim in Norway and then went north to attack merchant shipping, but she returned two months later without having achieved anything noteworthy. Afterwards, she went on a short training cruise, and the following winter returned to dock for repairs. In January 1943, *Tirpitz* returned to an earlier anchorage near Narvik and from there moved to Kaafjord, an inlet of the famous Altenfjord. She sailed to Spitzbergen, flying the flag of the Commander-in-Chief of the North Norway Naval Squadron (Admiral Oskar Kummetz) and, on 6 September 1943, took part in the bombardment of shore installations with

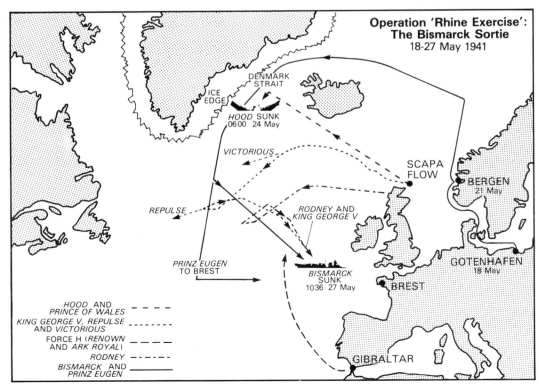

Operation 'Rhine Exercise': The Bismarck Sortie 18-27 May 1941

DENMARK STRAIT

ICE EDGE

HOOD SUNK 0600 24 May

VICTORIOUS

SCAPA FLOW

BERGEN 21 May

REPULSE

RODNEY AND *KING GEORGE V*

PRINZ EUGEN TO BREST

BISMARCK SUNK 1036 27 May

BREST

GOTENHAFEN 18 May

GIBRALTAR

HOOD AND *PRINCE OF WALES* – – – – –
KING GEORGE V, REPULSE AND *VICTORIOUS* · · · · · · ·
FORCE H (*RENOWN* AND *ARK ROYAL*) — — — —
RODNEY – · – · – ·
BISMARCK AND *PRINZ EUGEN* ————

Below: 'Cäsar' turret ('X' in British terminology) in action aboard *Tirpitz*. (Photo: Druppel)
Bottom of page: *Bismarck*. Designed between 1933 and 1936, she was launched in 1939 and commissioned after the start of the war. *Bismarck* went down in the North Atlantic with almost two thousand men; there were little more than a hundred survivors. (Photo: Author's Collection)

Scharnhorst and ten destroyers, which landed Army forces.

Tirpitz then returned to Altenfjord and was attacked by the famous British *X*-craft. This was, in fact, the second attack on *Tirpitz* by small submarines, for in October 1942 a pair of Royal Navy two-man human torpedoes ('Chariots') had been brought within striking distance, only to break away from their tow and sink. The *X*-craft attack on 22 September 1943 proved successful and caused considerable havoc: the rudder was damaged, all three propeller shafts were bent and some turbines were unseated from their mountings; cracks in the bottom caused flooding and even the rear 38cm gun turret was dislodged from its foundation. Repairs took five months, after which more trials were necessary. *Tirpitz* was just about ready for action when, on 5 April 1944, she came under attack from aircraft from the carriers *Victorious*, *Furious*, *Emperor*, *Searcher*, *Fencer* and *Pursuer*. More than a dozen bombs found

their target, killing over 100 crew and wounding a further 316. Again, the ship was put out of action for several months.

The lonely queen of the north was the target of two more air strikes in August 1944. *Tirpitz* was then given respite until mid-September, when she was attacked by RAF Lancasters. These aircraft carried special 12,000lb 'Tallboy' bombs—designed by Barnes Wallis, inventor of the bouncing bomb used by the 'Dambusters'—which put *Tirpitz* out of action completely. However, her crew went to some lengths to disguise the fact that she was not seaworthy, and routine carried on as before. Unable to move under her own steam, *Tirpitz* was towed out of Kaafjord by warships instead of tugs, to give the impression she was setting out with escorts. The deception paid off, but on 12 November RAF Lancasters launched another attack and she finally capsized at her anchorage off Haakoy Island, near Tromsö. Only about fifty of her crew were saved.

Tirpitz had been commissioned on 25 February 1941 by Kpt.z.S. Karl Topp, who left her during February 1943 to become a departmental head at

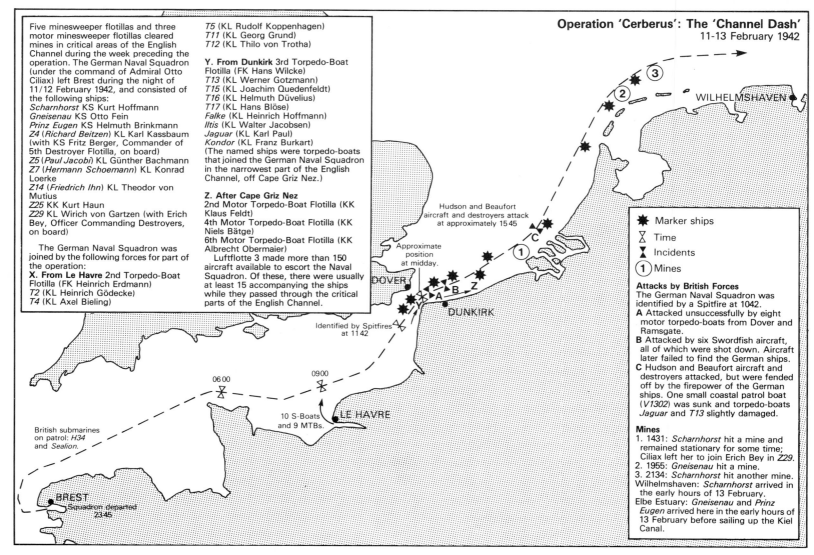

Five minesweeper flotillas and three motor minesweeper flotillas cleared mines in critical areas of the English Channel during the week preceding the operation. The German Naval Squadron (under the command of Admiral Otto Ciliax) left Brest during the night of 11/12 February 1942, and consisted of the following ships:
Scharnhorst KS Kurt Hoffmann
Gneisenau KS Otto Fein
Prinz Eugen KS Helmuth Brinkmann
Z4 (Richard Beitzen) KL Karl Kassbaum (with KS Fritz Berger, Commander of 5th Destroyer Flotilla, on board)
Z5 (Paul Jacobi) KL Günther Bachmann
Z7 (Hermann Schoemann) KL Konrad Loerke
Z14 (Friedrich Ihn) KL Theodor von Mutius
Z25 KK Kurt Haun
Z29 KL Wirich von Gartzen (with Erich Bey, Officer Commanding Destroyers, on board)

The German Naval Squadron was joined by the following forces for part of the operation:
X. From Le Havre 2nd Torpedo-Boat Flotilla (FK Heinrich Erdmann)
T2 (KL Heinrich Gödecke)
T4 (KL Axel Bieling)

T5 (KL Rudolf Koppenhagen)
T11 (KL Georg Grund)
T12 (KL Thilo von Trotha)

Y. From Dunkirk 3rd Torpedo-Boat Flotilla (FK Hans Wilcke)
T13 (KL Werner Gotzmann)
T15 (KL Joachim Quedenfeldt)
T16 (KL Helmuth Düvelius)
T17 (KL Hans Blöse)
Falke (KL Heinrich Hoffmann)
Iltis (KL Walter Jacobsen)
Jaguar (KL Karl Paul)
Kondor (KL Franz Burkart)
(The named ships were torpedo-boats that joined the German Naval Squadron in the narrowest part of the English Channel, off Cape Griz Nez.)

Z. After Cape Griz Nez
2nd Motor Torpedo-Boat Flotilla (KK Klaus Feldt)
4th Motor Torpedo-Boat Flotilla (KK Niels Bätge)
6th Motor Torpedo-Boat Flotilla (KK Albrecht Obermaier)
Luftflotte 3 made more than 150 aircraft available to escort the Naval Squadron. Of these, there were usually at least 15 accompanying the ships while they passed through the critical parts of the English Channel.

Operation 'Cerberus': The 'Channel Dash'
11-13 February 1942

WILHELMSHAVEN

Hudson and Beaufort aircraft and destroyers attack at approximately 1545

Approximate position at midday.

DOVER

DUNKIRK

Identified by Spitfires at 1142

06 00   09 00

10 S-Boats and 9 MTBs.   LE HAVRE

British submarines on patrol: *H34* and *Sealion*.

BREST
Squadron departed 23 45

★ Marker ships
✕ Time
▼ Incidents
① Mines

Attacks by British Forces
The German Naval Squadron was identified by a Spitfire at 1042.
A Attacked unsuccessfully by eight motor torpedo-boats from Dover and Ramsgate.
B Attacked by six Swordfish aircraft, all of which were shot down. Aircraft later failed to find the German ships.
C Hudson and Beaufort aircraft and destroyers attacked, but were fended off by the firepower of the German ships. One small coastal patrol boat (*V1302*) was sunk and torpedo-boats *Jaguar* and *T13* slightly damaged.

Mines
1. 1431: *Scharnhorst* hit a mine and remained stationary for some time; Ciliax left her to join Erich Bey in *Z29*.
2. 1955: *Gneisenau* hit a mine.
3. 2134: *Scharnhorst* hit another mine.
Wilhelmshaven: *Scharnhorst* arrived in the early hours of 13 February.
Elbe Estuary: *Gneisenau* and *Prinz Eugen* arrived here in the early hours of 13 February before sailing up the Kiel Canal.

the Supreme Naval Command. He was replaced as commander by Kpt.z.S. Hans Meyer who remained in office until May 1944, when he became Chief of the Operations Department at the Supreme Naval Command. Wolf Junge took his place until November 1944, when he was made Admiralty Staff Officer, and the ship's First Officer, Robert Weber, was given command.

BATTLECRUISERS

Gneisenau

In Britain, *Gneisenau* and *Scharnhorst* tend to be classified as battlecruisers, but in Germany they were referred to as battleships. *Gneisenau* was originally the flagship for the Fleet Commander, Vizeadmiral Wilhelm Marschall. During October 1939, she operated against shipping running between Britain and Scandinavia, but without any noteworthy success. Still under the command of Kpt.z.S. Erich Förste, her second cruise—in November 1939—took her into the Atlantic, south of Iceland. Her main objective was to draw Allied forces away from the pocket battleship *Admiral Graf Spee*, which was operating farther south in Atlantic waters. On 23 November *Gneisenau* attacked and sank the British auxiliary cruiser *Rawalpindi*. Afterwards, she ran into bad weather, and serious storm damage forced her to return to Kiel for repairs.

Erich Förste was promoted to Chief of Staff at the Naval Construction Yard in Wilhelmshaven, and he was replaced as *Gneisenau's* Commander by Kpt.z.S. Harald Netzbandt who took her back into the North Atlantic—again as flagship to the Fleet Commander. This time, *Gneisenau* was accompanied by *Scharnhorst* and the heavy cruiser *Admiral Hipper*. During the Norwegian Campaign she served west of the Lofoten Islands as flagship to Vizeadmiral Günther Lütjens, Commander-in-Chief Reconnaissance Forces. There, she scored two hits on HMS *Renown*, and received light damage in return.

Her next cruise, during early June 1940, took her from Wilhelmshaven into the Arctic seas off Norway, where *Gneisenau, Scharnhorst, Admiral Hipper* and several destroyers searched for an Allied convoy. Although failing to find the convoy, they did manage to sink several ships, including the aircraft carrier HMS *Glorious*.

Gneisenau returned to Trondheim, where she remained until 20 June 1940. She did not go to sea during this brief spell in port, except possibly for trials, but when she did put out, with *Admiral Hipper*, *Gneisenau* was hit by at least one torpedo from the British submarine *Clyde* and was forced to return to Trondheim for emergency repairs. Five days later she and the cruiser *Nürnberg* left for Kiel, to complete repairs in the naval dockyard. *Gneisenau* was out of action until 28 December 1940, when, under the command of Kpt.z.S. Otto Fein, she tried to break out into the Atlantic. (Her previous commander, Harald Netzbandt had been made Chief of Staff for the Fleet Command.) But, again, luck was not on *Gneisenau's* side: heavy weather forced her to return for minor repairs. Eventually, at the end of January 1941, she managed to get out into the Atlantic to operate in the waters off Iceland. From there she went to Brest, arriving on 22 March. While in port she was damaged by aerial torpedoes, thus forcing her to stay put.

Gneisenau took part in the famous 'Channel Dash', ending up in Kiel, where, on 26-27 February 1942, she was further damaged by the RAF. In April 1942, she was moved to Gotenhafen and withdrawn from active service for a large-scale refit. This idea was scrapped a year later and, at the end of the war, she was scuttled to block the harbour approaches. Her hulk was scrapped by the Russians between 1947 and 1951.

Scharnhorst

Scharnhorst was commanded by Kpt.z.S. Otto Ciliax until October 1939, when the Navy's re-organization programme promoted him to Chief of Staff at Naval Group Command West. Kpt.z.S. Kurt Caesar Hoffmann replaced him as *Scharnhorst's* commander. During that first winter, *Scharnhorst* joined *Gneisenau* and *Admiral Hipper* for several combined operations. In June 1940 she and *Gneisenau* went into action against merchant shipping. On the 8th, *Scharnhorst* received a torpedo-hit from the destroyer HMS *Acasta* and, in addition to damaged gun turrets, both the central and starboard engines were put out of action. Her commander had no alternative but to limp back to port. *Scharnhorst* tried to get back into the Atlantic with *Gneisenau* on 28 December 1940, but when *Gneisenau* was damaged by heavy seas, *Scharnhorst* accompanied her back to port. Their next attempt to break out into the Atlantic was successful and, on 8 February 1941, both ships passed through the Denmark Strait. After this cruise they both went to Brest, arriving there on 22 March. Once in port the ships were attacked by aircraft, and *Scharnhorst* was extensively damaged by several bombs.

During the famous 'Channel Dash' of 11-13 February 1942, *Scharnhorst* was flagship to Commander-in-Chief Reconnaissance Forces (Vizeadmiral Otto Ciliax). However, her old commander was out of luck: the ship ran onto two mines and remained stationary in the Channel for about thirty minutes, until her engineers managed to re-start the engines and she reached Germany under her own steam.

Scharnhorst's commander, Kurt Caesar Hoffmann, was then put at the disposal of the Naval Station Baltic and later he was made

Commanding Admiral in Holland. Meanwhile, *Scharnhorst* had been partly repaired and moved to Gotenhafen, where she was safe from the RAF. She then spent some time as a training ship under the command of Friedrich Hüffmeier. Later, during March 1943, he took her to Altenfjord in northern Norway to join *Tirpitz* and other warships for the Spitzbergen raid. *Scharnhorst* saw no further significant action for the rest of 1943. Hüffmeier was made a departmental head at the Supreme Naval Command and was replaced by Kpt.z.S. Fritz Intze, who took the ship on an operation in the Arctic seas at the end of 1943. After attempting to intercept convoy JW55B, *Scharnhorst* was engaged by several British cruisers. She managed to break away, only to run into a group of 4 destroyers, 1 battleship and 1 cruiser.

Finally, at 1945 on 26 December 1943 *Scharnhorst* went down. Many of her crew were lost in the icy cold waters of the North Atlantic, and fewer than forty survivors were picked up.

Below: *Scharnhorst* shortly after being commissioned in January 1939. She was built with a straight stem as seen here, but this was later modified to 'clipper' bows. (Photo: Bundesarchiv, Koblenz)

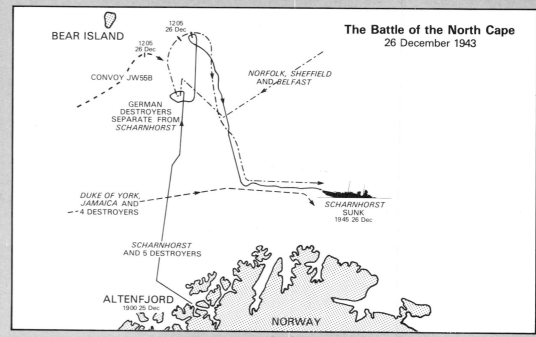

The Battle of the North Cape
26 December 1943

BEAR ISLAND

12 05 26 Dec

12 05 26 Dec

CONVOY JW55B

NORFOLK, SHEFFIELD AND BELFAST

GERMAN DESTROYERS SEPARATE FROM *SCHARNHORST*

DUKE OF YORK, JAMAICA AND 4 DESTROYERS

SCHARNHORST SUNK 1945 26 Dec

SCHARNHORST AND 5 DESTROYERS

ALTENFJORD
1900 25 Dec

NORWAY

POCKET BATTLESHIPS

Deutschland (later renamed *Lützow*)

(The name of the world's first pocket battleship was changed from *Deutschland* to *Lützow* in February 1940. Another cruiser, named *Lützow*, had been built for the German Navy, but this vessel was sold to Russia and never served with the Kriegsmarine.)

Deutschland left Germany for the North Atlantic before the start of the war, and did not return to Wilhelmshaven until late in 1939. From there she sailed up the Kiel Canal into the Baltic. *Lützow* took part in the invasion of Norway and, on 9 April 1940, she sailed through the Great Belt with the heavy cruiser *Blücher*. Both ships came under heavy fire from Norwegian forces in Oslo Fjord, where *Lützow* was seriously damaged and *Blücher* sank. The pocket battleship managed to crawl on to her destination, Oslo, and shortly afterwards headed towards Horten, where better repair facilities were anticipated. Her commander was ordered to take the ship to Kiel. A day later, on 10 April, the unescorted *Lützow* was attacked by HM Submarine *Spearfish*, whose torpedoes put paid to both propellers. She had to be towed back to Germany, where she remained for over a year undergoing repairs. It was June 1941 before she put to sea again—but not for long. Trials in Trondheim Fjord were interrupted by a single British aeroplane, which fooled the escorts into thinking it was a German aircraft and then scored a good torpedo hit. *Lützow* went back to port for further repairs and it was another year before she saw action again. But once again she was out of luck: *Lützow* ran aground, water seeped into some of her compartments, and she returned to dock for still more repairs. December 1942 found her back in Norway, first mooring in a fjord near Narvik and later taking up anchorage in Altenfjord. Later, she put out from there and saw action off Bear Island in the Battle of the Barents Sea. There was no noteworthy action after this and, eventually, in September 1943, she returned to Germany.

She sailed to Gotenhafen in October and from there on to Libau, where she underwent a complete refit. *Lützow* was then used as a training ship and did not see active operational service until the end of 1944, when she participated in the German evacuation of the eastern provinces—the largest

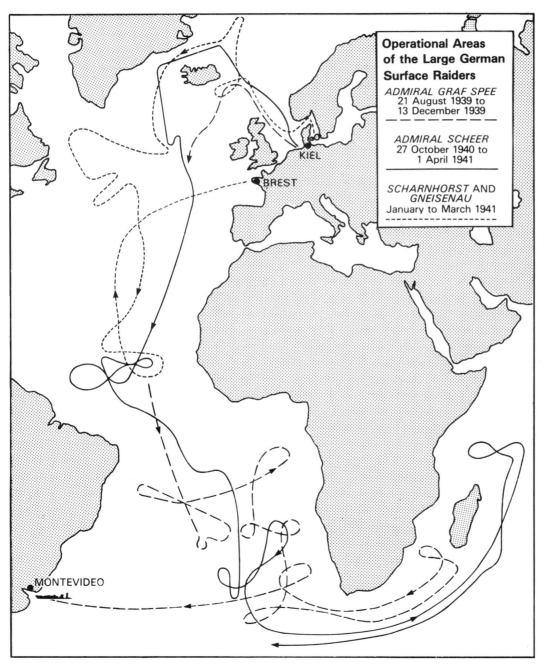

Operational Areas of the Large German Surface Raiders

ADMIRAL GRAF SPEE
21 August 1939 to
13 December 1939

ADMIRAL SCHEER
27 October 1940 to
1 April 1941

SCHARNHORST AND *GNEISENAU*
January to March 1941

KIEL

BREST

MONTEVIDEO

operation of its kind in history. After arriving at Swinemünde from Hela, on 16 April 1945, *Lützow* was hit by several bombs, and she sank on an even keel in shallow water. Most of her guns remained above the water, and some of them were used until a serious fire on 4 May 1945 put everything out of action and she was blown up by German forces. After the war, the wreck was raised by the Russians.

Deutschland/Lützow had various commanders, all of whom held the rank of 'Kapitan zur See' (Captain)—with the exception of the First Officers who temporarily commanded her, holding the rank of 'Fregattenkapitän' (Captain, junior grade). Her first wartime commander was Paul Wenneker, who left in November 1939 to spend the remaining war years as the German Naval Attaché in Japan. His successor, August Thiele, was originally meant to take command of an auxiliary raider, but these plans were scrapped and he ended up commanding *Lützow* for five months. Leo Kreisch moved command from the light cruiser *Nürnberg* to *Lützow* in March 1941, but he was absent for the last five months of that year, and the First Officer, Fregattenkapitän Bodo Knoke, took over from him. Kreisch returned during December 1941, but the following month he was made head of a training establishment in Rumania. He was succeeded by Rudolf Stange, formerly a section leader with the Supreme Naval Command. After serving on *Lützow*, Stange went back there as Chief of Staff for Naval Group Command South. Another First Officer, Horst Biesterfeld, took command from November 1943 until January 1944. He then became an admiralty staff officer, and Bodo Knoke, promoted to Kapitän zur See, returned as commander. Knoke stayed until the end, but he was absent for a short period during November 1944, when Kpt.z.S. Herhardt Böhmig held command.

Admiral Scheer

This pocket battleship first saw action in the Second World War when she shot down a British aeroplane while lying in the Schillig Roads off Wilhelmshaven. Her commander at the time was Kpt.z.S. Hans-Heinrich Wurmbach. In 1940 she was withdrawn from active service for a general refit: the solid, rather typical pocket battleship control-tower and bridge were replaced by a lighter type of mast, and she was also given a clipper bow.

After trials, she eventually broke out into the Atlantic—during October 1940—under command of Theodor Krancke and went into action against convoy HX84. During this engagement she sank the British auxiliary cruiser HMS *Jervis Bay*. Afterwards, *Admiral Scheer* refuelled from the supply ship *Nordmark* and headed south, crossing the equator on 16 December 1940. She captured the refrigerated freighter *Duquesa*, which replenished the food stores of *Admiral Scheer* plus those of the raiders *Thor* and *Pinguin* and the supply ship *Nordmark*. All these ships met up on Boxing Day 1940 to exchange Christmas greetings. *Admiral Scheer* continued on her own and managed to capture another ship—this time the Norwegian tanker *Sandefjord*, which was taken to France by a prize crew. There was another meeting with *Nordmark* and, later, with the auxiliary cruiser *Atlantis*, commanded by Bernhard Rogge. Two other captured ships, *Speybank* and *Ketty Brovig*, were also present at this gathering on the high seas, plus the blockade-breaker *Tannenfels*.

Admiral Scheer then moved off on her own to operate in the Indian Ocean, off Mozambique, where she received orders to return home. On her way back, she was sighted by a reconnaissance aircraft from the British cruiser *Glasgow*, and a massive search operation was launched to engage the German pocket battleship. *Admiral Scheer* managed to dodge through the net of six cruisers and the aircraft carrier *Hermes* and, early in March 1941, she met up with the auxiliary cruisers *Kormoran* and *Pinguin*. She also rendezvoused

with *U124*, under the command of Kptlt. Wilhelm Schulz, which had brought some vital spare parts for *Scheer's* radio. She then headed north, crossing the equator on 15 March 1941 and arriving in Bergen fifteen days later. During this successful cruise, she had sunk fourteen ships and one British auxiliary cruiser, and had captured two other ships.

After a complete overhaul, *Admiral Scheer* operated in the Baltic under the command of Kpt.z.S. Wilhelm Meendsen-Bohlken, who, towards the end of the war, was made Fleet Commander. There was no noteworthy action, and eventually the ship sailed to Trondheim, from where she continued up the coast to Narvik and joined a task force in search of convoy PQ17. She remained in the Arctic, near Bear Island, and after very little action she returned to Wilhelmshaven, passing through the Kiel Canal in November 1942.

After a refit, the ship came under the command of Fregkpt. Ernst Gruber, who had been the Communications Officer on the ill-fated *Blücher*. In February 1943, he was succeeded by Kpt.z.S. Richard Rothe-Roth, under whom *Admiral Scheer* served as a training ship in the eastern Baltic. From October 1944, when under the command of Kpt.z.S. Ernst Thienemann, she helped the Special Combat Units 'Rogge' and 'Thiele'. (These two units were created very hurriedly to help fight Russian forces in the East; they were named after their commanders, Bernhard Rogge of the legendary *Atlantis*, and August Thiele, who commanded the pocket battleship *Deutschland*,

later renamed *Lützow*, shortly after the start of the war.) Towards the end of the war, *Admiral Scheer* headed west from Pillau, laden with a thousand refugees and wounded, bound for Kiel. There she was bombed and capsized on 9/10 April 1945.

Admiral Graf Spee

This famous pocket battleship left Wilhelmshaven in August 1939, shortly before the outbreak of war. She remained in an isolated part of the South Atlantic until the end of September, when her commander, Kpt.z.S. Hans Langsdorff, was given orders to attack merchant shipping. This resulted in a relatively successful campaign, during which she sank nine merchant ships amounting to over 50,000 GRT.

The Battle of the River Plate began on 13 December, when *Graf Spee* came into contact with British cruisers. After a brief engagement, she put into the neutral south American port of Montevideo, where it was hoped some of the damage could be repaired. However, the Germans thought the town to be blockaded by superior British forces and, at 1815 on 17 December 1939, *Graf Spee* left Montevideo to be scuttled an hour later in the shallow waters of La Plata estuary. Langsdorff committed suicide and some of his crew remained in South America; only a few managed to escape back to Germany. Today, the wreck of *Admiral Graf Spee* can still be seen above the waterline, and one of her anchors lies in the town, forming a memorial to the Battle of the River Plate.

Below: *Admiral Hipper* in Kiel after the war, shortly before being towed to Heikendorfer Bay to be scrapped. She came to Kiel early in 1945 with a full load of refugees from the east. Bomb damage, as seen in this photograph, put her completely out of action. The rangefinder for her after heavy artillery control can be seen by the tripod mast; the domes visible on her starboard side are artillery control-towers with rangefinders. (Photo: Imperial War Museum)

HEAVY CRUISERS

Admiral Hipper

Admiral Hipper was undergoing a refit when war broke out. Trials lasted until the latter half of January 1940, and she was not ready for action until the end of that month.

In February 1940, *Hipper* sailed—under the command of Kpt.z.S. Hellmuth Heye—into the North Sea to operate with the battleships *Gneisenau* and *Scharnhorst*. Two months later she took part in the invasion of Norway, carrying mountain troops from Cuxhaven to Trondheim. During this voyage, *Hipper* was attacked by the destroyer HMS *Glowworm*. Both ships collided, causing *Hipper* to take on water and *Glowworm* to sink. The troops were then unloaded and the ship returned to Wilhelmshaven for repairs, after which *Admiral Hipper* operated in Norwegian, Arctic and Icelandic waters, only returning to Wilhelmshaven in autumn 1940. Heye was replaced as commander by Wilhelm Meisel, who tried to take the heavy cruiser to France via Norway and the Denmark Strait, but engine failure forced their return, and it was December before Meisel finally managed to get *Hipper* through the narrow gap between Iceland and Greenland. They finally arrived in Brest towards the end of January 1941. By the end of April, *Hipper* was back in Germany, where she remained in dock for the rest of the year.

During mid-March 1942, the ship moved to Trondheim, where she anchored next to the battleship *Tirpitz*. She remained in northern waters and, at the end of 1942, took part in the action against convoy JW51B. (It was the outcome of this operation that prompted Hitler's threat to "throw the surface fleet into the dustbin".) Kpt.z.S. Hans Hartmann replaced Meisel as commander of *Hipper* in February 1942. *Hipper* returned to Germany, accompanied by the light cruiser *Köln*, at the end of March 1943. She was decommissioned on 1 April 1943. At that time she was temporarily under the command of her First Officer, Kpt.z.S. Krauss. A year later she was recommissioned by Kpt.z.S. Hans Hengist, who had previously commanded the light cruiser *Emden*. However, *Hipper* was not fully operational and was only used for training purposes. At the end of the war, Hengist took his ship to Gotenhafen in the eastern Baltic, where he

picked up one and a half thousand refugees and took them to Kiel. There, *Hipper* was immobilized by bombs and, on 3 May 1945, she was scuttled.

Blücher

Blücher's first war operation was also her last. She left Swinemünde in April 1940 to take part in Operation 'Weserübung' (the invasion of Norway and Denmark), and arrived off the coast of

Norway without any noteworthy incidents. However, while trying to reach the Norwegian capital, she was seriously damaged by shore batteries in Oslo Fjord and sank shortly before 0730 on the morning of 9 April. On this ill-fated operation, *Blücher* had been carrying Hermann Boehm, the Commanding Admiral for Norway designate, and the commander of her task force, Konteradmiral Oskar Kummetz, who had to move

accounts suggest that *Prinz Eugen* landed the first shells.

After this action, *Prinz Eugen* was dismissed by the Fleet Commander (aboard *Bismarck*), and she sailed towards the South Atlantic to operate on her own. She appeared to have started her first lucky spell but, after refuelling from a supply ship, she developed engine trouble and had to return to port. *Prinz Eugen* arrived in Brest on 1 June 1941, only to suffer the torment suffered by all the German surface fleet stationed in France—being bombed by the RAF.

Six months later, *Prinz Eugen* took part in the 'Channel Dash', ending up at Trondheim, where she was torpedoed by HM Submarine *Trident*, causing considerable damage to the stern. Emergency repairs kept her afloat, and the heavy cruiser managed to limp back to Kiel under her own steam. She was in dock until October 1942, and thenceforward remained in German waters until the end of the war. *Prinz Eugen* was used as a training ship and, later, as an experimental vessel for testing new apparatus and weapons. She next saw action in June 1944, providing support for the Army against the Russians. On 15 October 1944, while travelling at twenty knots, she accidentally rammed the light cruiser *Leipzig*, a well-documented event, for there was ample time to take photographs during the fourteen hours that the two ships remained locked together.

With repairs completed, *Prinz Eugen* left Swinemünde during April 1945 and made for Copenhagen, where she remained until after the cease-fire, when she was moved to Wesermünde. *Prinz Eugen* left Europe for Boston on 13 January 1946, arriving there on 22 January. She was damaged during the atom bomb tests at Bikini Atoll but, unlike some other warships, she remained afloat, and was anchored at Kwajalein Atoll until November 1947 when she was scrapped.

Prinz Eugen had four different commanders. Kpt.z.S. Helmuth Brinkmann commissioned her on 1 August 1940 and remained in charge for two years. He then became Chief of Staff at the Naval Group Command South, and was replaced by Kpt.z.S. Hans-Erich Voss, who remained in office until February 1943, when he was made Permanent Naval Representative at Hitler's headquarters. Werner Eckhardt took command from March 1943 until January 1944, when he was succeeded by Hans-Jürgen Reinicke.

over to the heavy cruiser *Lützow* (ex-*Deutschland*). *Blücher's* commander, Kpt.z.S. Heinrich Woldag, only outlived his ship by a few days, for on 17 April he was killed in an air crash.

Prinz Eugen

In many ways *Prinz Eugen* was an unlucky ship. Firstly, she was damaged by bombs in Kiel before

being commissioned and then, during her shake-down cruise, she ran onto a mine. After repairs, she left Gotenhafen on 18 May 1941, calling at Bergen before successfully breaking out into the Atlantic with the battleship *Bismarck*. *Prinz Eugen* took part in the action against the British battleships *Hood* and *Prince of Wales* and the cruisers *Norfolk* and *Suffolk*. Although *Bismarck* is credited with sinking *Hood*, German eye-witness

LIGHT CRUISERS

Emden

Named after the famous First World War cruiser, *Emden* was the first large ship to be built for the Reichsmarine, with a design based on that of a promising cruiser from the Imperial Navy. Her armament came well within the limits of the Versailles Treaty, thus making it inadequate for modern warfare; but, although it had been designed with a view to increasing her firepower later, such a refit was never carried out and, as a result, *Emden* did not see much action during the war.

She was originally commissioned on 15 October 1925. Later, she was completely withdrawn from service for a lengthy overhaul until September 1934, when Karl Dönitz recommissioned her with a completely new crew. *Emden* then went on a long ambassadorial tour to the Far East. Although used as a training ship for most of her remaining life, she did see a few brief periods of operational service including participation in the Norwegian Campaign of spring 1940, and her meagre armament was used to bombard shore batteries during the invasion of Russia in 1941. However, her apparently uninteresting war service came to a dramatic climax during the winter of 1944/45, while she was undergoing a refit in Königsberg. After a great deal of her machinery, including parts of her engines, had been dismantled and taken ashore, thus leaving the ship partly immobilized, her commander (Kpt.z.S. Wolfgang Kähler) received orders to put to sea at once, to avoid being overrun by the advancing Russians. After instructing his men to gather as many replacement parts for her machinery as possible, Kähler managed to get the ship underway. *Emden* slowly crawled out to sea, laden with about a thousand refugees, including the stone coffin of Field Marshal Paul von Hindenburg, accompanied by his widow. The old ship made her way west at a painfully slow speed, but she reached Kiel where she was beached. *Emden* was eventually blown up by German forces shortly before British troops arrived. (Wolfgang Kähler, *Emden's* last commander, should not be confused with Otto Kähler, who commanded the auxiliary cruiser *Thor*.)

Emden held several records, besides that of being the first large warship of the Hitler era.

Below: *Karlsruhe*. Launched in 1927, she was the third ship in the German Navy with this name. The first *Karlsruhe* had been launched in Kiel in 1912, and went down during combat with HMS *Bristol* in 1914; the second was launched two years later in 1916, and was scuttled towards the end of the First World War. (Photo: Author's Collection)
Bottom of page: A close-up of one of *Köln's* after gun turrets.

This photograph was taken after the ship had actually been sunk. It was possible to use some of her armament because she was resting on a level seabed, and the guns engaged the advancing land forces. The wooden platform was built either to enable repair work to be carried out or, more probably, to allow the men to manhandle ammunition into the turret. (Photo: Imperial War Museum)

Firstly, members of her crew were the first casualties of the German Navy to be sustained aboard ship in the Second World War. During an air attack while the ship was lying at anchor in the estuary of the River Jade, one of the aircraft was shot down and crashed onto *Emden's* deck killing several men. Secondly, she must be the only German ship to have had one of her crew eaten by a lion! At least, one man disappeared while on the Far East tour, and a rather satisfied lion was the only plausible explanation. Thirdly, *Emden* was the last warship upon which Grand Admiral Raeder set foot as Supreme Commander-in-Chief of the Navy.

Karlsruhe

Karlsruhe was undergoing a refit when the war began, and was not recommissioned until November 1939. She then underwent several trials before taking part in the invasion of Norway. On 9 April 1940, the British submarine *Truant* torpedoed her, putting paid to both engines and rudder, as well as most of her electrical equipment. Torpedo-boats then took off her crew and, at 2250, *Karlsruhe* was sunk off Kristiansand by two torpedoes from the torpedo-boat *Greif*. *Karlsruhe's* commander was Kpt.z.S. Friedrich Rieve.

Köln

At the start of the war, *Köln* served in the Baltic off Norway. She became the flagship to Commander-in-Chief Reconnaissance Forces, seeing service in the North Sea. Later, in spring 1940, she took part in the Norwegian Campaign and the invasion of Russia. She sailed to Narvik via Oslo during August 1942, and remained in these northern waters until returning to the Baltic in the spring of 1943. Then she was decommissioned before being towed to Königsberg for a refit. In October/November 1944 she returned to operate in the waters around Denmark and Norway, as flagship for the Flag Officer for Destroyers. On the last day of 1944, *Köln* was put out of action by bombs; emergency repairs were carried out in Oslo, before she returned to Wilhelmshaven. Once there, she was subjected to further air attacks, which rendered her completely unseaworthy. However, some of her guns remained above the water and were used to bombard enemy troops after she was finally decommissioned on 5 April 1945.

Königsberg

While being used by the Artillery Inspectorate before the war, *Königsberg* had a revolutionary new radio rangefinder (i.e., a radar set) installed on her forward control tower. This efficient device differed slightly from British radar inasmuch that it was designed for use as an artillery rangefinder after the target had been sighted. *Königsberg*, under command of Kpt.z.S. Kurt Caesar Hoffmann, was operating off the Polish coast at the end of August 1939. On the day before the outbreak of war, she encountered two Polish destroyers: nerves on both sides must have been very tense as the destroyers trained their torpedo tubes on *Königsberg*, which had her guns aimed at the destroyers. However, nothing developed from this 'sabre rattling', and the three ships parted company peacefully.

On 10 April 1940, whilst taking part in the Norwegian Campaign, *Königsberg* was sunk by three dive-bombers. Her wreck remained off Bergen until 1943, when it was raised and scrapped. Her commander, Kpt.z.S. Heinrich Rufus (who had relieved Hoffmann of command in September 1939) was understandably distressed at her loss, because she had been the second ship to sink under him, although on neither occasion had he been at fault: before the war, Rufus had commanded the sail training ship *Niobe* until she capsized in a strong squall.

Leipzig

Leipzig was torpedoed by HM Submarine *Salmon* in mid-December 1939, while laying mines off Newcastle. Heinz Nordmann, her commander, managed to take her back across the North Sea, but she was attacked by another submarine, *Ursula*, en route. The lookouts aboard *Leipzig* actually spotted the submarine and fired a salvo of torpedoes towards her, but these missed their target and went on to sink a German escort. *Leipzig* was repaired and, at the same time, converted to a training ship. Some of her damaged boilers were removed to provide extra space for accommodation.

Shortly after leaving Gotenhafen on 15 October 1944, *Leipzig* was involved in a dramatic collision with the heavy cruiser *Prinz Eugen*. This happened some distance out, after she had stopped to change from diesel propulsion on the middle shaft to turbines on the two outer propeller shafts. This

photograph, taken at Swinemünde some time before 1935, shows the old battleships Schlesien *on the left and* Schleswig-Holstein *on the right. (Photo: Bundesarchiv, Koblenz)*

was quite a complicated procedure, usually taking at least twenty minutes; in the process, *Leipzig* drifted into bad weather and also into the wrong shipping lane—right in the path of *Prinz Eugen*. The resulting collision tore a deep hole in *Leipzig*, effectively putting her out of action for the rest of the war. However, her guns remained in use, and were used against the Russian Army. After the war, she was moved to Wilhelmshaven, where she was loaded with gas ammunition and, on 16 December 1946, scuttled in the North Sea.

Nürnberg

At the start of the war, *Nürnberg* served as flagship to the Commander-in-Chief Reconnaissance Forces. She was hit by a torpedo from the British submarine *Salmon* at about the same time that this submarine scored a hit on *Leipzig* (mid-December 1939). She was out of action undergoing repair until the summer of 1940, when she went north to serve in the Arctic seas. In August 1940, *Nürnberg* returned to Germany. She remained in home waters until November 1942, when she returned to Norway. *Nürnberg* was in Wilhelmshaven at the end of the war, under the command of Kpt.z.S. Giessler; after the cessation of hostilities, she was

handed over to the Russian Navy, who then commissioned her under the name of *Admiral Makarov*.

OLD BATTLESHIPS

These veteran predreadnoughts saw action at the Battle of Jutland in the First World War, and they both saw action during the Second World War. *Schleswig-Holstein* fired the first shots of the war at sea when she opened the bombardment of the Polish-held Westerplatte (a narrow spit of land between the mainland and the open Baltic) near Danzig. Although both ships were used during the invasion of Norway and Denmark, for most of the war they served as training or accommodation ships.

Schlesien saw active service again during the Battle of Gotenhafen in March/April 1945, when she ferried numerous refugees as far as Swinemünde; there she was scuttled on 4 May 1945.

Schleswig-Holstein was sunk by bombs on 19 December 1944. She went down on an even keel in shallow water in Gotenhafen. Her guns remained in use for some time, but a serious fire finally put her out of action completely. On 25 January 1945, her flags were lowered for the last time.

Below: Destroyer *Z20, Karl Galster*, shortly before the start of the war. (Photo: Druppel)

DESTROYERS

The German Navy used the term 'Zerstörer' (destroyer) somewhat differently from their British counterparts: German torpedo-boats of the First World War were large enough to act as destroyers, and the first new German destroyers built after that war were very much larger than British destroyers. Destroyers were used during the Polish Campaign for laying defensive mines near the German coast and later for mining British sea lanes. These mining operations were certainly the most important carried out by German destroyers during the winter of 1939/40. (At the time, in fact, German mines laid close to British harbours were usually accredited to U-boats, to prevent the Royal Navy from expecting enemy surface ships infiltrating her sea lanes.)

Two German destroyers were indirectly sunk by the Luftwaffe during that first winter of the war. This incident occurred on 22 February 1940, when Kommodore Friedrich Bonte sailed to the Dogger Bank area with the 1st Destroyer Flotilla. Details of this movement were not passed on to German aircrews, and so the flotilla was attacked. *Leberecht Maass*, commanded by Korvkpt. Fritz Bassenge, received a direct hit, which exploded inside her small launch. This saved the rest of the ship, but shortly afterwards the destroyer ran onto a mine laid by a British submarine in a German mine-free area. *Max Schultz*, commanded by Korvkpt. Claus Trampedach, suffered a similar fate during the same attack. She too ran onto a mine while trying to avoid the air attack. Both commanders and most of the crews were lost.

Almost all available destroyers, as well as other small craft, were used during the invasion of Norway and Denmark—so many, in fact, that at one time there were hardly any ships left in German waters. The Norwegian fjords became a bloody battleground for the destroyers; although it was a successful campaign overall, Germany lost many of her small ships during the confused fighting. As a result, the destroyer arm had to be drastically reorganized.

After the Norwegian Campaign, destroyers dealt with various tasks over a wide operational area. After the Polish Campaign of 1939, there were virtually no destroyers in the Baltic until the end of 1944, when the 6th Destroyer Flotilla was sent east on security and mining operations.

The main operations areas for destroyers were as follows.

● Sunk in operation area.
✳ Moved to another operation area, but sunk before the end of the war.
N Sunk near Narvik during the invasion of Norway in April 1940. No symbol means the boat survived the war.

The Polish Campaign, 1939:

Z1 ✳	Z11✳	Z16 ✳
Z8 ✳	Z14	
Z9 ✳	Z15	

Norwegian Waters:

Z2 ●N	Z12 ●N	Z19 ●N
Z6 ✳	Z13 ●N	Z20 ✳
Z8 ✳	Z15	Z21 ●N
Z9 ●N	Z16 ✳	Z22 ●N
Z10	Z17 ●N	
Z11●N	Z18 ●N	

Arctic/Northern Seas:

Z4	Z20	Z29
Z6	Z23 ✳	Z30
Z7 ●	Z24 ✳	Z31
Z10	Z25	Z33
Z14	Z26 ●	Z34
Z15	Z27✳	Z38
Z16●	Z28 ✳	

Skagerrak:

Z4	Z14
Z6	Z20

North Sea:

Z3 ●	Z12✳	Z19✳
Z4	Z13✳	Z20
Z6	Z14	Z21✳
Z8 ✳	Z15	Z22✳
Z9 ✳	Z16✳	Z34●
Z10	Z17✳	
Z11✳	Z18✳	

Western Waters (English Channel and French Atlantic Coast):

Z4	Z14	Z27●
Z5	Z15	Z32●
Z6	Z16 ✳	Z37●
Z7 ✳	Z20	ZH1 ●
Z8 ●	Z23●	
Z10	Z24●	

The Baltic, late 1944:

Z5	Z28	Z36 ●
Z10	Z31	Z39
Z20	Z34 ✳	Z43 ●
Z25	Z35●	

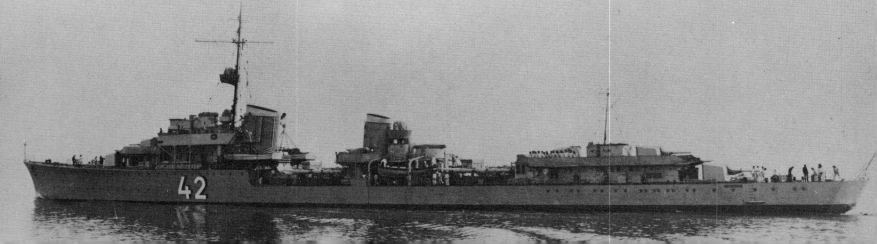

AUXILIARY CRUISERS

Atlantis

In March 1940, *Atlantis*, the first auxiliary cruiser of the Second World War, left German waters disguised as a Russian freighter. Shortly before she was permitted to start aggressive action, on 29 April 1940, her appearance was changed to resemble that of a Japanese ship. Four days later, she bagged her first victim in the still bustling shipping lanes between Capetown and Freetown. *Atlantis* kept to the shipping lanes and sailed south, eventually laying mines near Cape Agulhas, the most southerly point of Africa. After completing this operation, on 10 May, she changed her identity to that of a Dutch ship, and sailed into the Indian Ocean, which remained her hunting ground for the rest of the year. In December 1940, she met up with the auxiliary cruiser *Pinguin* and her prize, the tanker *Storstad*. *Atlantis* then sailed on to the Kerguelen Islands for a general overhaul of her machinery.

At the end of January 1941, *Atlantis* encountered the pocket battleship *Admiral Scheer*, which passed within a few hundred yards of the raider, and in April she met the auxiliary cruiser *Kormoran*. Another, far more dramatic meeting took place in the South Atlantic in mid-May, when *Atlantis* was suddenly surprised by the aircraft carrier HMS *Eagle* and the battleship HMS *Nelson*. Either the two warships did not spot *Atlantis* in the darkness or the four and a half miles between them was sufficient to deceive the Royal Navy, for she was not challenged. In such situations, the auxiliary cruiser had to rely completely on her disguise, because her armament was barely sufficient to take on even a small cruiser. Meanwhile, further problems were brewing on the high seas, because the German supply ship *Babitonga* had been sunk by a British cruiser. As a result, the auxiliary cruiser *Orion* had almost run out of fuel, and Bernhard Rogge (commander of *Atlantis*) had no choice other than to hand over some of his 'liquid gold'. This meeting took place on 1 July, after which *Orion* headed for home and *Atlantis* continued hunting in southern waters. Another supply ship, *Münsterland*, reached *Atlantis* and the auxiliary cruiser *Komet* in mid-September 1941.

At about this time, *Atlantis* received orders to cease operating as an auxiliary cruiser and to concentrate on supplying U-boats, which were starting operations in the southern seas. By this time, however, it was possible for Royal Navy Intelligence to understand a fair proportion of the Germans' secret code, and the heavy cruiser HMS *Devonshire* was dispatched to intercept a German refuelling rendezvous. *U68*, commanded by Korvkpt. Karl-Friedrich Merten, and *U126*, commanded by Kptlt. Ernst Bauer, had just been supplied some 470 miles north-west of Ascension Island when the cruiser appeared. *U68* saw the ensuing action, but was too far away to help, and *U126* crash-dived. The commander of *U126* was aboard *Atlantis* when *Devonshire* appeared, and the boat dived without him. Once submerged with no commander (who was the only person in the submarine trained to carry out an attack) and untrimmed because of the newly loaded stores, *U126* was no threat to the British cruiser. *Atlantis*, was scuttled and abandoned while under fire from *Devonshire*, but Rogge and a large proportion of the crew were picked up by the two U-boats. Later, these survivors were taken aboard the supply ship *Python*, but she was sunk and another rescue operation had to be mounted to bring the men back to France. When *Atlantis* was scuttled, she had been at sea for 622 days without putting into port and had covered some 112,500 miles.

Coronel

Coronel was used as a minelayer before being converted to an auxiliary cruiser during the winter of 1941/42. She underwent trials and, during January 1943, tried to break out into the Atlantic. She sailed from the central Baltic around Denmark and stopped near the island of Sylt for four days, before heading south through the English Channel. But luck was not on her side: one of the escorts hit a mine and *Coronel* twice ran aground. This caused considerable delay, making it impossible for her to pass through the Strait of Dover under cover of darkness, so she remained in Dunkirk until the next night. *Coronel* left Dunkirk on the night of 8 February 1943, when she came under attack from British forces and was forced to go back to Dunkirk for repairs. *Coronel* was then ordered back to Germany, where she was refitted as an auxiliary minesweeper and served as such in the Baltic.

Hansa

In 1940 this ship was under construction for the Glen Line in Copenhagen when it was commandeered by the Germans. *Hansa* was first employed in the Baltic as a target ship for U-boat training and only later fitted out as an auxiliary cruiser. Most of this work was done in Rotterdam, with only the armament and the finer details being added in Hamburg. However, this was never completed because the ship was damaged during an air raid, and conversion plans were therefore scrapped. The ship was subsequently used for target practice and training in the Baltic.

Komet

Komet, the smallest German auxiliary cruiser, was fitted with specially strengthened bows to negotiate polar pack ice, and undertook one of the most dramatic voyages of the Second World War. Leaving Gotenhafen, in the eastern Baltic, she called at Bergen in Norway on 9 July 1940, and then sailed around the North Cape to go through the Siberian sea passage into the Pacific Ocean. *Komet* crossed the Kara Sea with the help of two Russian icebreakers, *Stalin* and *Lenin*. A third icebreaker later took over, but proved too slow. Diplomatic relations were also rapidly deteriorating between Russia and Germany, so the auxiliary cruiser continued alone on the three and a half thousand mile voyage, arriving in the Bering Strait (between Russia and America) on 5 September 1940. A good quarter of this distance had been made more difficult by thick ice.

Komet then sailed south into warmer waters to meet the supply ship *Kulmerland*, which had sailed from Japan. They were joined by the auxiliary cruiser *Orion* and also by another supply ship *Regensburg*. *Komet* and *Orion* then operated together for a short period.

Komet's first success against enemy shipping came on 25 November 1940, when she sank the New Zealand ship *Holmwood*. *Komet* then called at Nauru Island, north-east of Australia, during the last days of 1940, to set prisoners ashore. (Another part of the island group was later bombarded by *Orion*; the ships had parted company by this time and were operating separately.)

All German auxiliary cruisers, despite having a fairly free hand, were under the direct control of the Naval High Command, who instructed *Komet* to meet *Pinguin* and supply ships before heading south to look for whaling ships. *Komet* did not remain long in whaling waters before being instructed to head for home, with strict orders to avoid further conflict. She went to France, sailed up the English Channel and eventually arrived in Hamburg after 516 days at sea. All this time she

had been under command of Vizeadmiral Robert Eyssen.

Komet did not manage to break out into the Atlantic for a second time. On 14 October 1942, she came under attack from the Royal Navy's *MTB236*, and was sunk near Cape de la Hague. Her last commander, Kpt.z.S. Ulrich Brocksien, went down with his ship.

Kormoran

Kormoran left Gotenhafen on 3 December 1940 under the command of Fregkpt. Theodor Detmers and passed into the South Atlantic through the Denmark Strait. A meeting with *U124*, commanded by Kptlt. Wilhelm Schulz, took place during early March (when a considerable volume of cargo was passed from the U-boat to the cruiser).

Kormoran had been experiencing some problems with her radar, and this equipment was dismantled and given to the heavy cruiser *Admiral Scheer* to take back. (These radar sets were not used for locating enemy ships, as in the Royal Navy, but more as artillery rangefinders after the target had been sighted. Radar impulses could be picked up by the target long before there was a response on the German radar screen, so that poorly-equipped auxiliary cruisers could accidentally give their presence away to superior enemy forces.) *Kormoran* supplied *U105*, commanded by Kptlt. Georg Schewe, and *U106*, commanded by Kptlt. Jürgen Oesten, with fuel and provisions before meeting the auxiliary cruiser *Atlantis* and passing into the Indian Ocean. She was supplied by the *Kulmerland* shortly before encountering the Australian cruiser *Sydney*. *Kormoran* played her disguised role to the last, managed to fool her adversary, get within range and sink the cruiser after a short duel. HMAS *Sydney* also landed four hits on *Kormoran*, one of which exploded in the engine room, causing considerable damage. Over seventy of the crew were killed and the ship had to be scuttled, bringing her voyage of 350 days to an end. Most of the survivors managed to reach the Australian mainland.

Michel

This ship was originally commandeered by the Naval High Command with a view to fitting it out as a hospital ship, and only much later was it

considered for conversion to auxiliary cruiser. *Michel* left Germany on 9 March 1942 and passed through the Strait of Dover during the night of 13/14 March. Then she sailed into the South Atlantic, where she had her first success on 19 April 1942, sinking the 7,000-ton motor-tanker *Patella*, which was loaded with oil. The raider carried a small motor torpedo-boat (*LS4*)—in addition to the usual antiquated armament—which was first used against the enemy on 22 April 1942, when the merchant ship *Connecticut* was stopped and sunk.

Michel met the auxiliary cruiser *Stier* on 29 July, and then operated alone until she was ordered home in January 1943. But the presence of several Allied ships near the French coast prompted the Naval High Command to reconsider their decision, and *Michel* was instructed to make for Japan. She called at Djakarta and Singapore before arriving at Kobe, where she was refitted from 2 March to 21 May 1943. On 4 June 1943, *Michel* set sail on her second cruise from Yokohama, by which time she was the only German auxiliary cruiser left on the high seas. But her days were numbered. On 17 October 1943, she was sunk by the United States submarine *Tarpon*.

Michel's first commander had been Kpt.z.S. Hellmuth von Ruckteschell. He was replaced by Kpt.z.S. Günther Gumprich, who commanded her from May 1943 until she was sunk.

Orion

Orion, the second auxiliary cruiser to leave Germany during the Second World War, sailed from Kiel on 30 March 1940. *Atlantis* was waiting for suitable conditions before breaking out into the South Atlantic via the Denmark Strait and, as the Naval High Command did not want to run the risk of two cruisers bumping into British forces at the same time, *Orion* was ordered to remain in coastal waters for another week. Eventually, on 6 April, she headed west disguised as the Dutch freighter *Beemsterdijk*.

Orion had not gone very far before the Naval High Command issued another revision of orders to her commander, Fregkpt. Kurt Weyher. Instead of heading straight for the Pacific, he was instructed to sink some merchant ships. The Germans hoped this would fool the Royal Navy into thinking that a pocket battleship was on the prowl, in which event they might draw some forces

Right: The auxiliary cruiser *Orion* on 23 August 1941, after her successful cruise. She looks very much like a merchant ship, and there is no clue that she is armed with six 150mm guns as well as several smaller weapons. Her large Zeiss rangefinder is also well hidden. (Photo: Bundesarchiv, Koblenz)

away from Norway, where Germany was anticipating a heavy sea battle during the invasion of that country. The auxiliary cruiser eventually passed Cape Horn on 27 May 1940, and she arrived off Auckland on 13 June to lay mines in the Hauraki Gulf. The most noteworthy victim of this enterprise was the freighter *Niagara*, which was carrying a vast hoard of gold ingots. Later, *Orion*

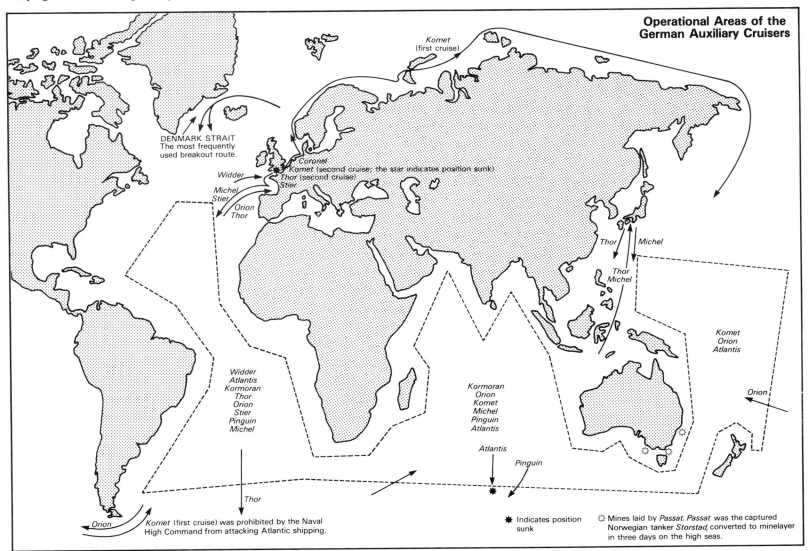

Operational Areas of the German Auxiliary Cruisers

Komet (first cruise)

DENMARK STRAIT
The most frequently used breakout route.

Widder
Michel
Stier
Orion
Thor

Coronel
Komet (second cruise; the star indicates position sunk)
Thor (second cruise)
Stier

Thor *Michel*

Thor
Michel

Komet
Orion
Atlantis

Orion

Widder
Atlantis
Kormoran
Thor
Orion
Stier
Pinguin
Michel

Kormoran
Orion
Komet
Michel
Pinguin
Atlantis

Atlantis

Pinguin

Thor

Orion

Komet (first cruise) was prohibited by the Naval High Command from attacking Atlantic shipping.

✱ Indicates position sunk

✿ Mines laid by *Passat. Passat* was the captured Norwegian tanker *Storstad,* converted to minelayer in three days on the high seas.

Opposite page:
Top left: Cadets scrambling up the masts of *Niobe*. (Photo: Author's Collection)
Top right: Korvkpt. Kümpel, commander *Niobe* in 1931. (He was replaced by Heinrich Ruhfus, who survived the sinking off the island of Fehmarn and later commanded the light cruiser *Königsberg*, which also sank under his feet during an air attack.) Kümpel is wearing a frock coat and the old pattern of cap, with the Weimar Republic eagle in the cockade. The U-boat Badge of the First World War and the Wounded Badge can be seen below the 1914 Iron Cross. Just visible on his right breast is the

Iron Halfmoon, a star-shaped badge with a half moon on the inside, which was awarded by Turkey for his services there during the First World War. It was roughly equivalent to the Iron Cross (1st Class). Kümpel does not feature in records of the Second World War because he committed suicide shortly before. (Photo: Author's Collection)
Below left: *Niobe* was originally a Danish four-masted freighter, and was converted into a sail training ship with this sail arrangement in 1923. (Photo: Author's Collection)
Below right: The old sailing ship *Westwärts* serving as accommodation ship in Norway. (Photo: Author's Collection)

arrived at Lamutrek Atoll to meet the supply ships *Kulmerland* and *Regensburg*, as well as the raider *Komet*. Afterwards, both auxiliary cruisers operated along the east coast of New Zealand. *Orion* eventually headed west, only to find herself in real difficulties; her designated supply ship had been sunk, she was low on fuel and her crew had not sighted a suitable ship—with fuel—to capture. In the end, *Atlantis* supplied her with sufficient 'liquid gold' to enable her to pass north through the Atlantic to France. She arrived there on 23 August 1941, having left Kiel some 511 days earlier. *Orion* went on to Germany, where she was converted to a repair and workshop ship. In 1944, she was commissioned as the artillery training ship *Hektor*. Her end came on 4 May 1945, when she was bombed off Swinemünde by Allied aircraft.

Pinguin

Pinguin—although not named until she was approaching the South Atlantic—left Gotenhafen on 15 June 1940, with some 350 mines below decks and a cunning mining expert on the bridge. Kpt.z.S. Ernst-Felix Krüder, her commander, lived up to his reputation by capturing the Australian-bound Norwegian tanker *Storstad* and converting her into an auxiliary minelayer in three days. Renamed *Passat*, she was then taken along her planned route and was used to lay mines off Melbourne, Sydney and Adelaide. Afterwards, both ships met up again, with *Passat* acting as an additional set of eyes for *Pinguin*. Her name now changed back to *Storstad*, the tanker was sent back to Europe with a 'prize crew' and prisoners from *Pinguin* and *Atlantis*.

Pinguin sailed on into Antarctic waters and captured three whale factory ships plus their fleets of small hunters. She then headed north again into warmer waters, and met the heavy cruiser *Admiral Scheer*, which provided her with food, fuel and men to take the prize whaling ships back to Europe. Repairs to the engine room were carried out at the Kerguelen Islands in March 1941, during which time *Pinguin* was joined by *Komet*. Krüder then went on the prowl for another ship suitable for conversion to auxiliary minelayer, but his luck had run out. *Pinguin* crossed the bows of the heavy cruiser *Cornwall* on 8 May 1941—her 357th day at sea. One of *Cornwall*'s shells exploded among the remaining mines, detonating them and blowing *Pinguin* to smithereens.

Stier

Stier was taken over by the German Navy during November 1939 to be used as an icebreaker. The following summer, she was converted to a minelayer and employed as such in the Bay of Biscay until the latter half of 1941, when it was decided to refit her as an auxiliary cruiser. She eventually left Kiel early in May 1942 to pass through the Baltic-North Sea Canal and on to Rotterdam. At this stage, she was still known under her old identity of Sperrbrecher *171*. After arriving in the South Atlantic, *Stier* spent several weeks operating with the auxiliary cruiser *Michel*, and then headed south alone, reaching a point roughly half way between the equator and the South Pole. The necessity to overhaul parts of her engines led *Stier* to explore the waters around Gough Island, but no suitable anchorage could be found and the repair attempt was abandoned. Instead, *Stier* took fuel from the supply ship *Charlotte Schliemann* and headed for Japan. On 27 September 1942 she engaged the US armed freighter *Stephen Hopkins* which, although eventually sunk, severely damaged *Stier*. So, after a total of 140 days at sea, she was abandoned and scuttled.

At the time *Stier* sank, *Michel* had been relatively close and had even picked up the ship's SOS; but her commander, not convinced by the signal and suspecting a trap, quickly sailed out of the area. Some of *Stier*'s crew were later picked up by the supply ship *Tannenfels*. (In order to understand the action taken by *Michel*'s commander, one should be aware of the extraordinary events that dictated it. Commanders of German auxiliary cruisers employed a great deal of cunning in catching their quarry, including sending false messages to Allied merchant ships persuading them to change course towards the predator. One such message had even been weighted and dropped onto a ship from a seaplane. The ship's crew obeyed—not having noticed the swastika on the aeroplane! So, expecting to be treated in a like manner, raider commanders treated all signals with the utmost suspicion.)

Thor

Thor left Kiel early in June 1940 on what may well appear to have been a general inspection of British auxiliary cruisers, for she came into conflict with three of them: HMS *Alcantara*, HMS *Carnarvon*

Castle and, later, HMS *Voltaire*. *Thor* encountered the first of this trio, the 22,000-ton *Alcantara*, on 28 July 1940. In the ensuing skirmish, *Thor* was slightly damaged by two hits and broke off the action. She faired better against *Carnarvon Castle*: during this engagement, on 5 December 1940, *Thor* hit the British vessel many times and forced her to break off the action. *Thor* completed her 'round' of British auxiliary cruisers with a flourish when, on 4 April 1941, *Voltaire* sank under a barrage of artillery fire. *Thor* also met the heavy cruiser *Admiral Scheer* in the South Atlantic before returning to the Bay of Biscay during April 1941. The German raider reached Hamburg on 30 April 1941, ending a 329-day cruise, during which *Thor* had either sunk or captured 12 ships. She managed to break out into the South Atlantic from Kiel a second time on 30 November 1941 and sailed on to the Indian Ocean, eventually arriving in Yokohama on 9 October 1942. *Thor* was moored next to the supply ship *Uckermark* when an explosion and subsequent fire gutted both ships. *Thor*'s second voyage had lasted 321 days, during which time she had captured or sunk 10 ships.

Widder

Widder sailed from Cuxhaven on 5 May 1940 and, before breaking out into the central Atlantic, had a minor skirmish with HM Submarine *Clyde*. Engine trouble eventually forced her to make for France, where she arrived some 180 days after leaving Germany. But, despite the engine trouble, the voyage had not been a wasted one, for *Widder* had sunk 10 enemy ships. Afterwards, her commander, Kpt.z.S. von Ruckteschell, became commander of the auxiliary cruiser *Michel*.

SAIL TRAINING SHIPS

A tremendous shock wave echoed throughout Germany when the sail training ship *Niobe* sank off the Baltic island of Fehmarn on 26 July 1932, taking sixty-nine lives with her. Peacetime accidents of such magnitude were rare, and there had not been a similar disaster since 16 December 1900, when the training ship *Gneisenau* went down in a gale off Malaga for the loss of about a hundred lives. The loss of *Niobe* triggered off several reactions. The general public, in good Prussian tradition, needed a scapegoat, but the court

Left: The sail training ship *Gorch Fock*. She had a small diesel engine for moving in confined waters. On one occasion, the ship came into Kiel with the aid of this engine and shortened the newly extended Blücher Pier, cutting through the telecommunication and power cables. (Photo: Author's Collection)

martial found everybody, including the captain, completely innocent. *Niobe* was thought to have been uncapsizable, but nature had obviously been stronger than anticipated. In naval circles, there was a great debate about the future of sail training ships, which ended with the Navy determining to build better ships. As a result, a new design, *Gorch Fock*, was laid down at the Blohm & Voss shipyard in Hamburg. She was launched on 3 May 1933, and two similar vessels followed: *Horst Wessel* on 13 June 1936 and *Albert Leo Schlageter* on 30 October 1937. The quality of these ships can be assessed by the fact that they not only survived the war, but still sail the oceans to this day.

The sinking of *Niobe* had some far-reaching effects on naval history, for it deprived the German Navy of a whole year's intake of officer cadets, who were lost at a time when the Navy was starting to expand. Admiral Raeder, Supreme Commander-in-Chief of the Navy, wrote to Germany's civil shipping companies, requesting their best men to volunteer for the Naval officer corps. It was by this route that many famous men joined the Navy, among them Günther Prien, the hero of Scapa Flow, and 'Ajax' Bleichrodt, also one of the top U-boat commanders.

Horst Wessel went to the United States in May 1945 and, under the name of *Eagle*, is still sailing. During the war, *Albert Leo Schlageter* ran onto a mine in the Baltic and had to be towed to Swinemünde; she was repaired after the war and went first to the United States, then to Brazil, and finally to Portugal. *Gorch Fock* was scuttled at Stralsund during May 1945; she was later salvaged by the Russians and renamed *Tovarisch*. (The Federal German Navy's sail training ship *Gorch Fock*, which is similar to the original, was launched by Blohm & Voss at Hamburg in 1958. It has been stated that *Gorch Fock* was named after one of Hitler's early supporters, but, as the gentleman in question died long before the Nazi Party was founded, this is obviously untrue. In fact, Gorch Fock was a poet, who went down with his ship, SMS *Wiesbaden*, on 31 May 1916 during the Battle of Jutland.)

U-BOATS
In Germany, the different submarine classes were referred to as 'Types', which were identified by a number—usually written as a roman numeral.

Below: *U109*, under command of 'Ajax' Bleichrodt, coming into port after its 12th operational cruise. On the deck is a 105mm quick-firing gun. Note the vents along the side of this Type IXB boat; they are a good distinguishing feature when comparing with Type VII.

Below centre: *U532*, under command of Fregkpt. Ottoheinrich Junker, running into Liverpool after the war. He surrendered the boat while on his way back from Japan. The large 105mm

quick-firing gun has been removed from the deck of this Type IXC boat, because it became obsolete during the summer of 1943. The three men on the bows are wearing a most interesting uniform combination: the jackets are the Field Grey tunics, which can be determined because of the four pockets and visible buttons. The naval jacket usually had concealed buttons and only two pockets.

Below right: *U883* in Wilhelmshaven at the end of the war. It is

interesting to compare the deck structure of this boat with the other two photographs on this spread. This is Type IXD$_2$. Guns were fitted to both B and C versions, and they are more or less identical; but the D$_2$ had a different deck because it was thought that this design made it possible for the boat to dive slightly more quickly. A capstan can be seen on deck, between the men; behind them are two retractable bollards. (Photo: Imperial War Museum)

Numbers were designated to projects before they reached the drawing-board and, as many of the ideas were never considered for construction, some numbers did not appear. Each Type started as a basic design, and many of them were modified as time went on. Such modifications were distinguished by a letter after the number.

The most important of the German submarines was Type VIIC; more than 600 were commissioned, making it the largest class of submarine ever built. Throughout the war, they were used for a wide variety of duties, remaining in production long after they became obsolete in 1943. Several of

them were taken over by Allied navies after the war and used for active service until the end of the 1950s.

The other Type that played an important role in the Battle of the Atlantic was Type IX, which, although similar to Type VII, was considerably larger. These were designed as 'flagships' for U-boat packs, the idea being that they would carry the task force commander, who would conduct the convoy battles at sea. The extra space enabled the boats to carry the additional staff and communications equipment necessary. However, such a system of command was hardly ever utilized, and

most of the actions were led directly from U-boat headquarters on land, with the most senior U-boat commander usually taking command of the whole pack if and when conditions demanded it.

All existing operational U-boats became obsolete in 1943. They were to be replaced by electro-submarines, which were an interim measure until Walter's true submarines could be commissioned. There were two operational types: Type XXI, which was a large ocean-going boat to replace Type VII; and Type XXIII, which was a small coastal submarine to help fill the gap until bigger boats could be built.

U-boat types in commission during the war

Type IA: Ocean-going boats based on the design of of the Turkish submarine *Gür*; only two boats, *U25* and *U26* were launched.

Type II: Small coastal submarines based on the UBII Class of 1915, UF of 1918 and on the prototype *Vesikko*, which was built for Finland by the German Submarine Development Bureau; most of these were used for training during the war.

Type VII: Ten experimental prototypes were launched between June and December 1936, based on the UBIII design of 1915/1916 and on

the prototype *Vetehinen*, which had also been built for Finland before the Second World War.

Type IX: Developed from the *U81* design of 1915, the first three versions (Types IXA, B and C) were straightforward conventional submarines. Type IXD, however, was not planned as a fighting submarine, but rather as a long-distance cargo carrier, without torpedo tubes. Torpedo tubes were later added and another long-distance fighting version built as Type IXD$_2$. These long-range boats could cover distances up to about 32,000 nautical miles and were used for voyages to the Far East. Once there, only the boats'

defensive armament was retained and they took on cargo which was then ferried back to Europe.

Type XB: Type XA, a design based on Type I, was not very successful and was never built, but the plans were modified to build a minelayer. These boats had a capacity of about 88 mines, but were often used as supply vessels for other fighting U-boats.

Type XIV: These boats had no torpedo tubes, but were designed and built as supply submarines.

Types XXI and XXIII: These were the electro-submarines, which only became operational shortly before the end of the war.

The German Fleet: Warship Data

= Horizontal ditto mark.

	Battle-cruisers	Battleships		Pocket Battleships			Heavy Cruisers	Light Cruisers	
	Scharnhorst, Gneisenau	Bismarck	Tirpitz	Deutschland	Admiral Scheer	Admiral Graf Spee	Admiral Hipper Blücher and Prinz Eugen	Emden	Karlsruhe
Displacement, standard (tons):	31,850	41,700	43,000	11,700	12,000	=	14,050	5,600	6,650
full load (tons):	38,900	50,900	52,600	16,000	16,000	=	18,200	6,990	8,350
Waterline length (metres):	226	242	=	182	=	=	195	150	169
Overall length (metres):	235	251	=	188	=	=	206	155	174
Beam (metres):	30	36	=	20.7	=	21.7	21.3	14.3	16.6
Draught (metres):	9.9	10.5	10.2	7	=	=	7.7	5.9	6
Machinery:	12 boilers in 3 sets	12 boilers in 3 sets	=	8 × 9-cylinder diesel	=	=	12 boilers in 3 sets	10 boilers	2 sets of boilers + 2 × 10-cylinder diesel
Number of shafts:	3	3	=	2	=	=	3	2	=
Maximum SHP:	160,000	138,000	=	54,000	=	=	132,000	46,500	66,800
Maximum speed (knots):	31.5	31	=	28	=	=	32	29	30
Cruising speed (knots):	17	19	=	20	=	=	20	18	19
Range (nautical miles):	10,000	8,100	9,000	10,000	9,000	=	6,800	5,300	5,700
Crew:	1,800	2,090	2,600	1,150	=	=	1,600	636	850
Deck armour (mm):	50-105	50-120mm	=	18-40	18-45	=	30	20	40
Side armour (mm):	45-350	up to 320mm	=	up to 60	up to 80	=	80	50	50
Armament:									
20mm:	10-38	12-52	=	10-28	=	=	28	0	0?
37mm:	16	16	=	8	=	=	12	4	8 twins
88mm:	0	0	0	0	=	=	0	3	6 twins
105mm:	14	16	=	6	=	=	12	0	0
150mm:	12	=	=	8	=	=	0	8	9
203mm:	0	=	=	0	=	=	8	0	0
280mm:	9	0	0	6	=	=	0	0	0
380mm:	0	8	=	0	=	=	0	0	0
Torpedo tubes:	6	8	=	8	=	=	12	4	12
Aircraft catapults:	2, later 1	1 double	=	1	=	=	1	0	1[1]
Aircraft carried:	4	6	=	2	=	=	3	0	2[1]

1. Removed in 1942. 2. 2 sets boilers on outside shafts + 4 × 7-cylinder diesel on centre shaft.

Königsberg	Köln	Leipzig	Nürnberg
=	6,650	6,515	6,520
8,130	8,130	8,250	8,380
=	=	166	170
=	=	177	181
15.3		16.2	16.4
=		5.7	5.7
=		2	=
			=
		3	=
=	=	60,000/12,400	=
32	=	32	=
=	=	19	=
=	=	5,700	=
=	=	850	896
=	=	20-25	=
=	=	50	=
0?	0?	10	4
=	=	8	8
=	=	6	6
0	0	0	0
=	=	9	9
0	0	0	0
0	0	0	0
0	0	0	0
=	=	12	12
=	=	1	1
=	=	2	2

Left: The light cruiser *Köln* was launched in 1928 and used as a training ship before participating in the Spanish Civil War. (Photo: Author's Collection)
Right, top to bottom:
Battleship *Bismarck*. (Photo: Author's Collection)
Battleship (although regarded by the Royal Navy as a battle-cruiser) *Scharnhorst*. (Photo: Druppel)
Pocket battleship *Admiral Scheer*. Note the torpedo tubes below the triple 280mm turret. The rather solid looking, typical early command-tower was replaced by a tubular tripod structure at the start of the war. (Photo: Bundesarchiv, Koblenz)
Heavy cruiser *Admiral Hipper* in 1939, before she was modified with 'clipper' bows and a funnel cap. The new bows made her ride heavy seas better, but it did not improve her machinery, which had a tendency to break down. The catapult and hangar for three Arado 196 seaplanes can be seen just aft of the funnel. (Photo: Bundesarchiv, Koblenz)

Destroyers

Type:	1934	1934	1934	1934	1936	1936A	1936A	1936A	1936B	1936B	1936A (Mob.)	1936B
Number:	*Z1* to *Z4*	*Z5* to *Z8*	*Z9* to *Z13*	*Z14* to *Z16*	*17-Z22*	*Z23, Z24*	*Z25* to *Z27*	*Z28*	*Z29* to *Z34*	*Z35, Z36*	*Z37* to *Z39*	*Z43* to *Z45*
Displacement, standard (tons):	2,232	2,171	2,270	= (larger by	2,411	2,603	2,543	2,595	2,603	2,527	2,600	2,527
full load (tons):	3,156	3,100	3,190	31 tons)	3,415	3,605	3,545	3,519	3,597	3,507	3,597	3,507
Waterline length (metres):	114	116	=	=	120	122	=	=	122	108	=	122
Overall length (metres):	119	121	=	=	123-125	127	=	=	127	112	=	127
Beam (metres):	11.3	11.3	=	=	11.8	12	=	=	12	11.3	=	12
Draught (metres):	4.2	4.2	=	=	4.5	4.7	4.4	5	4.6	4.3	4	4
Maximum speed (knots):	38.2	38.2	=	=	36	=	=	=	36	=	=	=
Cruising speed (knots):	19	19	=	=	19	=	=	=	19	=	=	=
Range (nautical miles):	4,400	=	=	=	4,850	5,000	=	5,900	5,900	6,200	5,900	=
Crew:	325	=	=	=	313	332	321	327	321	332	332	321
Armament:[1]												
20mm:	8	=	=	=	7	14	=	=	14	16	up to 14	15
37mm:	4 to 14	=	=	=	4	4	=	=	4	=	4	=
127/128mm:	5	=	=	=	5	0	0	0		0	4	0
150mm:	0	0	0	0	0	5	=	=	0	5	0	5
Torpedo tubes:	8	=	=	=	8	=	=	=	8	=	=	=
Mines carried:	60	=	=	=	60	=	=	=	60	76	60	76

1. The exact number of guns varied during the war. 2. Not completed. 3. Plus 3 × 55mm and 14 × 30mm guns. 4. Not of German standard diameter. 5. Plus 3 × 105mm guns.

Auxiliary Cruisers

	Atlantis	*Coronel*	*Komet*	*Kormoran*	*Michel*	*Orion*	*Pinguin*	*Stier*	*Thor*	*Widder*
Crew:	350	=	270	400	400	376	420	324	345	363
Approx. displacement (tons):	17,600	12,700	7,500	19,900	11,000	15,700	17,600	11,000	9,200	16,800
Length (metres):	155	134	115	164	132	148	155	133	122	152
Beam (metres):	18.7	17.9	15.3	20.2	16.6	18.6	18.7	17.3	16.7	18.2
Draught (metres):	8.7	8	6.5	8.5	7.4	8.2	8.7	7.2	7.1	8.3
Maximum SHP:	7,600	5,100	3,900	16,000	6,650	6,200	7,600	3,750	6,500	6,200
Maximum speed (knots):	16	16	14.5	18	16	14	17	14	18	14
Armament:										
20mm:	4	?	4	5	4	4	=	=	4	=
37mm:	2	?	2	4	4	6	2	=	2	4
75mm:	1	0	0	0	1	1	=	0	0	1
150mm:	6	6	6	6	6	6	=	6	6	=
Torpedo tubes:	4	4	6[1]	6[1]	6[1]		6	2[3]	4	=
Aircraft carried:	2	2	2	2	2	1	2	2	1	2
Mines carried:	92	0	30[2]	360[2]	0[2]	228	380	?	?	?

1. 4 tubes above waterline, 2 below. 2. *Komet, Kormoran* and *Michel* also carried, respectively, *MTB2* (*LS2*), *MTB3* (*LS3*), and *MTB4* (*LS4*). These were 11.5-ton, 45-knot boats, with a range of 300 nautical miles at 30 knots. Each had 2 × 457mm torpedo tubes, 3-4 mines and a crew of six. 3. Below the waterline.

Right, top to bottom:
1934-type destroyer *Z6, Theodor Riedel*. (Photo: Druppel)
1934-type destroyer *Z10, Hans Lody*. (Photo: Druppel)
1936B-type destroyer *Z33*. (Photo: Druppel)
Bottom of page: 1936-type destroyer *Z21, Wilhelm Heidkamp*, commanded by Korvkpt. Hans Erdmenger, shortly before the start of the war. (Photo: Bundesarchiv, Koblenz)
Early destroyers tended to be bow heavy, partly due to their heavy armament, and this problem was overcome in later types by building clipper bows to provide extra forward buoyancy.

1936C[2]	1942C[2]	1942C[2]	Ex-Royal Netherlands Navy	Ex-French Navy	Ex-Greek Navy	Ex-Norwegian Navy
Z46 to Z50	Z51	Z52 to Z56	ZH1	ZF2[2]	ZG3	ZN4/ZN5[2]
2,574	2,053	2,818	1,604	2,070	1,414	1,278
3,596	2,632	3,700	2,222	2,910	2,088	1,694
121	108	126	105	111	98	94
126	114	132	107	113	101	101
12.2	11	12.6	10.6	11.1	10.4	10.6
4.4	4.4	4.9	3.5	3.4	3.2	3.2
37.5	36	37.5	37.5	=	32	=
=	19	=	19	=	19	=
6,000	13,500	16,000	5,400	4,700	4,800	3,100
320	247	320	230	245	225	162
6	12	0[3]	0	10	4	6
6	8	0	4	4	4	2
	4	6	5	0	4	0[5]
	0	0	0	5	0	0
6	6	8	8	8[4]	8	4
60	50	60				

Torpedo-Boats

Type:	1935	1937	Fleet Torpedo-Boats, 1939	Fleet Torpedo-Boats, 1941	Fleet Torpedo-Boats, 1944	Fleet Torpedo-Boats, 1940[4]	1923	1923	1924
Name:	T1 to T8[1] / T9 to T12	T13 to T21	T22 to T36	T37 to T51[3]	T52 to T60[3]	T61 to T64,[3] T67 to T70[3]	Seeadler, Möwe	Albatros, Falke, Greif, Kondor	Wolf, Jaguar, Leo... Luchs, Iltis, Tiger
Displacement, standard (tons):	844	853	1,294	1,493	1,418	1,931	924	=	933
full load (tons):	1,088	1,098	1,754	2,155	1,794	2,566	1,290	=	1,320
Waterline length (metres):	82	82	97	=	=	=	85	86	89
Overall length (metres):	84	85	102	=	=	=	87	88	93
Beam (metres):	8.6	8.9	10	=	=	=	8.4	=	8.7
Draught (metres):	2.9	3.1	3.2	=	=	=	3.7	=	3.5
Maximum speed (knots):	34.5	34.5	32.5	34	37.2	34.8	32	33	34
Cruising speed (knots):	19	19	19	19	19	19	17	=	=
Range (nautical miles):	2,400	3,000	2,100	2,350	4,500	6,000	3,600	=	3,100
Crew:	119	=	206	210	222	231	122	=	129
Torpedo tubes:	6	=	=	=	6	=	Variable	6	=
Mines carried:	30	=	50	?	=	=	?	?	?
Armament:					=				
20mm:	8	7	7-12	9	0	8	Variable	4	=
37mm:	0	1	4	4	10	4	?	?	?
105mm:	1	1	4	4	4	0	3	=
127mm:	0[2]	0	0	0	0	4	0	0

1. *T1* to *T8* were some 5-10 tons heavier than *T9* to *T12*. 2. Armament modified during the war. 3. Not completed. 4. *T65, T66, T71* and *T72* were also planned but not completed.

Motor Torpedo-Boats (Schnellboote)[1]

Number:	S1	S2 to S5	S6 to S9	S10 to S13	S14 to S17	S18 to S25	S26 to S29	S30 to S37	S38 to S53 S62 to S99 S101 to S135 S137	S100, S136, S138 to S150 S159 to S169 S171 to S185 S187 to S194	S151 to S158	S170, S186, S195 to S218
Crew:	14	=	21	=	=	16	21	23	=	=	21	23
Launched:	Pre-war	1937/38	1933/34	1934/35	1936/37	1938/39	1940	1940	1942/43	1942/44	1941/42	1944
Displacement (tons):	50	=	80	78	97	85	95	82	95	=	55	95
Length (metres):	28	32.5	35	=	=	=	35	33	35	=	28	35
Beam (metres):	4.3	5	=	=	=	=		5	=	=	4.3	5
Draught (metres):	1.4	1.4	1.7	1.4	1.6	1.6	1.6	1.5	2	=	1.6	2
Maximum speed (knots):	33	=	36.5	35	38	40	39	36	39	=	32	39
Range at cruising speed (nautical miles):	350	=	600	600	600	700	700	800	700	=	350	750

1. Almost all these boats could cruise at a speed only a few knots below their maximum. They were armed with two torpedo tubes, plus light anti-aircraft guns; some had machine-guns too. 2. Excluding Nos. *229* to *300* and *308* to *700*.

Right: The Motor Torpedo-Boat Arm was not established until April 1942. The first boats were commissioned from about 1931 onwards and there is a distinct difference between the earlier boats (as seen here) and later versions. (Photo: Bundesarchiv, Koblenz)

Below: *T157*, one of the old torpedo-boats built for the Imperial Navy, having a rough time in bad weather during November 1933.

Old Torpedo-Boats[1]

T107, T108, T110, T111	T151, T153, T155, T156, T157, T158	T185	T190	T196
750	650	760	750	=
875	800	860	=	875
75, later 80	73	74	=	=
7.5	=	8	=	=
3	=	3	=	=
31	30	=	30	32
17	=	=	=	19
2,000	3,500	1,400	=	1,850
85	=	=	100	=
2	1	0	2	2
0	0	0	0	0
1	0	0	1	2
0	0[2]	0	0	0

1. These boats, which were not used as torpedo-boats, were launched before the First World War. They were used for a variety of purposes after 1918, mainly as tenders and for training or similar work. 2. Plus 1 × 88mm.

Below: *M18,* commanded by Otto Köhler, was one of the lucky ships in the German Navy. On one occasion, finding themselves in an impossible situation, the Commander and First Officer started to say their last prayers as two torpedoes hit: but they went straight through the hull and failed to explode. On another occasion *M18* was rammed, first in the bows and shortly afterwards in the stern. (Photo: Author's Collection)

Minesweepers

	M1 to M260	M261 to M500[1]	M601 to M612, M801 to M806[2]
Crew:	90-120	60-80	107
Displacement (tons):	682/875	545/775	580/820
Length (metres):	67/68	58/62	63/68
Beam (metres):	8.3	8.5	9
Draught (metres):	2.6	2.8	2.7
Maximum speed (knots):	18.3	16.8	16.7
Range (nautical miles):	5,000	4,000	3,600
Armament:			
20mm:	6	7	8
37mm:	2	1	2
105mm:	2		2
Torpedo tubes:	0	2	0
Mines carried:	30	?	24

1. Not all numbers were commissioned. 2. Nos. *M613* to *M800* were never built.

Motor Minesweepers (Räumboote)

	R1	R2 to R7 R9 to R16	R8	R17 to R24	R25 to R40	R41 to R129	R130 to R150	R151 to R290[1]
Launched:	1930	1932	1934	1934	1938	1939	1943	1940
Crew:	40	18	18	34	34	34	34	
Displacement (tons):	45	60	63	115	110	125	150 t	110
Length (metres):	42.5	24.5	26	27.8	37	34.5	37.8	35.4
Beam (metres):	5.2	4.4	4.5	4.5	5.5	5.6	5.8	5.6
Draught (metres):	2.5	?	1.1	1.3	1 +	1.4	1.4	1.4
Maximum speed (knots):	17	17	?	21	23.5	20	19	23
Range (nautical miles):	800(?)	800	?	900	1,100	900	900	1,100

Armament: 1-4 × 20mm AA guns, 3-6 × 37mm AA guns, plus variations.

1. Nos. *R291-R300* were not completed.

Below: A flotilla of R-boats, or Räumboote, photographed after the end of the war. (Photo: Imperial War Museum)
Bottom of page: These minesweepers were built for the Imperial Navy and remained in German hands after the end of the First World War. Although somewhat antiquated, they formed the backbone of the Reichsmarine's minesweeping squadrons. Seen here are *M133* followed by *M50* and *M129*. (Photo: Author's Collection)

First World War Minesweepers[1]

Crew:	51
Displacement (tons):	515/700
Length (metres):	56–60
Beam (metres):	7–8
Draught (metres):	2–3
Maximum speed (knots):	10
Range (nautical miles):	up to 3,400
Armament:	1 × 105mm
	3 × 20mm (plus variations)

1. This group consisted of successful First World War minesweepers which survived the Treaty of Versailles and remained in German hands. Between the wars they were converted from coal to oil fuel and used for a variety of different tasks, mainly as tenders, experimental craft or for training. During the Second World War they were converted back to burn coal and again used for numerous duties. Probably all of them were used as minesweepers sometime between 1939 and 1945. Some of these ships were known under a traditional name and all of them were renumbered during the Second War. (See page 97.)

Training Ships	Schlesien Schleswig-Holstein	Albert Leo Schlageter	Gorch Fock	Horst Wessel
Launched:	1906	1937	1933	1936
Crew:	c. 800	298	265	298
Displacement (tons):	14,900	1,634	1,500	1,634
Length (metres):	126	89	74	89
Beam (metres):	22.2	12	12	12
Draught (metres):	7.7	5	48	4.8
Maximum SHP:	16,000	750	520	520
Maximum speed (knots):	16	10[1]	8[1]	8[1]
Range (nautical miles):	5,900	3,500[1]	3,500[1]	3,500[1]
Armament (1944):	4 × 280mm	8 × 20mm AA	=	=
	6 × 105mm			
	10 × 40mm AA			
	20 or more 20mm			

1. Engines only.

Purpose-Built Escorts (Geleitboote)[1]

	F1 to F10
Crew:	120
Displacement (tons):	770 to 1,150
Length (metres):	73/76
Beam (metres):	8.8
Draught (metres):	3.2
Maximum speed (knots):	28
Range (nautical miles):	1,500
Armament:	2 × 105mm
	4 × 37mm
	8 × 20mm

1. Larger boats (G1-G24) were projected, but they were never built.

Right: The sail training ship Gorch Fock. (Photo: Author's Collection)
Left: A close-up of the bridge of the old battleship Schlesien. This picture was taken before the start of the war, but after her 1927 refit. (Photo: Author's Collection)
Below right: The first escort boat (F1) before being commissioned. She is still flying her maker's flag (Krupps/Germania Werft, Kiel). The new national flag is at the bow, and the flag at the stern appears to be the older national flag (three horizontal stripes of black, white and red). Initially, she was armed with two 105mm quick-firing guns, and anti-aircraft armament was added later. (Photo: Author's Collection)

U-boats

Type:	Type IIC[4]	Type VIIC[5]	Type IXC[5]	V80[6]	Type XVIIA[6]	Type XXIII[7]	Type XXI[7]
Crew:	25	44-56	about 48	4	12	14	57
Displacement, surface (tons):	314	770	1,120	71	240	235	1,620
submerged (tons):	460	1,070	1,540	80	280	275	2,100
Length (metres):	44	67	76	22	34	35	77
Beam (metres):	5	6	7	2	3½	3	8
Draught (metres):	4	5	5	3	4½	4	6
Maximum speed, surface (knots):	13	17	18	4	9	10	15.5
submerged (knots):	7.5	7.5	7	28	26	12	17
Cruising speed, surface (knots):	8	10	10	—	—	6	10
submerged (knots):	4	4	4	—	—	4-10	5-10
Range at cruising speed, surface (nautical miles):[1]	5,650	8,500	13,450	—		4,450	15,500
submerged (nautical miles):	56	80	63	50nm at full speed	80nm at full speed	35nm at 10 kts 200nm at 4 kts	110nm at 10 kts 365nm at 5 kts
Maximum diving depth (metres):	150	250	200	—	—	150m	over 250
Torpedo tubes, bow:	3	4	4	—	2	2	6
stern:	0	1	2	—	0	0	0
Torpedoes carried:[2]	5	14	22	—	4	2	24
Mines carried:[2]	18	39	66	—	—	—	—
Guns:							
105mm:[3]	0	0	1	—	0	0	0
88mm:[3]	0	1	0	—	0	0	0
37mm AA:	0	1[8]	—[8]	—	0	0	0
20mm AA:	2 to 4	2 twin[8]	—[8]	—	0	0	4

1. Range would be increased if the boat ran on the diesel-electric drive method, using the other set to charge the batteries. 2. This number of mines and torpedoes could not be carried at the same time. 3. Not for anti-aircraft use. 4. Small coastal boats, used mainly for training. 5. The boats that carried the burden of the Atlantic campaign. 6. Experimental submarines with Walter turbine. 7. Electro-boats. Type XXIII was a coastal design; Type XXI was a large boat, intended to replace Type VIIC. 8. Usual armament, see p. 48.

Below: A group of Type VIIC boats moored next to the much larger Type IXC. Both these boats were employed in the Battle of the Atlantic, and this photograph clearly shows the different deck structures of the two types. (Photo: Imperial War Museum)

Miscellaneous vessels.

Top left: Fisheries Protection Vessel *Elbe* in 1933. Two special fisheries protection boats were launched in 1931, but *Weser* and *Elbe* were used as escort ships for motor minesweepers during the war. (Photo: Author's Collection)

Top centre: The Aviso *Grille*, which served as headquarters for the Admiral Polar Seas between May 1942 and June 1944, at Narvik. (Photo: Druppel)

Top right: Armed Fishing Vessel (KFK) 285. This boat was also known as Vorpostenboot 1534, and she saw service with the German Minesweeping Administration after the war. She was later renamed *Christel*. (Photo: Imperial War Museum)

Bottom left: The hospital ship *Rostock* was converted from Sperrbrecher *19*. She survived the war, and was still afloat during the mid-1960s under the name of *Marhonda*. (Photo: Imperial War Museum)

Bottom right: Cuxhaven, in the Elbe estuary, shortly after the war, with a variety of auxiliary craft in the harbour, including auxiliary minesweepers and patrol boats. (Photo: Imperial War Museum)

Rank, Uniform Awards and Insignia

Right: The layout of a naval locker allocated to a Matrosen-Stabsgefreiter. Boxes similar to the one at the bottom (on right) can still be seen. They were strongly made from wood with metal (often brass) reinforced corners and a lockable sliding lid. Although they look quite interesting and appear as if they were used for holding valuables, they were in fact only used for carrying shoe-cleaning materials and had a lockable lid so that they could be attached to the outside of kitbags. (Photo: Author's Collection)

Ranks

The basic ranks in 1938 and their approximate British equivalents were as follows.

Seamen:

Matrose	Ordinary Seaman
Matrosen-Gefreiter	Able Seaman
Matrosen-Obergefreiter	Leading Seaman
Matrosen-Hauptge-freiter	Leading Seaman (4½ years service)[1]

Junior NCOs:[2]

-maat[3]	Petty Officer
Ober-maat[3]	Chief Petty Officer

Warrant Officers:[4]

Bootsmann[5]	Boatswain[1]
Oberbootsmann[5]	Chief Boatswain[1]

Commissioned Officers:

Fähnrich zur See	Midshipman/Cadet
Oberfähnrich zur See	Sub-Lieutenant
Leutnant zur See	Lieutenant (Junior)
Oberleutnant zur See	Lieutenant (Senior)
Kapitänleutnant	Lieutenant-Commander
Korvettenkapitän	Commander
Fregattenkapitän	Captain (Junior)
Kapitän zur See	Captain
Kommodore	Commodore (Captain in a post usually held by a Rear-Admiral)
Konteradmiral	Rear-Admiral
Vizeadmiral	Vice-Admiral
Admiral	Admiral
Generaladmiral	No equivalent
Grossadmiral	Admiral of the Fleet

The following two titles are a little out of the ordinary and may not be easily recognized.

Kraftfahrer	Driver with rank of Ordinary Seaman
Kraftfahr . . .	Driver with rank given at the end of the word
Feldwebel	Same rank as Bootsmann (used for land-based units)

1. Ranks introduced later included Matrosen-Stabsgefreiter and Matrosen Stabsobergefreiter (more senior ranks of Leading Seaman), Stabsbootsmann (a senior rank of Boatswain) and Stabsoberbootsmann (a senior rank of Chief Boatswain).
2. Unteroffiziere ohne Portepee.
3. A man's trade sometimes prefixed the word 'maat'; a list of such trades can be found accompanying the illustrations on page 147.
4. Unteroffiziere mit Portepee (Senior NCOs).
5. If he had a special occupation, a man's trade could be used instead of the word 'Bootsmann'. Such words had several different endings, such as: Maschinist, Steuermann, Funkmeister, Feuerwerker.

Rank Insignia

The German Navy used a far wider range of rank insignia than any other branch of the armed forces. These fell into four basic types: Seamen, Petty and Chief Petty Officers, Warrant Officers and Commissioned Officers.

Seamen:

Seamen wore their badges of rank as chevrons on the left sleeve. These chevrons were often combined with trade insignia as a one-piece badge. Seamen also wore plain cornflower blue collar patches on the pea jacket as a further indication of rank.

Petty and Chief Petty Officers:

Petty Officer grades displayed their rank by means of an anchor on the left sleeve, upon which their trade badge was superimposed. Flat, woven, gold braid was worn on the collar of the pea jacket and on the cuffs of the uniform jacket. The collar patches on the pea jacket had a single bar of silver cord for Petty Officers and two bars for Chief Petty Officers. The silver colour was changed to gold on 1 December 1939.

Warrant Officers:

Warrant Officers displayed their rank by means of shoulder straps. These straps were in dark blue cloth with flat gold braid edging and various combinations of aluminium pips to denote ranks.

Commissioned Officers:

On the blue uniforms, rank groups were shown on the peaks of the caps, and specific ranks were indicated by rings on the jacket sleeves. On white summer uniforms and greatcoats (and also on the reefer jackets towards the end of the war), there were no sleeve rings; rank was shown by the peak of the cap and by shoulder straps.

Sleeve rings were made from flat, woven, gilt wire braid. The peaks of the caps were covered with dark blue cloth on which a pattern of oakleaves was embroidered in gilt wire.

Shoulder straps were based on the Army pattern, being made from matt silver braid on a dark blue cloth base. Admirals had a triple cord, the centre one in gilt and the outer cords in silver. Aluminium pips were used to denote specific ranks. Only the highest rank of Grand Admiral had crossed admiral's batons instead of the pips.

The Field Grey Uniform (Feldgraue Bekleidung):

Seamen wore chevrons on the left sleeve and field grey coloured shoulder straps, with their unit designation embroidered in yellow cotton thread.

Petty Officers and Warrant Officers wore shoulder straps similar to those worn by Warrant Officers on the blue uniform, but slightly wider with gilt braid on a field grey base.

Officer styles of shoulder straps followed those for the blue uniform, but the base colour was dark green. Officers from Leutnant to Kommodore wore silver-wire-embroidered collar patches with two yellow stripes. Admirals wore collar tabs based on the design for Army generals, but the gold wire was based on blue instead of red.

No peak embroidery was worn on the cap for the field grey uniform.

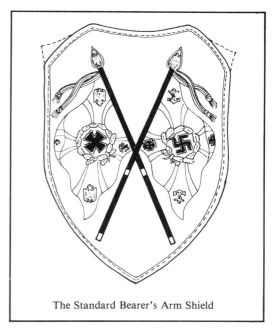

The Standard Bearer's Arm Shield

The Standard Bearer's Arm Shield

This embroidered shield insignia was worn by Naval Standard Bearers on the upper left arm. It was produced as shown on a white backing for the summer uniform, and on a dark blue backing of a slightly differing shape (indicated on this illustration by a broken line) for wear on the winter uniform.

Rank Insignia

Worn on the pullover, uniform jacket and pea jacket.

Matrosen-Gefreiter

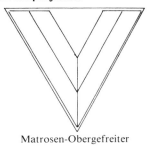

Matrosen-Obergefreiter

Matrosen-Hauptgefreiter

Matrosen-Stabsgefreiter

Matrosen-Stabsobergefreiter

Shoulder straps worn on the white summer jacket, white mess jacket, greatcoat and U-boat clothing; also, unofficially, on the reefer jacket towards the end of the war. Sleeve rings worn on the reefer jacket, mess jacket and frock-coat.

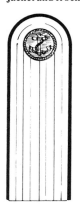

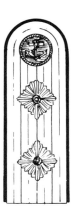

Shoulder strap and sleeve ring for Leutnant zur See

Shoulder strap and sleeve rings for Oberleutnant zur See

Shoulder strap and sleeve rings for Kapitänleutnant

Shoulder strap and sleeve rings for Korvettenkapitän

Shoulder strap and sleeve rings for Fregattenkapitän

Shoulder strap and sleeve rings for Kapitän zur See

Shoulder strap and sleeve ring for Kommodore

Shoulder strap and sleeve rings for Konteradmiral

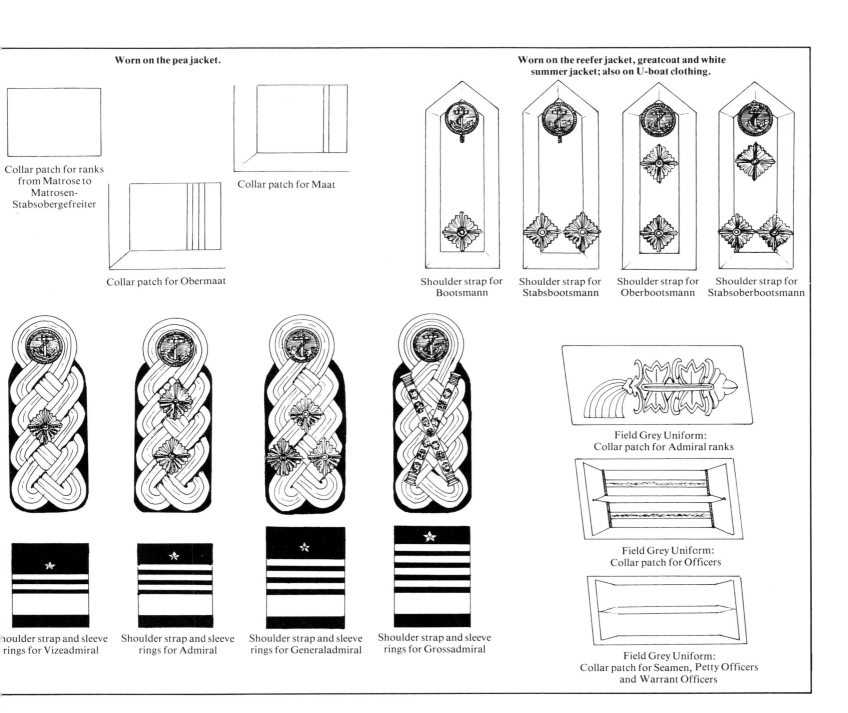

Worn on the pea jacket.

Collar patch for ranks
from Matrose to
Matrosen-
Stabsobergefreiter

Collar patch for Obermaat

Collar patch for Maat

**Worn on the reefer jacket, greatcoat and white
summer jacket; also on U-boat clothing.**

Shoulder strap for
Bootsmann

Shoulder strap for
Stabsbootsmann

Shoulder strap for
Oberbootsmann

Shoulder strap for
Stabsoberbootsmann

houlder strap and sleeve
rings for Vizeadmiral

Shoulder strap and sleeve
rings for Admiral

Shoulder strap and sleeve
rings for Generaladmiral

Shoulder strap and sleeve
rings for Grossadmiral

Field Grey Uniform:
Collar patch for Admiral ranks

Field Grey Uniform:
Collar patch for Officers

Field Grey Uniform:
Collar patch for Seamen, Petty Officers
and Warrant Officers

Trade Badges (Laufbahnabzeichen)

Trade badges or Laufbahnabzeichen for Seamen and Petty Officers were worn on the upper left arm; those for Warrant Officers on the shoulder strap; and those for Commissioned Officers on both arms.

Trade badges for Seamen consisted of a circular piece of navy blue badge cloth, approximately 6cm (2¼ in) in diameter, with the appropriate insignia machine-embroidered in golden yellow cotton thread. For wearing during the summer months (April to September) or in tropical waters, the insignia was machine-embroidered in cornflower blue on a white linen disc, and the edges were bound to prevent them from fraying. Lower-deck ratings wore a specialist badge to denote their specific duty (e.g., specializing in anti-aircraft gunnery within the naval artillery branch) below the trade badge.

Trade badges for Petty Officers were identical to those for Seamen, but were superimposed on an anchor. The design was also machine-embroidered in golden yellow thread on blue badge cloth, forming an oval of about 9cm × 7cm (3½ in × 2¾ in). The summer version was of similar design, but embroidered in blue cotton on a white linen base. Insignia for Chief Petty Officers was the same, but with the addition of a single chevron below the anchor.

Petty Officers and Chief Petty Officers could, at their own expense, purchase fine quality versions of their trade insignia in gilt metal alloy. This was fixed to a badge-cloth base by four prongs, which fastened behind a metal backing plate. It was covered on the reverse side with black linen.

Warrant Officers wore their trade insignia in gilt metal alloy on their shoulder straps.

Commissioned Officers wore their trade insignia, hand-embroidered in gilt wire, on a small blue cloth patch immediately above their sleeve rings. They also wore gilt metal trade insignia on the shoulder straps of appropriate uniforms.

Trade Badges

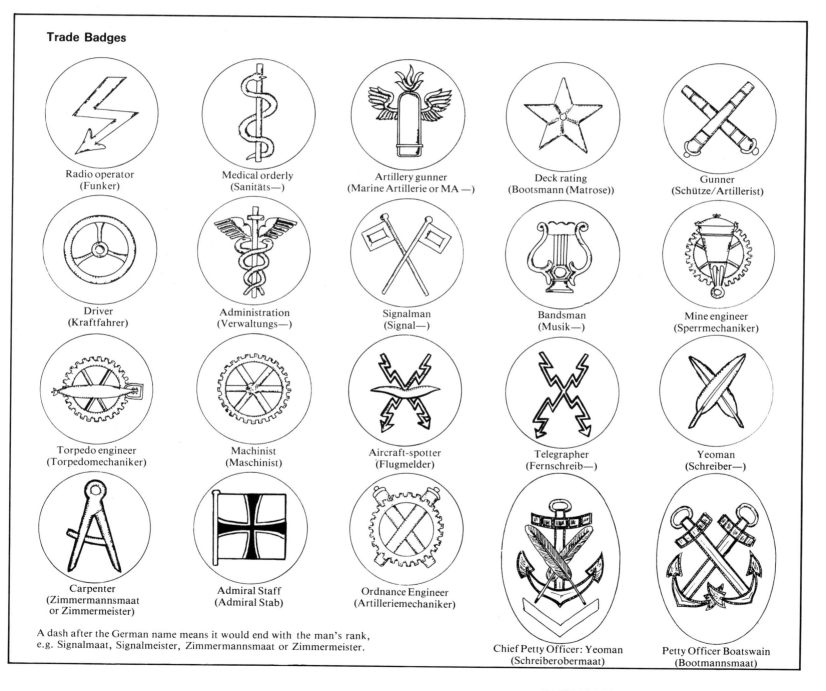

Radio operator
(Funker)

Medical orderly
(Sanitäts—)

Artillery gunner
(Marine Artillerie or MA —)

Deck rating
(Bootsmann (Matrose))

Gunner
(Schütze/Artillerist)

Driver
(Kraftfahrer)

Administration
(Verwaltungs—)

Signalman
(Signal—)

Bandsman
(Musik—)

Mine engineer
(Sperrmechaniker)

Torpedo engineer
(Torpedomechaniker)

Machinist
(Maschinist)

Aircraft-spotter
(Flugmelder)

Telegrapher
(Fernschreib—)

Yeoman
(Schreiber—)

Carpenter
(Zimmermannsmaat
or Zimmermeister)

Admiral Staff
(Admiral Stab)

Ordnance Engineer
(Artilleriemechaniker)

Chief Petty Officer: Yeoman
(Schreiberobermaat)

Petty Officer Boatswain
(Bootmannsmaat)

A dash after the German name means it would end with the man's rank,
e.g. Signalmaat, Signalmeister, Zimmermannsmaat or Zimmermeister.

Clothing

The Pullover Shirt (Bluse):

This was the most commonly worn item of clothing in the German Navy. The blue, winter version was made in navy blue melton cloth, with button fastening cuffs, and was worn with a cornflower blue collar, edged with three white bands and a black silk. The national emblem, in yellow silk weave or in yellow cotton embroidery, was worn over the right breast, and rank/trade badges on the left sleeve. Navy blue trousers made from the same material were worn with this shirt.

A white version of the pullover was worn during the summer months (April to September) or in tropical waters. The appearance of this was slightly more elaborate, with cornflower blue cuffs, trimmed in white and fastened by gilt anchor buttons. The insignia for this version were in cornflower blue on white backing.

A further version of the pullover, in a very strong white woollen cloth, was used as working rig. Much simplified, this version had a plain collar and was of a closer fit than the normal pullover.

The Uniform Jacket (Dienstjacke or Paradejacke):

Worn as service dress, this elaborate jacket resembled the officers' mess jacket and was worn by Sailors and Petty Officers only. It was worn over the pullover, with the pullover's collar outside the jacket. The jacket was fastened by means of a small chain link.

The insignia on this jacket were worn in the normal manner, with national emblem over the right breast and trade/rank badge on the sleeve. The cuffs for Petty and Chief Petty Officers were decorated with flat, woven, gilt wire braid.

The Pea Jacket (Überzieher):

Designed to be used over the service dress or over the pullover, this jacket was worn by all grades of seamen and petty officers in place of the greatcoat. A warm garment, it was made from thick, blue, melton cloth, was double-breasted and fastened by five anchor buttons. The national emblem and rank/trade badges were worn in the usual manner, and collar patches were also worn (it being the only form of naval clothing, apart from the field grey naval artillery dress, to use collar patches). The pea jacket for Petty and Chief Petty Officers had flat, woven, gilt wire braid around the collar.

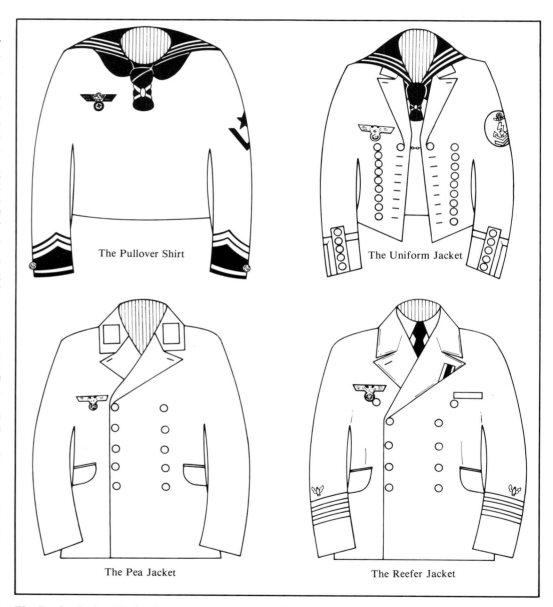

The Pullover Shirt

The Uniform Jacket

The Pea Jacket

The Reefer Jacket

The Reefer Jacket (Jackett):

The reefer jacket was worn by all ranks above Chief Petty Officer as parade dress, service dress or as walking-out uniform. It was made of navy blue cloth of smarter, but similar, style to the pea jacket. The top button of the double-breasted five-button front was usually left undone.

The national emblem, sewn over the right breast, was machine-embroidered in yellow cotton thread for Warrant Officers and hand-

Left: Aboard *M104* of the 2nd Minesweeper Half Flotilla. This shows a common combination of clothing, with the white summer trousers and matching caps being worn with the standard blue pullover shirts. (Photo: Author's Collection)

Below left: The uniform jacket for the lower ranks. (Photo: Author's Collection)

Below: The sailors' mess deck in *M104*. The men appear to be wearing their working rig over the naval pullover—hence the white jacket with large navy-blue collars. (Photo: Author's Collection)

Bottom: The typical rig of the German seaman—blue trousers, a pullover shirt and a cap with the name of his ship or unit.

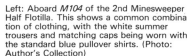

Below: The pea jacket. The collar of the pullover was worn on the outside of the jacket. Note the plain, cornflower-blue collar patches and the trade insignia. This photograph was taken during 1933, and the hat band inscription reads *Schiffsstamm-division der Nordsee*. (Photo: Author's Collection)

embroidered with gilt wire for Commissioned Officers.

Warrant Officers had shoulder straps with this jacket to indicate their rank, and Commissioned Officers also wore sleeve rings. It was not uncommon to find officers also wearing shoulder straps during the latter months of the war, but this was purely a fad and was against the written regulations. It was usual for all ranks to wear a white shirt and black tie under this jacket.

The White Summer Jacket (Weisses Jackett):

This smart uniform jacket was worn by Commissioned and Warrant Officers during the summer months (April to September) and in tropical waters. It was single-breasted, fastened by four gilt anchor buttons, with an open collar and with four pleated patch pockets. Rank was indicated by shoulder straps, and the national

emblem was made from gilt metal with a pin-back attachment. All insignia and the buttons could easily be removed for cleaning. Earlier versions of the jacket had a high collar and six button fasteners at the front. White trousers, white shirt and black tie were usually worn with this jacket.

The Mess Jacket (Messejacke):

Two types of mess jackets were produced, but exclusively for officer ranks. The standard type was made from fine quality blue material, with four buttons at the front, and fastened with a small chain. Rank was indicated by sleeve rings. The jacket was usually worn with a matching waistcoat (often replaced by a white one for formal dress occasions), a stiff white shirt and a black bow tie.

A white version of this mess jacket was produced for wear in tropical waters and during

the summer months. It was identical in design to the other garment, but rank was indicated by means of shoulder straps instead of the sleeve rings.

The Greatcoat (Mantel):

The greatcoat was worn by all ranks from Warrant Officer upwards. It was double-breasted with seven button fastenings, and there were a further seven buttons on the half belt. It had deep turn-back cuffs and was usually buttoned up to the top unless left open to display a neck decoration (such as the Knight's Cross). The coat had corn-flower blue lapels for Admirals; ranks were indicated on all coats by shoulder straps only, there being no sleeve rings.

Grand Admiral Karl Dönitz had the habit of wearing his coat open and he carried his gloves, instead of wearing them. One day, while sitting

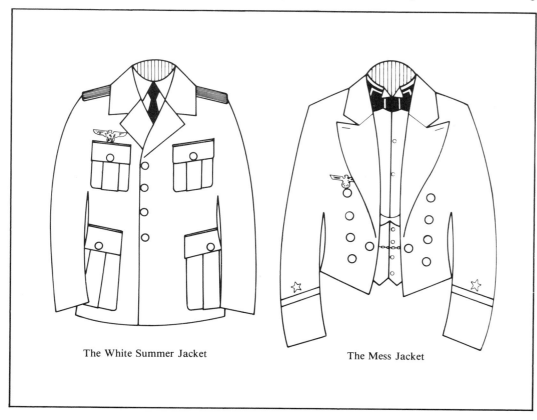

The White Summer Jacket

The Mess Jacket

Below: The greatcoat.
Top left: The author's parents and grandfather. The naval coat on the right can be compared with the Water Police version on the left. (Photo: Author's Collection)
Top right: Otto von Schrader, Admiral of the Norwegian West Coast, addressing the men shortly before awarding Iron Crosses. (*M1*, in the background, has been squeezed next to a warehouse and camouflaged to prevent her being spotted from the air.) Admirals usually wore their coats open to show the cornflower-blue lapels, while other ranks had theirs buttoned right up to the top. (Photo: Author's Collection)
Bottom of page: Awarding Iron Crosses (2nd Class) to crew members of *U37*. The photograph was taken during April 1940, and shows Dönitz with his Flag Lieutenant (H. J. von Knebel Doeberitz). (Photo: Bundesarchiv, Koblenz)

among a group of junior officers, he invited questions and was asked why he wore his coat and gloves against the written regulations. Looking the man straight in the eye, Dönitz replied: "I look just like every other sailor, and somehow you have got to notice that I am in charge."

The Field Grey Tunic (Feldbluse):
A field grey tunic, with high collar and four patch pockets, was worn by naval artillery land units, by Seamen undergoing initial training and also by numerous sailors towards the end of the war, because crews from obsolete ships were drafted into land units. (This explains why so many photographs of what are obviously land uniforms show naval badges.)

Below: Adolf Kirchner of the Naval Artillery. On the left he wears the field grey uniform, which was his walking out uniform. Note that the trousers were not intended for wearing inside boots. He is also wearing an Army-style cap; the naval version, which was more boat-shaped, can be seen in the right-hand photograph. This shows his everyday working uniform, with the rank insignia of Matrosen-Hauptgefreiter.

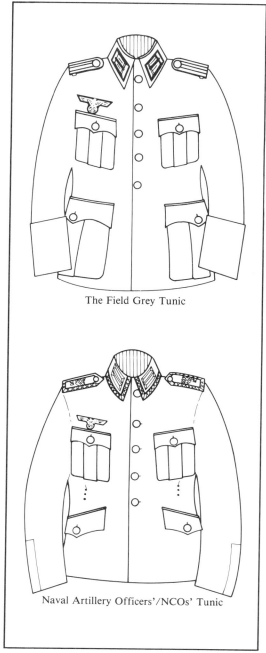

The Field Grey Tunic

Naval Artillery Officers'/NCOs' Tunic

Right: The frock coat. Admiral Erich Raeder inspecting officers before the war. The men are wearing frock coats with brocade belts. Note that the epaulettes worn by Erwin Wassner in the photograph on page 173 are not worn here. (Photo: Author's Collection)

Various styles were available. From photographic evidence, it appears that Officers tended to wear Army-pattern tunics. Non-commissioned ranks wore a similar tunic, but of inferior quality, with a shorter skirt and a 'slash' rather than patch pockets. Both the collar and shoulder straps were edged with gilt braid, whereas lower ranks had none on either. The jacket for lower ranks had a plain collar and a much shorter skirt.

Buttons were identical for all ranks. Normal anchor buttons and the national emblem were worn as mentioned before, but the motif was on a dark blue-green backing for Officers and on the field grey cloth for the lower ranks. Collar patches were yellow, and were similar to the Army pattern. There were two types of collar patches: one for lower ranks and NCOs and another for commissioned officers up to the rank of Captain.

Collar patches for Admirals were embroidered in gilt wire on a blue backing, and were identical to those worn by Army Generals.

The Frock Coat ('Gehrock', later 'Rock'):

This was a three-quarter length coat worn only by officers. It was slightly shorter than the greatcoat but considerably longer than any naval jacket. It also differed from the jacket and greatcoat in that both shoulder straps and sleeve rings were worn. A black leather belt or an elegant silver brocade belt was usually worn on the outside of this garment.

Epaulettes could be attached to the shoulder straps, but these were usually only worn by an Officer in foreign waters or at the Officer's own wedding (for which there was also a special pair of trousers with a broad golden band along the outside seams of the legs).

The frock coat was worn for official functions and for walking-out on Sundays by Officers only. The early design of the coat was called 'Gehrock' (frock coat), but the style was changed later and it became known simply as 'Rock' (coat).

The Cloak ('Umhang', nickname 'Spanier'):

This was rather like an elaborate opera cloak. It was secured with a small chain attached to two lion-head buttons, and the whole cloak was lined with silver-grey silk. Pre-war garments such as this received a new lease of life during the war when many were 'requisitioned' by the men's wives for making into dresses.

Informal dress.
Left: The men from *U377* demonstrate another type of uniform — one that has become so dirty after a long spell at sea (where there were no washing facilities) that it is hardly recognizable. The men could just squeeze a few changes of underwear into the boat, but that was about all. This photograph must have been taken after the summer of 1943 because two twin AA guns are just visible and, generally, U-boats carried only one gun up to this time. Just to the left of the attack periscope is Heinrich Böhm (see page 163). (Photo: Author's Collection)
Right: Two different types of working rig aboard a mine-sweeper, 1933. The three men on the right are members of the Training Division of the North Sea (*Schiffsstamm-division der Nordsee*) and the others are minesweeper crew members.
Below right: Afternoon coffee aboard *M18*. When thinking about the identification of uniforms, it is important to remember that there were two basic types: the uniforms they should have worn and those they actually did wear. The men would often wear private clothing, and the jumper knitted by grandma was often warmer than the one issued by the Navy.

Left: Eagle symbols to be found in the heraldry of the German Navy. Top, the eagle of the Reichsmarine; centre, the eagle of the Kriegsmarine; bottom, the political eagle of the NSDAP often used by the Kriegsmarine.

War Badges

A vast range of war badges was created from 1939 until 1945. Many of them were designed by well-known artists, engravers and designers to reflect the branch of service to which the wearer belonged. All naval units were eligible for some type of award, although not every department was covered by an individual badge. Crews of supply ships, which supported raiders such as *Atlantis, Thor* and *Pinguin*, were eligible for the Auxiliary Cruiser Badge.

Method of wear:

These war badges were produced in two basic forms: either as a badge (Abzeichen) to be worn on the breast, or as a clasp (Spange) worn above the left breast pocket (or in that position, if there were no pockets). The only exceptions to this rule were the seven grades of awards for the Midget Weapons Unit (Kleinkampfverband), which were fixed to the sleeve. All these badges ranked lower than decorations; an Iron Cross, for example, was worn above the war badge.

Attachment:

The majority of these badges were made of metal, although in some cases cloth variants could be purchased at the wearer's expense. The first mentioned were attached to the uniform by means of a hinged pin fitting, of which there were two common types: the early badges were mostly produced with a broad flat pin, which passed through thread loops sewn on the tunic; later examples had round pins and could be pushed through the material of the tunic. These pins ran either vertically or horizontally.

Materials:

During the early stages of the war, these badges were generally made from a bronze alloy (called Tombakbronze) or brass, with a very high quality gilt finish. Later, they were produced in a fine-grain zinc and, towards the end of the war, in very poor quality pot metal known in Germany as war metal (Kriegsmetall). The gilt finish of these later types wore off remarkably quickly and it is not uncommon to find these badges today in mint condition, but with hardly any traces of their original gilt colouring. Later, when the Germans were short of materials, specimens were finished in poor-quality paint.

It should also be noted that not all these badges were produced in Germany. Consequently, it is possible to find several deviations from the original design, as well as a variety of production standards.

The Awards:

A certificate or some type of document usually accompanied the badge itself at the award ceremony. These pieces of paper ranged from fairly plain designs to most impressive and elaborate works of art. There was no real attempt to standardize the documents, as was the case with certificates for decorations, and it is quite possible that, towards the end of the war, no documents were awarded.

The badges themselves were handed over in anything from a brown paper bag or small box to an elaborate velvet-lined case. In many cases, the badge was pinned directly onto the recipient's tunic, without any box or case being given with it.

Miniature stick pin versions of these badges exist, for wearing as lapel pins on civilian clothing.

Variant Awards:

Naval war badges were also produced on a limited scale in occupied France. Their standard of finish was very high, the gilt areas of the badge being copper-plated and the contrasting areas silvered, rather than the usual gun metal colour. At least three types of war badges (E-boat, High Seas Fleet and Coastal Artillery) are known to have been produced in France, and it is quite possible that there were others.

The detail on these badges differed greatly from their German counterparts, the most striking difference being their smaller size. It can be assumed from their rarity that these badges were only produced on a small scale.

U-Boat Badge (Ubootskriegsabzeichen):

This was the first war badge introduced during the Second World War. It was instituted on 13 October 1939—the day that Günther Prien and *U47* started their famous attack on the battleship HMS *Royal Oak* in Scapa Flow. Paul Casberg designed the badge to follow the First World War pattern of a U-boat superimposed on an oval wreath of laurel; the only noteworthy change was the substitution of an eagle and swastika for the old imperial crown.

The basic requirement for the award of the badge was that the recipient had served on at least two operational cruises, although this could be waived for wounded men.

The badge itself measured 48mm × 40mm (about 2in × 1½in) and was worn on the left side of the tunic or shirt. It was usually made from gilt metal, but embroidered cloth versions can also be found.

A special gilted, solid silver version of this badge was produced by Schwerin of Berlin. It can be identified by the nine small diamonds that were set into the swastika. Unfortunately, this form is very rare: only 29 were awarded to outstanding U-boat commanders. It appears that Schwerin also made the badge in solid gold with the swastika and laurel wreath encrusted with diamonds. Only one was made, which was then awarded to Karl Dönitz.

The original version of the U-boat Badge was introduced on the orders of Grand Admiral Raeder, and the silver version was added later on by Grand Admiral Dönitz.

Destroyer Badge (Zerstörer Kriegsabzeichen):
The Destroyer Badge was instituted during June 1940 as an award for men engaged in the Battle of Narvik, during the Norwegian Campaign. In October of the same year, it was authorized for crews of other destroyers and for men serving in torpedo-boats who could fulfil one of the following conditions.
1. Participation in three engagements against the enemy.
2. Participation in twelve sorties without engaging the enemy.
3. Being wounded in action.
4. Service in a vessel that had been sunk by enemy action.
5. Especially meritorious service.
The designer, Paul Casberg, based the ship depicted upon the badge on the destroyer *Z21* (*Wilhelm Heidkamp*). The award was worn on the left side of the shirt or tunic and measured 54mm × 44mm (about 2in × 1¾in).

Badge for Minesweepers, Submarine-Hunters and other Security Forces:
In Germany this is called the 'Kriegsabzeichen für Minensuch, Ubootsjagd und Sicherungsverbände'. It was instituted on 31 August 1940 for crews of minesweepers, submarine-chasers and

escort vessels who could fulfil one of the following conditions.
1. Participation in three operational sorties.
2. Participation in one successful sortie.
3. Six months active service.
4. Being wounded in action.
5. Service in a vessel sunk by enemy action.
The badge, in gilt and measuring 55mm × 44mm (about 2in × 1¾in) was designed by Otto Placzek and worn on the left side of the tunic or shirt.

Motor Torpedo-Boat Badge (Schnellbootskriegsabzeichen):
This was instituted on 30 May 1941 for crews of torpedo and motor torpedo-boats to replace the Destroyer Badge for which they had been eligible.

(There was a split in the organization, with torpedo-boats leaving Destroyer Command and forming their own arm.) Conditions for its receipt remained similar.

The badge was originally designed by Wilhelm E. Peekhaus of Berlin to depict a silver-coloured, early type of motor torpedo-boat speeding through a gilt wreath. It was redesigned, with help from Kpt.z.S. Rudolf Petersen (Commander-in-Chief for Motor Torpedo-Boats) during January 1943 to show a more modern boat. The first design measured 45mm × 57mm (about 1¾in × 2¼in) and the later version 52mm × 60mm (about 2in × 2¼in).

A special badge, in gilted solid silver with nine diamonds on the swastika and depicting the early

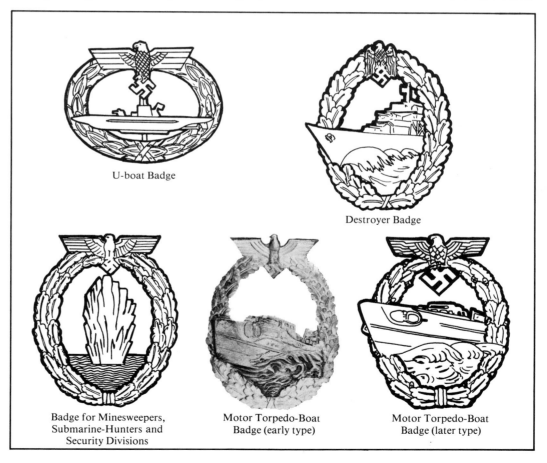

U-boat Badge

Destroyer Badge

Badge for Minesweepers, Submarine-Hunters and Security Divisions

Motor Torpedo-Boat Badge (early type)

Motor Torpedo-Boat Badge (later type)

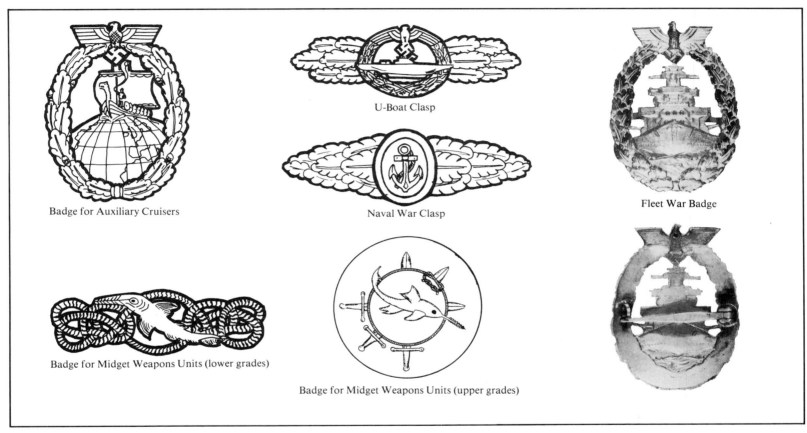

Badge for Auxiliary Cruisers

U-Boat Clasp

Naval War Clasp

Fleet War Badge

Badge for Midget Weapons Units (lower grades)

Badge for Midget Weapons Units (upper grades)

type of boat, was produced by Schwerin of Berlin. It was awarded eight times to outstanding motor torpedo-boat commanders, all of whom also held the Knight's Cross of the Iron Cross.

Auxiliary Cruiser Badge (Kriegsabzeichen für Hilfskreuzer):

This badge was instituted on 24 April 1941 for crews of auxiliary cruisers and also for the crews of their supply ships who had taken part in at least one long-distance cruise. It was designed by Wilhelm E. Peekhaus to show a gilt metal wreath with a silver-coloured globe, and was similar in size to the earlier version of the Motor Torpedo-Boat Badge.

A special edition of this badge was commissioned, with fifteen small diamonds and made from solid silver, but it was only awarded two or possibly three times. One was definitely given to Kpt.z.S. Bernhard Rogge, commander of the legendary *Atlantis*, and another went to Kpt.z.S. Ernst-Felix Krüder of the famous *Pinguin*. It is thought the badge was also awarded to Kpt.z.S. Hellmuth von Ruckteschell, who commanded several auxiliary cruisers, but it is not certain whether he actually received it.

U-Boat Clasp (Uboots Frontspange):

This clasp was introduced by Grand Admiral Dönitz in May 1944 to recognize further merit on the part of U-boat personnel who had already been awarded the U-boat Badge. No fixed criteria were laid down for this award, except that each application had to be approved personally by Dönitz.

The clasp was initially only made from bronze, but a silver grade was added during November 1944. They were designed and made by Schwerin of Berlin and measured 71mm × 24mm (about 2¾in × 1in).

Naval War Clasp (Marine Frontspange):

This clasp was introduced on 19 November 1944 for all crews other than U-boat personnel. Requirements were five times those needed for the appropriate war badge. The only original examples of this clasp extant are crude, and were probably made aboard the *Prinz Eugen*.

Badge for Midget Weapons Unit (Kampfabzeichen der Kleinkampfmittel):

This badge was introduced during November

Below: Certificate for the Blockade-Breakers Badge. Blockade-breakers were merchant ships, and these badges were not awarded by the military authorities. Blockadebrecher (Blockade-breakers) should not be confused with Sperrbrecher (Auxiliary minesweepers or barrier-breaking vessels). The former were merchant ships that tried to break through the enemy blockade and bring their cargoes to a German port; the latter were military vessels, quite often large cargo ships, equipped with special mine clearing gear to break through minefields outside their port.

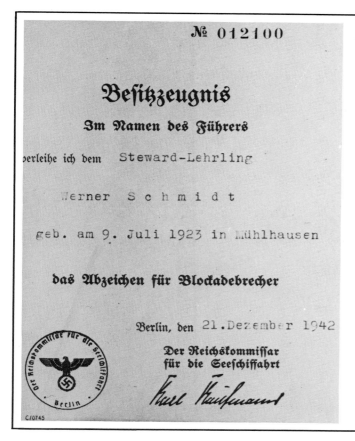

Badge for Blockade-Breakers

U-Boat Badge (First World War)

Wounded Badge

Motor-Boat Rescue Badge (Air Sea Rescue, controlled by the Luftwaffe). Probably not awarded; but photographs of the badge testify that at least some were manufactured.

1944. There were seven grades:

1. A yellow embroidered swordfish within a rope circle on a blue cloth backing; awarded for participation in one action. (This should not be confused with the emblem of the 9th U-boat Flotilla, which also depicted a swordfish.)
2. As above, but with the addition of a single sword, pointing forty-five degrees to the left; awarded for participation in two actions.
3. As above, but with two crossed swords; awarded for completing three actions.
4. As above, but with a third, vertical sword added; awarded for completing four actions.
5. A bronze metal clasp showing the swordfish superimposed on a knotted rope; awarded for participation in five actions.
6. As above, but made from a silver-coloured

metal; awarded after completing seven missions.
7. As above, but in a gilt metal; awarded after completing at least ten missions.

The cloth awards were worn on the upper right sleeve and the metal clasps on the left breast.

Fleet War Badge (Flottenkriegsabzeichen):

Introduced during April 1941 for crews of battleships and cruisers who could fulfil one of the following conditions:
1. Twelve weeks active service at sea.
2. Service in a ship lost at sea.
3. Being wounded in action.
4. Participation in one particularly successful cruise.

The badge, in gilt metal with the battleship in dark grey, was designed by the marine artist Adolf

Bock. It measured 44mm × 57mm (about 1¾in × 2¼in).

Blockade-Breakers Badge (Abzeichen für Blockadebrecher):

This was awarded to crews of merchant ships that were in foreign ports at the start of the war and managed to bring their vessels into a German-held port. Men serving in ships lost at sea by enemy action or men who prevented their ship from falling into enemy hands by scuttling were also eligible.

The badge was 51mm (2in) in diameter and was usually awarded together with a half-size miniature for wearing with civilian clothing. It was dark grey in colour, with the eagle and swastika silvered.

Right: The Sailor's cap. The white summer version bears the hat band legend 'Panzerschiff Admiral Graf Spee', while the dark blue version has the later legend 'Kriegsmarine'. The subject of these two photographs is Heinrich Böhm (who, after accidentally shooting a torpedo while carrying out maintenance work, was nicknamed 'Wilhelm'—after Wilhelm Tell—by his commander). The left-hand photograph shows Böhm in the uniform jacket, with the white gloves that were intended for wear with this walking out uniform. The right-hand picture shows him after promotion to Chief Petty Officer. (Note the collar insignia.) Bottom of page: Three examples of hat bands for wear with the sailors' cap. (Photos: Author's Collection). The ribbons at the back of the sailor's cap can be seen in the photograph on page 173.

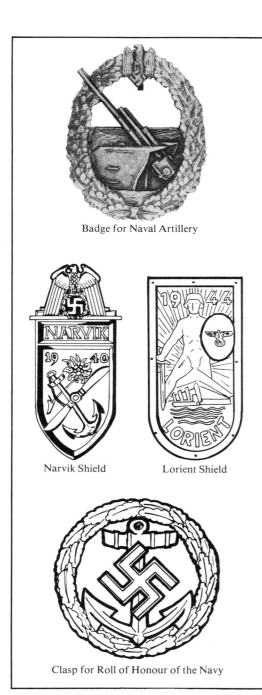

Badge for Naval Artillery

Narvik Shield   Lorient Shield

Clasp for Roll of Honour of the Navy

Naval Artillery Badge (Kriegsabzeichen für Marineartillerie):

This badge was awarded to crews of naval artillery batteries engaged in either anti-aircraft or coastal defence duties. It first appeared during June 1941 and was awarded on a points basis, a total of eight points being required for the badge. Two were given for shooting down an aeroplane unassisted, one point if helped by another gun, half a point for detecting enemy aircraft, and so forth. The badge, in gilt colour with a dark grey gun emplacement motif, was designed by Otto Placzek and measured 55mm × 42mm (about 2¼ in × 1¾ in).

The Narvik Shield (Narvikschild):

The Narvik Shield was designed by Professor Klein of Munich and was instituted during August 1940 for men involved in the Battle of Narvik between April and June of 1940. Two different versions were produced: a gilt metal badge for the Navy and a silver-coloured type for Army and Air Force.

Of a total of 8,577 distributed throughout the Navy, 2,670 went to destroyer personnel; 411 of these were posthumous awards.

The badge measured 92mm × 40mm (about 3½ in × 1½ in) and was fixed to a piece of navy blue backing cloth, which was sewn onto the upper left arm of the tunic.

The Lorient Shield (Lorientschild):

The idea to commemorate the stand of the Lorient garrison with a badge was only approved at local level and it probably never received official backing. Apparently, the shield was made from a variety of materials, and was somewhat crudely manufactured. There were four pairs of small holes around the edge for attaching to the sleeve.

Clasp for the Roll of Honour of the Navy (Ehrentafelspange der Kriegsmarine):

This clasp was intended to recognize those men whose names were recorded in the Ehrentafel der deutschen Kriegsmarine, a roll of honour recording heroic deeds by German seamen.

The clasp consisted of a gilt metal wreath of oakleaves with an anchor, upon which a swastika was superimposed. It was clipped to the ribbon of the Iron Cross Second Class and worn from the buttonhole. Very few were ever awarded.

Headgear

Headgear for the Kriegsmarine followed the traditional naval design, the principal innovation of the Third Reich period being the introduction of gilt wire embroidery on the peaks of officers' caps to indicate rank groupings.

The most frequently worn type of headgear among the lower ranks was the sailors' cap with tally ribbon. This consisted of a rigid band with a floppy, wide-brimmed top fitting over it. The colour was dark blue for winter, white for summer and for tropical waters. The hat band was fitted with a long ribbon, which had the name of the wearer's ship or shore establishment woven upon it in gilt wire gothic letters. Insignia, in the form of a gilt eagle and swastika over the national cockade, was worn on the front of the brim.

All these ribbons with names should have been withdrawn during the war and replaced by one bearing the legend 'Kriegsmarine', but this does not appear to have been strictly adhered to, although the Kriegsmarine hat bands became more common.

The sailors' cap became less popular as the war progressed, and it was gradually replaced by the forage cap or Schiffchen ('Schiffchen' meaning small ship, because of its shape). This was made from blue woollen cloth with a black lining, and it was worn by all ranks from Ordinary Seaman to Grand Admiral.

Lower ranks had the insignia woven in yellow silk on blue; officers had gilt wire instead of the silk, and also had gilt piping around the flap.

A forage cap was produced in the same pattern for the naval field grey uniform. This had the insignia woven in yellow on green for lower ranks and in gilt wire for officers, who also had the gilt piping around the flap. Some examples of the field-grey forage cap have an inverted, lemon-coloured chevron over the cockade.

The forage cap was also produced in white for summer months and for tropical waters, but it appears to have been worn but rarely. The insignia for this cap was blue on a white background.

A peaked field cap, very similar to those worn by the Afrikakorps and also in tan canvas with gold silk woven insignia, was used to a limited degree in the Mediterranean area.

The peaked cap, called 'Schirmmütze', was similar in basic appearance for all ranks. It had a leather peak, a woven mohair band and a wide-

1. A. Schiffsstammdivision der Nordsee. 1. A.

Panzerschiff Deutschland

1. Marineunteroffizierlehrabteilung. 1.

Below: Forage caps being worn by crewmen of *U377*. The officers' pattern was similar, but this had gilt piping and gilt insignia. The officer on the right is a Naval Official (Marine-beamter); note the plain leather peak to his cap and the silver chin cords. (Photo: Author's Collection)

brimmed floppy top in blue cloth. The chin strap was made from leather and fastened by two small anchor buttons. The insignia consisted of an embroidered eagle and swastika, either in yellow cotton or in gilt wire, on the front of the floppy top. A red/silver/black national cockade, surrounded by a wreath of oakleaves, was attached to the cap band, which was also embroidered in either yellow cotton or in gilt wire.

The peak of the cap was in plain leather for non-commissioned officers; those ranking from Leutnant zur See to Kapitänleutnant had a thin row of gilt wire oakleaves embroidered on the blue cloth of the peak; officers from Korvettenkapitän to Kommodore had a wider row of oakleaves; and Admirals had two wide rows of gilt wire oakleaves.

White covers, removable and fixed types, were worn on the peaked cap during summer months and also in tropical waters. Almost without exception, U-boat commanders wore a white top to their caps at all times.

The peaked cap for wearing with the field grey uniform was similar in design to the normal blue cap. It had a plain undecorated peak for all ranks, with the top in field grey and with dark green piping. The cap band was also dark green and, depending upon the manufacturer, either with or without the dark green piping. Silver cord chin straps were worn by officers and leather chin straps by NCOs. The insignia were similar to those

Belt Buckle for Lower Ranks

Officers' Pattern Belt Buckle

on the blue cap, but were embroidered in gilt on green for officers, while NCOs had plain metal badges.

Belts and Buckles

The belt buckle for the lower ranks of the German Navy was identical in design to the buckle worn by the Army and was made from iron with a brass plate. An aluminium buckle with gilt wash (a thin anodised coating) was used for parades; the front of this was pebbled and there was a separate centrepiece. Examples of this buckle with a dark blue painted finish also exist; these were used for front-line field service duty. All these buckles were usually worn with a brown leather belt.

There were several variations in the general appearance of the buckle. Officers normally wore a gilt finish, pebbled aluminium, double-clawed buckle; a circular buckle consisting of an oakleaf wreath surrounding an anchor, was worn for dress occasions, with a black and silver brocade belt. The buckle was cast in aluminium and had a gilt finish. A similar buckle, only much smaller, was worn with the blue canvas dagger or sword belt inside the greatcoat or jacket, while the brocade belt was worn on the outside.

Small Arms and Edged Weapons

There appears to have been no hard and fast rule about the issue of guns. They were often given to a ship or unit and distributed by the commander when required, and then collected again after use. Some men carried their own personal—but naval issue—pistols either for self defence or to ensure a quick death should they find themselves in an impossible situation faced with a slow and painful end.

Pistols:
The hand-guns used by the Navy were standard pieces issued to other branches of the armed services. There were no special naval pattern guns, like the naval P08 of the Imperial Navy. However, the Mauser HSc automatic appears to have been very popular during the Third Reich period.

Rifles and other small arms:
Standard issue infantry weapons, such as the Mauser Kar 98k, MP38/40, MG34/41, were issued to naval personnel when required. It appears that obsolete weapons, such as the Mauser Gewehr 98,

were issued to naval units, so that front-line Army units could be given preference for new weapons.

Bayonets:
The standard Mauser 98 bayonet, with either wood or bakelite grips and worn in a brown leather frog, was issued to naval personnel.

Daggers:
Two basic forms of naval daggers were produced, either with a beaten or an engraved scabbard. The dagger itself had a long double-edged blade, with two fullers, and was either plain or with a large variety of etch patterns of naval motifs. Blades were made in both plain and Damascus steel, although the latter were not usually issued by the Navy—they had to be purchased. The cross-piece, with anchor motif, was in gilt cast brass, as was the pommel, which was in the form of an eagle and swastika. The grip was in white celluloid with a gilt wire wrap over the wooden base. Special scabbard designs with ornate oakleaf designs were also produced.

The dagger was suspended from two black satin straps, which were fitted with gilt alloy, lion-head motif buckles. Administration officials had silver buckles.

(Naval daggers, virtually indistinguishable from the original, are still being produced today to meet the demand from collectors, and a new version with the swastika replaced by an anchor is being made for the Federal Navy.)

The Honour Dagger:
This highly ornate version of the naval dagger was instituted by Grand Admiral Raeder, and it is known to have been awarded at least six times. It was manufactured by the firm of Carl Eikhorn in Solingen. The swastika on the pommel was encrusted with small diamonds and the ivory grip had an ornate oakleaf wrap. The blade was made from Damascus steel with a raised gilt dedication on the ricasso. The scabbard was also very ornate, with fine oakleaf decorations.

The Sword:
The naval sword was traditional in appearance, with a gilt lion-head pommel, a white grip with gilt wire wrap and a fouled anchor on the folding shell guard. The scabbard was in black leather with gilt brass fittings.

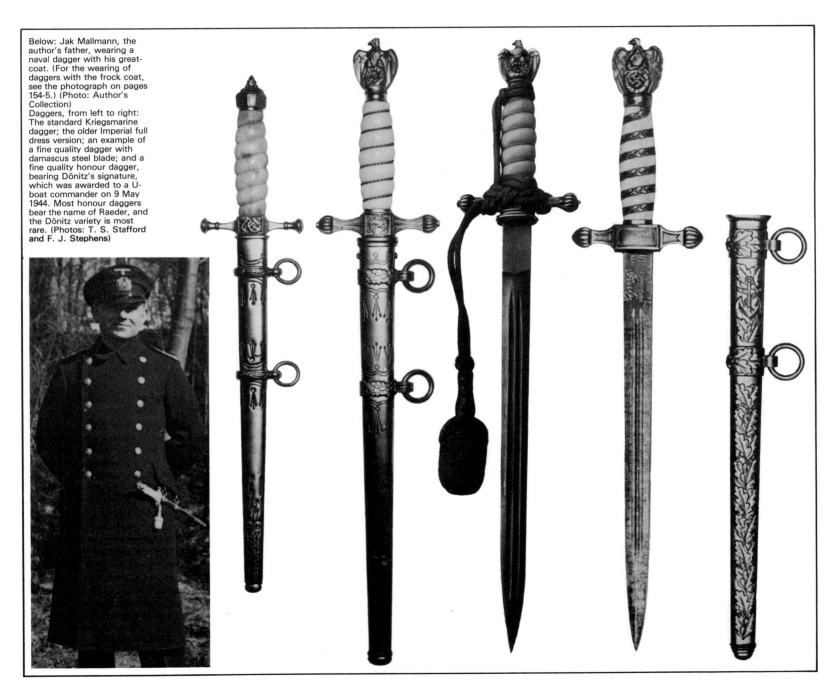

Below: Jak Mallmann, the author's father, wearing a naval dagger with his great-coat. (For the wearing of daggers with the frock coat, see the photograph on pages 154-5.) (Photo: Author's Collection)

Daggers, from left to right: The standard Kriegsmarine dagger; the older Imperial full dress version; an example of a fine quality dagger with damascus steel blade; and a fine quality honour dagger, bearing Dönitz's signature, which was awarded to a U-boat commander on 9 May 1944. Most honour daggers bear the name of Raeder, and the Dönitz variety is most rare. (Photos: T. S. Stafford and F. J. Stephens)

Below: The Marksmanship Lanyard with acorn attachment to indicate proficiency with rifle or machine-gun. The author's father, seen here aboard the steamer *Hansa* in May 1939, gained this lanyard on 17 August 1933 after 'drilling' holes through the centre of 10cm discs, holding the rifle freehand, without support, at a range of 100 metres. (One of these discs is still in existence, signed by the training officer.) This photograph also shows the uniform jacket with gilt braid decorations on the cuffs for petty and chief petty officers; the white summer pullover is being worn under the jacket with the collar on the outside. (Photo: Author's Collection)

Marksmanship Awards

Marksmanship was recognized by awarding a lanyard made from plaited blue cord, which was worn from the right shoulder. The type of weapon with which proficiency had been achieved was indicated by a miniature device hung from the end of the lanyard. An acorn, as shown in the diagram, indicated rifle and machine-gun marksmanship. Other symbols were as follows.

Shell: Deck guns, anti-aircraft and coastal artillery.
Shell with wings: Anti-aircraft machine-guns.
Torpedo: Torpedo shooting.

These awards were of gun metal colour for the first award and silver and gold for the second and third awards. The lanyard itself also differed for each higher award:

1st Award: Plain blue lanyard with a black miniature.
2nd Award: Blue lanyard with a silver inter-woven stripe and a silver miniature.
3rd Award: Blue lanyard with a silver inter-woven stripe and a gilt miniature.
4th Award: Blue lanyard with a silver inter-woven stripe and a gilt metal miniature.

Naval Officials (Marinebeamten)

Marinebeamten were officials who carried out administrative duties, and they were given status equivalent to the appropriate naval rank. Their uniforms were in the same style as those of regular officers, but the insignia were in a silver rather than a gold colour. Their trade speciality was indicated by a small embroidered badge on each sleeve, worn just above the sleeve rings: this insignia consisted of an eagle and swastika over the appropriate trade badge.

The peaked cap for officials was similar to the standard naval cap, but it also had the silver insignia. The peak was plain leather with wire chin cords, rather than plain leather ones, and admirals had gilt wire chin cords.

Naval officials were further distinguished by the use of coloured piping on uniforms where epaulettes were worn: black for technical personnel, carmine red for legal officials, and cornflower blue for administrative officials, pharmacists and all other non-technical personnel.

Naval chaplains were also classed as officials and wore the uniform of the Marinebeamten with a few minor changes. There was, for example, a silver wire, embroidered cross above the national cockade on the peaked cap. Collar patches, showing a cross surrounded by oakleaves in wire embroidered on purple velvet, were also worn on the reefer jacket.

Coastal Police (Marineküstenpolizei)

This was a coastal security unit performing similar duties to the United States Coastguards. The men wore standard naval uniforms with special police insignia in gilt colour. A gorget, bearing the luminous inscription 'Marineküstenpolizei', was worn when on duty, as was a cuff title with the same inscription. After 1943, the police pattern insignia was replaced by standard naval rank insignia.

Awards and Insignia for Individual Units

Some units created their own unofficial awards and badges, usually incorporating their own insignia in the design. There were two main types: lapel badges, worn in a similar manner to Air Force insignia; and non-portable badges in the form of shields, plaques or paintings on sides of ships. One example of lapel insignia was created by Korvkpt. Hans Bartels, commander of mine-sweeper *M1*. When he became Chief of Naval Defence Units in part of Norway, he instituted his own Pin of Honour, a small pin that was presented with an elaborate award document in colour. (See page 26.)

The 3rd Motor Torpedo-Boat Flotilla was one of the units that produced its own shield, which was finely cast in aluminium and hand-painted. The insignias or emblems painted directly on to the sides of the ships were either done by hand or, if the insignia were elaborate, the boat carried a sheet metal stencil. Officially, the Naval Command did not object to such insignias; they specified that they should be removed before the boat went to sea, but many boats disregarded the directive and proudly carried their badges into battle. Even so, the emblems had to be repainted frequently and, as a result, the exact details of the design tended to differ.

Naval Hitler Youth (Marine-Hitlerjugend)

The Naval Hitler Youth played an important part in the training of future recruits for both the Kriegsmarine and the merchant navy. They wore the standard naval rating's uniform with the following insignia:

1. An enamelled red, silver and black diamond-shaped Hitler Youth badge in place of the national insignia on the rating's cap.
2. A tally ribbon, in pale blue, with gilt block letters woven to show the district.
3. A Hitler Youth armband on the left arm.
4. Also on the left arm, above the armband, a woven triangular badge with the district designation.

Achievement Badge for Shipyard Workers (Werftleistungsabzeichen)

This was introduced during 1944 to recognize the U-boat men's appreciation of the work done by the maintenance fitters at their home bases. It is not known whether this was an official award, as very little information about it has come to light, and original examples of the badge are relatively scarce.

the reverse side was plain silver-coloured, with a hinged pin fitting to attach the cross to the left breast of the tunic. Variations exist with a screw back fitting, and some crosses also had brass centres (which were especially popular with naval personnel because they did not rust as quickly as the iron variety). Some of these brass-centred crosses were also convex in shape, which was popular during the First World War, but fairly rare during the Second.

One major and extremely rare variation was the Japanese-produced type. Obermaat Conrad Metzner and some twenty-five other men, all from the auxiliary cruiser *Michel*, were awarded the EK1 by Admiral Paul Wenneker, who was the Naval Attaché in Tokyo. These were made from pure Japanese silver with a copper centre.

Men who had won the EK1 in 1914 and were awarded it again during the Second World War wore the 1914 version on the left breast of the tunic and above this a clasp similar to that for the EK2, but this one had a hinged pin fitting and it was slightly larger, 45mm × 31mm (1¾in × 1¼in). The clasp was presented in a small black case lined with black velvet, and there was a silver clasp embossed on the lid.

Approximately 300,000 EK1s and Clasps were awarded during the Second World War.

The Knight's Cross:

The Knight's Cross of the Iron Cross was a new award introduced to bridge the previously enormous gap between the EK1 and the Grand Cross. It was almost identical to the EK2. (In fact, some antique shops have been known to sell 'doctored' 2nd Class Iron Crosses as Knight's Crosses.) The true Knight's Cross was slightly larger, at 48mm (nearly 2in), and the rim was made from genuine fine silver. The medal was worn from a red, white and black neck ribbon.

The Cross was awarded with a black oblong fitted case lined with black velvet, and accompanied by a most elaborate hand-finished citation. The wording was on velum and presented inside a large red and brown leather folder with a gilt metal eagle and swastika on the front. The original notification of the award was usually accompanied by a preliminary certificate of less imposing appearance.

It should be noted that many Knight's Cross holders had copies made, or they even wore an EK2 at the neck, for fear of losing their real medal in action. Ships' crews, especially submarines, often made their own Knight's Crosses for their officers, which could be worn until the proper presentation. Many men wore this home-made version in preference to the correct naval issue one.

318 Knight's Crosses were awarded to Kriegsmarine personnel; the majority of these went to U-boat men, as can be seen from the table.

Knight's Cross awards to the German Navy:

	Knight's Crosses	Higher Grades
OKM (Supreme Naval Command) and Staff Officers	18	3 (Oakleaves)
Battleships and cruisers	44	5 (Oakleaves)
Destroyers and torpedo-boats	44	9 (Oakleaves)
U-boats	145	28 (Oakleaves, Swords and Diamonds)
Minesweepers	37	4 (Oakleaves)
Coastal Security Craft	9	1 (Oakleaves)
Small battle groups	6	0
Coastal artillery and Anti-aircraft gunners	14	3 (Oakleaves)
Merchant navy	1	0

Contrary to popular belief, the Knight's Cross was not liberally awarded; the higher grades of the Knight's Cross were certainly just as rare as the higher Allied awards. Only two Knight's Crosses with Oakleaves, Swords and Diamonds were awarded to the Navy during the entire war.

Oakleaves to the Knight's Cross:

The Oakleaves were instituted on 3 June 1940, and consisted of a small pure silver cluster of three oakleaves, mounted on a replacement ribbon loop, which was clipped on to the Knight's Cross. The Leaves were awarded in a small black case lined in black velvet, and accompanied by an elaborate certificate and a white leather folder, similar to the one presented with the Knight's Cross. Fifty-three such awards were made to the Kriegsmarine during the war.

Swords and Oakleaves to the Knight's Cross:

The Swords were instituted on 21 June 1941, and they consisted of two small pure silver swords, 24mm (approx. 1in) long and crossed at an angle of

forty degrees. They were soldered to the bottom of a replacement set of oakleaves, and presented in a black case similar to the others. The certificate was also similar to the others, but the design was a little more elaborate. All five Swords awarded to the German Navy went to U-boat commanders:

Fregkpt. Otto Kretschmer (26 December 1941), the 5th set of Swords awarded to German Armed Forces.

Fregkpt. Erich Topp (17 August 1942), the 17th set of Swords awarded to the German Armed Forces.

Fregkpt. Reinhard Suhren (1 September 1942), the 18th set of Swords awarded to the German Armed Forces.

Kpt.z.S. Wolfgang Lüth (15 April 1943), the 29th set of Swords awarded to the German Armed Forces.

Fregkpt. Albrecht Brandi (9 May 1944), the 66th

set of Swords awarded to the German Armed
Forces.

Diamonds to the Knight's Cross:
This rare and beautiful hand-made version of
the Swords and Oakleaves was studded with real
diamonds on the front. Only two men in the
Kriegsmarine were awarded them: Albrecht
Brandi and Wolfgang Lüth.

The Distinguished Service Cross
(Kriegsverdienstkreuz or KVK)
This was awarded for distinguished service away
from the front, in place of an Iron Cross, which
was restricted to awards for special action against
the enemy. The Distinguished Service Cross was
also awarded in two classes (like the Iron Cross),
and there was a Knight's Cross with or without
swords. These medals were worn in a similar
manner to the corresponding Iron Crosses.

The Distinguished Service Cross is quite rare in
the Navy. The first Knight's Cross was awarded,
with swords, to Generaladmiral Carl Witzel on 5
October 1942, and the next one, to Oberfunk-
meister Klaus Hoelck, was not authorized until 21
February 1944. Another fifteen or so were
awarded in 1944, and only about eleven in 1945.

In photographs, especially poor-quality prints,
it could be possible to mistake the Knight's Cross
for the Pour le Mérite of the First World War. The
Knight's Cross of the Distinguished Service Cross
had a distinct disc bearing a swastika in the centre,
and there was no such disc in the Pour le Mérite.
There were about sixteen men serving during the
Second World War who also held this famous First
World War medal.

The German Cross (Deutsches Kreuz)
This large dominant medal was introduced in 1941
to acknowledge effort above the degree normally
recognized by the Iron Cross (1st Class), but not
sufficient to merit a Knight's Cross. The German
Cross was large, 63mm (2½in) in diameter, a
heavy and most impressive pin-backed medal,
which was worn on the right breast of the tunic.

It consisted of a central silver-coloured disc with
a black swastika in enamel, surrounded by a
wreath of oakleaves, bearing the date '1941'.
Radiating out from this was a sunburst star. The
Cross was also manufactured in cloth, with a metal
central core surrounded by embroidery.

Below: Kpt.z.S. Erwin Wassner seen here as commander of the light cruiser *Karlsruhe* shortly before receiving the Head of State of Peru on board in 1932. The Pour le Mérite, or Blue Max, can be seen around his neck; the Iron Cross and U-boat badge are also from the First World War. He is wearing the frock coat with epaulettes, which were only worn in foreign waters or for the officer's own wedding. Erwin Wassner is a most interesting character. He came to Britain shortly after this photograph was taken and negotiated the early naval agreements. He died in 1937 and his body was taken back to Germany by a British warship. (Photo: Author's Collection)

The Spanish Cross (Spanienkreuz)

This award appears occasionally in wartime photographs. It was presented as a result of some noteworthy participation in the Spanish Civil War during 1937. The Cross consisted of a Maltese cross with a central swastika between the four arms, and there were small Luftwaffe-type flying eagles.

The Knight's Cross of the Distinguished Service Cross compared with the Pour le Mérite of the First World War.

Biographical Notes

The people in this section have been selected because their names appear fairly frequently in post-war literature, but little tends to be known about their careers. This is not, therefore, intended as a roll-call of the most famous men. (Certain outstanding people have been omitted because they held a few easily distinguishable offices and it is not too difficult to trace their careers from books listed in the Bibliography on p. 212.)

The rank shown at the head of each entry in the following section was the last position held by that individual in the Kriegsmarine.

Backenköhler, Otto   Admiral
1892-1967. Chief of Staff of the Baltic Naval Station and later of Fleet Command. He later held several posts connected with weapons and armament.

Bastian, Max   Admiral
1883-1958. President of the National War Court until November 1944.

Behncke, Paul   Admiral
13.8.1866-4.1.1937. Born near Lübeck, he joined the Imperial Navy at Easter 1883. At the start of the First World War, he occupied several influential positions, and became commander of the Third Battle Squadron of the High Seas Fleet, with which he saw action at the Battle of Jutland. He was awarded the Pour le Mérite (The Blue Max) in 1917. Although Behncke held several important posts at the end of the First World War, today he is probably best remembered as the first Commander-in-Chief of Germany's post-First-World War Navy, a position he held from 1920 until his retirement in September 1924.

Bey, Erich   Konteradmiral
23.3.1898-26.12.1943. Born in Hamburg, he joined the Navy after the start of the First World War. At the outbreak of the Second World War, Bey was Flag Officer for Destroyers and Commander of the 6th Destroyer Flotilla. Later, still holding these posts, he also commanded the North Norway Naval Squadron. Bey was killed in action during the Battle of the North Cape.

Boehm, Hermann   Generaladmiral
18.1.1884-11.4.1972. Boehm joined the Imperial Navy in 1903. He was Fleet Commander until October 1939, when he worked in the Supreme Naval Command, and was later made Commanding Admiral for Norway.

Bonte, Friedrich   Kpt.z.S. and Kommodore
1896-10.4.1940. Bonte commanded the 2nd Destroyer Flotilla and was later made Flag Officer for Torpedo-Boats, a title he held briefly until the reorganization of October 1939 changed it to Flag Officer for Destroyers. He was killed off Narvik while taking part in the Norwegian Campaign.

Brandi, Albrecht   Fregkpt.
20.6.1914-6.1.1966. Born in Dortmund, Brandi served under Hans Bartels, as First Officer of the minesweeper *M1* at the start of the war. Afterwards he went to submarine school, and served in three U-boats: *U617, U380* and *U967*. Brandi had the distinction of being only the second naval man to receive the Knight's Cross of the Iron Cross with Oakleaves, Swords and Diamonds, a feat he achieved while commander of *U967*. (The other award went to Wolfgang Lüth.) Brandi then served as Admiralty Staff Officer, before being made commander of the Midget Weapons Unit in Holland.

Brinkmann, Helmuth   Vizeadmiral
12.4.1895-. Born in Lübeck, Brinkmann was Chief of the Naval Defence Department at the Supreme Naval Command until July 1940, when he joined the heavy cruiser *Prinz Eugen* as her first commander. After this, he was Chief of Staff for Naval Group Command South. In November 1943 he was made Commanding Admiral for the Black Sea, and he returned to Germany towards the end of the war to take up the post of Commanding Admiral for the Baltic and North Sea. Brinkmann was discharged from the Navy towards the end of November 1947.

Burchardi, Theodor   Admiral
1892-. Burchardi was commander of the cruiser *Köln*, and went on to become Chief of Staff at the Naval Construction Yard in Kiel. Subsequently, he held several posts connected with coastal defence.

Canaris, Wilhelm   Admiral
1.1.1887-9.4.1945. Born in Dortmund, Canaris was appointed Chief of the Abwehr in January 1935. He held this position until July 1944, when he was appointed Chief of the Special Staff for War Economy and War Economic Measures. On 23 July, Canaris was arrested for complicity in the Bomb Plot and sent to Flossenburg concentration camp, where he was executed shortly before the end of the war.

Carls, Rolf   Generaladmiral
18.5.1885-15.4.1945. Born in Rostock, Carls joined the Imperial Navy in 1903 and, at the start of the First World War, was serving aboard the cruiser *Breslau*. Subsequently, he served on the battleship *König*, commanded *U9* and, later, *U124*. After the war he was made Chief of the Training Division at the Supreme Naval Command and was then given command of the old battleship *Hessen*. From 1933 until his appointment in the following year to the posts of Commander-in-Chief Battleships (Linienschiffe) and C-in-C of German Naval Forces in Spanish waters, Carls was Chief of Staff of the Fleet Command. He was Fleet Commander from 1937 until 1938, when he became Commanding Admiral for the Baltic; at the same time he held the post of Commander-in-Chief of the Naval Group Command East. Afterwards, he became Chief of the larger Naval Group Command North, which he commanded until March 1943. Both Rolf Carls and Karl Dönitz were nominated to succeed Grand Admiral Raeder. Hitler chose Dönitz and Carls later resigned, possibly to prevent friction among the naval leadership. He was killed by enemy action in 1945.

Ciliax, Otto   Admiral
30.10.1891-12.12.1964. Ciliax commanded the battlecruiser *Scharnhorst* until October 1939, when he became Chief of Staff at Naval Group Command West. This was followed by a spell as Commander-in-Chief Battleships. He then worked with the Torpedo Inspectorate. Ciliax was promoted to Admiral on 1 February 1943 and, in the following month, was made Supreme Commander-in-Chief of the Supreme Naval Command for Norway. He was discharged in February 1946.

Densch, Hermann   Admiral
1887-24.8.1963. Born in Königsberg, Densch held the post of Commander-in-Chief Reconnaissance Forces until October 1939, when he was made

Commanding Admiral for the North Sea Naval Station, later known as Supreme Naval Command North Sea. After that he worked in Berlin as a Naval Commissioner.

Dönitz, Karl   Grossadmiral/Head of State 16.9.1891-. Born at Grünau, which was then a small village south-east of Berlin and is now part of the city, Dönitz joined the Navy as an officer cadet on 1 April 1910 at Kiel-Wyk. After his initial training, he spent a year aboard the training ship SMS *Hertha*, and was later posted to the cruiser *Breslau*, then the fastest and most modern cruiser in the Imperial Navy. *Breslau* operated in the Mediterranean with the battlecruiser SMS *Goeben*, as the core of the German Mediterranean Naval Squadron, commanded by the famous Admiral Souchon. However, the squadron was never fully developed and, at the outbreak of the First World War, *Goeben* and *Breslau* were the only two German ships in this theatre. They managed to evade the numerically superior forces hunting them and made their way to neutral Turkey, where the ships were eventually handed over to the Turkish Navy, an action that helped bring Turkey into the war on Germany's side.

Dönitz married Ingeborg Weber, daughter of General Weber, in May 1916. In October of that year, the newly-weds returned to Germany and took up residence in Kiel. Dönitz was made First Officer of *U39*, commanded by the ace submariner Walter Forstmann, and a year later was given command of *UC25*. Later, he was transferred to the larger and faster *UC68*, which was depth-charged and sunk by HMS *Snapdragon*. Fortunately, Dönitz and some of his crew managed to evade a watery grave and, instead, were taken prisoner. Dönitz was first held in a prison camp on Malta and later at Redmires, near Sheffield, England. He eventually returned to Germany in July 1919 in a poor state of health.

Dönitz remained in the Navy, and was given an administrative position in the Personnel Department. In March 1920, he took command of the old torpedo-boat *T157*. In 1921, the Dönitz family, now with the addition of a daughter, Ursula (born 1917), and son, Klaus (born 1920), moved to Swinemünde—one of the major torpedo-boat bases. Two years later, they moved back to Kiel when Dönitz was appointed adviser at the Torpedo, Mine and Artillery Inspectorate. The

family moved again in 1923—by which time another son, Peter, had arrived (born 1922)—this time to Berlin, where Dönitz was adviser at the Naval Office. In 1927, on Dönitz's appointment to the post of Navigation Officer of the cruiser *Nymphe*—flagship for the Commander-in-Chief Seaforces Baltic—the family returned to Kiel. The position of C-in-C Seaforces Baltic was held by Admiral Wilfried von Loewenfeld, whom Dönitz had known since he joined the training ship *Hertha*.

In 1928, Dönitz became Chief of the 4th Torpedo-Boat Half Flotilla, which consisted of four brand new boats: *Albatros, Kondor, Möwe* and *Greif*. This gave Dönitz a golden opportunity to show what he could do, since the crews were also new and Dönitz was free to train them as he wished.

During 1930, Korvkpt. Karl Dönitz was appointed to the post of First Admiralty Staff Officer at the Naval Station in Wilhelmshaven. There, he won a naval scholarship to visit any country of his choice and, as a result, went to Ceylon and several other countries in the Far East. This was an interesting experience for him, especially as it came just before the National Socialists' rise to power. He revisited the region in 1934 as commander of the light cruiser *Emden*, the first large ship built after the First World War. Then, after a lengthy refit, she was commissioned with a completely new crew.

A year later, he held the rank of Fregatten-kapitän and returned to Germany with *Emden*, hoping to take the ship on another cruise to the Far East. Instead, however, he was ordered to take command of the U-boat flotilla in Kiel. He expanded this initially small group of half a dozen coastal submarines to become what has been described as the fourth branch of the armed forces: Army, Air Force, Navy and U-boat arm.

Dönitz succeeded Grand Admiral Erich Raeder as Supreme Commander-in-Chief of the Navy in January 1943. On 30 April 1945 at 1835, Dönitz received a radio signal from Berlin, telling him that Hitler had appointed him second Führer of the Third Reich. Dönitz did not want to accept this office, and he carefully considered the alternatives —including suicide—but in the end he concluded that it was his duty to accept the office of Head of State. Dönitz and his entire staff were arrested by British forces on 23 May 1945, when the German

Below: Generaladmirals Hans-Georg von Friedeburg and Oskar Kummetz (see page 178) followed by a British officer. Von Friedeburg is wearing the German Cross (Deutsches Kreuz). below the eagle on his right breast. The badge at the bottom is a silver version of the Spanish Cross, without swords. Some 26,000 Spanish Crosses were issued and only 327 of this silver type were awarded, so it is quite rare. (Photo: Imperial War Museum)

Top right: Kurt Freiwald behind his desk, while serving in the Federal Navy. Freiwald commanded the first operational U-boat after the First World War. He also served as adjutant to both the Grand Admirals and in 1943 he went on a refresher course and then took *U181* into the Indian Ocean. He remained in Singapore until 1946, and then spent another year as a prisoner-of-war before being released. (Photo: Author's Collection)

Below right: Konteradmiral Eberhard Godt is not very well known in Britain, yet he was Supreme Commander-in-Chief of the Operations Department or U-boat Command throughout the war. He was responsible for the co-ordination and planning of the battles in the Atlantic. The badge with the large swastika, below the eagle, is the War Order of the German Cross. (Photo: Author's Collection)

government was dissolved and the armed forces disbanded. Dönitz stood trial at Nuremberg and was sentenced to ten years imprisonment.

Eyssen, Robert   Konteradmiral
2.4.1892-31.3.1960. Eyssen was Chief of the Military Department at the Supreme Naval Command Defence (OKM Wehr) and later commanded the auxiliary cruiser *Komet*. Afterwards, he worked as liaison officer, followed by a spell as Chief of the German Naval Office in Oslo, then went to the Regional Defence Office in Vienna.

Fischel, Hermann von   Admiral
1.1887-1950. Born in Kiel, von Fischel was Chief of the General Naval Office. Later, he became head of the Command that tested new warships (Erprobungskommando für Kriegsschiffneubauten). This was followed by a period as Sea Commander at Ostende. Afterwards, von Fischel held several posts connected with coastal defence. Von Fischel died a prisoner-of-war in Russia during 1950.

Freiwald, Kurt   Kapitän zur See
29.10.1906-. Born in Berlin, Freiwald was one of the Third Reich's very early U-boat commanders. In fact, in 1935 he commanded their first operational boat, *U7*. He was made adjutant to Generaladmiral Raeder in October 1938 and later became adjutant to Karl Dönitz—the other Supreme Commander-in-Chief of the Navy. Freiwald returned to submarine school during the summer of 1943, and afterwards took command of the long-distance boat, *U181*, in which he sailed to Japanese-held bases in the Far East.

Friedeburg, Hans-Georg von   Generaladmiral
15.5.1895-23.5.1945. Friedeburg joined the staff of the Flag Officer for U-boats in 1937. It was intended that he should take over the U-boat arm, thus releasing Dönitz for a post with cruisers, but the war started before such plans could be implemented and, instead, Friedeburg became Chief of the U-boat arm's large Organization Department. Von Friedeburg held the title of Commanding Admiral for U-boats from February 1943 until April 1945, when he was made Supreme Commander-in-Chief of the Navy. It was von Friedeburg who negotiated surrender with the Allies—led by Montgomery—and, with others, signed the official surrender document. Von Friedeburg, who was described by his colleagues as "the perfect gentleman—correct to the last degree", committed suicide in May 1945.

Fuchs, Werner   Admiral
1891-. Admiral Fuchs was Chief of the Fleet Department at the Supreme Naval Command (Flottenabteilung), and especially dealt with new construction problems. He was made Chief of the Office for Warship Construction shortly before the start of the war. Fuchs worked in ship construction for most of the war until 1944, when he held the post of Flag Officer for Reserves. (No doubt he was moved because, during 1943, ship construction was placed under the control of the Ministry of Armament.)

Godt, Eberhard   Konteradmiral
5.8.1900-. This man—almost unknown throughout the war and after—was the driving force behind the all-important Operations Department of the U-boat arm. Born in Lübeck, he joined the Navy at the end of the First World War and, after commanding a U-boat during the 1930s, became a staff officer. Later, he was made head of the Operations Department, at that time still a small, relatively unimportant post. But, as the war progressed, both the department and Godt's responsibility grew. The post was later redesignated 2nd Chief of Naval War Staff, although most men referred to the department as 'U-boat Command' (Ubootsführung). Eberhard Godt was the driving force behind nearly all the convoy battles, directing the U-boat commanders from the U-boat arm's nerve centre—the Operations Room. He was made Konteradmiral on 1 March 1943, when his office was renamed Commander-in-Chief for Submarines (Operations)—Befehlshaber für Unterseeboote (Operationen) or B.d.U. (Ops).

Heye, Hellmuth   Vizeadmiral
1895-1970. At the outbreak of the Second World War, this colourful character was commander of the heavy cruiser *Hipper*. He then held several administrative posts, and in 1944 he was made Admiral for the Midget Weapons Unit.

Krancke, Theodor   Admiral
30.3.1893-18.6.1973. Krancke was born in Magdeburg and was Chief of the Naval Academy shortly before the start of the Second World War, and was later made Chief of Staff for the Commander-in-Chief Security Forces of the North Sea. Afterwards, he took command of the pocket battleship *Admiral Scheer* and, simultaneously, held the post of Chief of Staff for the Commanding Admiral in Norway. From January 1942 until March 1943, Krancke was the Permanent Representative of the Supreme Commander-in-Chief of the Navy at Hitler's headquarters. He then moved on to become Supreme Commander-in-Chief of the Naval Group Command West. Shortly before the war ended he held the post of Supreme Commander-in-Chief of Naval Command Norway.

Kranzbühler, Otto   A rank in the Naval Legal
Service equivalent to Kpt.z.S.
8.7.1907-. Born in Berlin, Kranzbühler's main claim to fame was in being Dönitz's defence counsel at Nuremberg. Dönitz was given a list of German lawyers willing to act for him at the Trials, but he rejected them all because of their inexperience regarding maritime law. Dönitz had retained the memory of Kranzbühler's adept handling of a pre-war collision case, and the Grand Admiral decided he was the one person capable of defending him. Not surprisingly, Kranzbühler was difficult to find, and he had to be virtually dug out of the ruins of the Third Reich. Although Dönitz was convicted, after the trial he reaffirmed his belief that he could not have hoped for a better lawyer.

Kretschmer, Otto   Fregkpt.
1.5.1912-. Otto Kretschmer, the 'Tonnage King', was the most successful U-boat commander of the Second World War. He sailed on sixteen operational war cruises and sank 238,000 GRT, which included one destroyer and at least 41 merchant ships. (An earlier figure puts the number of ships sunk at 44, and the gross registered tonnage at 266,629.) Kretschmer was born near Leignitz (now called Legnica, lying west of Wroclaw (Breslau), and joined the Navy in 1930. At the start of the war, Kretschmer commanded the small boat *U23* and later took over *U99*. Both *U99* and *U100* (Kptlt. Joachim Schepke) were sunk simultaneously on 17 March 1941: *U100* was located on the surface by Type 286 radar fitted in HMS *Vanoc*; and *U99*'s lookouts failed to spot

HMS *Walker* until the U-boat had run across the destroyer's bows. Kretschmer was not on the bridge at the time, and the duty officer gave the order to dive, after which *U99* was saturated with depth charges and only just managed to re-surface. Fortunately, quite a number of her crew got out before she sank—including Otto Kretschmer who spent the remaining war years in a prison camp and was not released until the end of 1947. He was awarded the Knight's Cross with Oakleaves and Swords. (A detailed account of Kretschmer's career has been drawn by Terence Robertson in *The Golden Horseshoe*.)

Kummetz, Oskar Generaladmiral
21.7.1891-. Oskar Kummetz was born in East Prussia and was Chief of Staff of the Fleet Command until October 1939, when he joined the Torpedo Inspectorate. During the invasion of Norway, he held the position of Commander of Task Force Oslo and, after this, held the office of Commander-in-Chief Cruisers and Commander-in-Chief North Norway Naval Squadron. Shortly before the end of the war, he was Supreme Commander-in-Chief of the Supreme Naval Command Baltic.

Lüdde-Neurath, Walter Korvkpt.
15.5.1914-. Although Walter Lüdde-Neurath had a most distinguished naval career, his name did not become famous until the end of the war, when he was the last adjutant to Grand Admiral Dönitz. After the war, he recorded a valuable set of records, outlining the events leading to the end of the Third Reich. (See Bibliography, p. 212.)

Born in Hüningen, just north of Basel, he joined the Navy in 1933. His wartime duties included the posts of Watch Officer and Torpedo Officer aboard the destroyer *Karl Galster*. He then became First Officer of *Z30*, and went on to command the torpedo-boats *Greif, Möwe* and the destroyer *Richard Beitzen*. Lüdde-Neurath next held the post of First Admiralty Staff Officer with the Flag Officer for Destroyers, shortly after which he became Dönitz's adjutant.

Lüth, Wolfgang Kpt.z.S.
15.10.1913-14.5.1945. Wolfgang Lüth was one of two men in the German Navy to be awarded the Knight's Cross of the Iron Cross with Oakleaves, Swords and Diamonds. (The other medal was awarded to Albrecht Brandi.) This famous U-boat commander was born in Riga, and died after being accidentally shot by one of his own guards. Apparently, he failed to reply to the guard's challenge—and paid the penalty. Lüth commanded *U9, U138, U43* and *U181*. He was also chief of the 22nd U-boat Flotilla and, towards the end of the war, was head of the naval school in Mürwik.

Lütjens, Günther Admiral
5.1889-27.5.1941. Lütjens was born in Wiesbaden, and held the post of Flag Officer for Torpedo-Boats from October 1937 until October 1939, after which he was made Commander-in-Chief Reconnaissance Forces. He was Fleet Commander from the spring of 1940 until he went down with the battleship *Bismarck* in May 1941.

Marschall, Wilhelm Generaladmiral
1886-20.3.1976. Born in Augsburg, Marschall joined the Navy in 1906. He was Commander-in-Chief Pocket Battleships at the start of the war, and Fleet Commander from October 1939 until June 1940. At the same time, he was Commander-in-Chief Naval Forces West (Seebefehlshaber West). After this he became an inspector with Education Units and, from August 1942 until a year later, when the post was renamed Commander-in-Chief Naval Group Command West, he held the office of Commanding Admiral France. Wilhelm Marschall was made the Führer's Special Naval Delegate for the Danube after his spell of duty in France, returning to the Supreme Naval Command shortly before the end of the war. He was discharged from the Navy in June 1947.

Meckel, Hans Fregkpt.
15.2.1910-. Meckel was a U-boat commander at the submarine arm's refounding in 1935, after which he held the post of Admiralty Staff Officer for the Flag Officer for U-boats. In 1944, he became Chief of the Radar Division.

Puttkammer, Karl-Jesko von Konteradmiral
Von Puttkammer was 39 years old when he moved from the destroyer *Hans Lody* to Berlin, just before the start of the war, to become a liaison officer at Hitler's headquarters. He was Hitler's Naval Adjutant from October 1939 until the end in April 1945.

Raeder, Dr. h.c. Erich Grossadmiral/Admiral Inspekteur
24.4.1876-1960. Erich Raeder was born in Hamburg-Wandsbek, the eldest son of a language teacher, who was also the headmaster of a grammar school. He joined the Navy as an officer cadet in 1894 and, after three and a half years training, 'passed out' as best student of his year. Raeder first served in the Far East aboard the battleship *Deutschland*, the flagship of Prince Heinrich of Prussia (Commander-in-Chief of the 2nd Cruiser Division). Later, Raeder was made Wachoffizier (Watch-Keeping Officer) of the battleship *Kaiser Wilhelm der Grosse*. Afterwards he went to the Naval Academy, from where he travelled to Russia in order to improve his Russian. (He also spoke fluent English and French.) Raeder held several interesting land-based positions before being made Navigation Officer of the armoured cruiser *Yorck*. Then, also in the capacity of Navigation Officer, he was transferred to the Kaiser's yacht *Hohenzollern* (a post he disliked, because the ship spent most of its time lying at anchor).

In 1912, Raeder was appointed to the post of First Admiralty Staff Officer to the Commander-in-Chief Reconnaissance Forces (a position first held by Admiral Hans Bachmann, who was replaced by the famous cruiser pundit, Admiral Franz Ritter von Hipper). Raeder saw several important actions from the command bridge of the battlecruiser SMS *Seydlitz*, including the Battle of Jutland. He was given command of *Köln* shortly before the end of the war, but did not spend much time aboard the small cruiser because of his appointment as Naval Representative to the Armistice Commission.

After the war, he was transferred to 'Archives', because of his suspected involvement in the Kapp Putsch while he was Chief of Staff to Admiral von Throtha. However, it was not long before his innocence was established and he returned to normal duties, initially as Commander-in-Chief of Sea Forces North Sea and later as Commanding Admiral in Kiel. He then succeeded Admiral Hans Zenker as Chief of the German Navy, a position he held until his resignation in January 1943. This position was known by a variety of names which could lead to some confusion. He still held the honorary rank of Admiral Inspekteur der Kriegsmarine after his resignation, but this involved no

Below: Wolfgang Lüth (left) and Erich Topp. Lüth and Albrecht Brandi (see page 174) were the only men in the Navy to receive the Knight's Cross with Oakleaves, Swords and Diamonds, and Erich Topp was among the five who were awarded the Swords and Oakleaves. Lüth was the second and Topp the third most successful U-boat commanders in respect of tonnage sunk. (Photo: Author's Collection)

Centre: Grand Admiral Dr. h.c. Erich Raeder during the spring of 1942. (Photo: Bundesarchiv, Koblenz)
Right: Bernhard Rogge, as commander of the auxiliary cruiser *Atlantis*, was one of the two men who were definitely awarded the Auxiliary Cruiser Badge with Diamonds (see page 160). Around his neck is the Knight's Cross with Oakleaves, awarded for his magnificent service aboard the *Atlantis*. On his lapel is

the Clasp (1939) to the Iron Cross (2nd Class) of the First World War. The large Iron Cross on his breast is the 1914 version (1st Class), and above it is the 1939 Clasp. The badge next to the Iron Cross is the famous Auxiliary Cruiser Badge. The real badge with diamonds was not often worn because it was too valuable, and a replica often took its place. (Photo: Author's Collection)

command duties. Raeder received a ten-year sentence at the Nuremberg Trials.

Rösing, Hans-Rudolf   Kpt.z.S.

28.9.1905-. Rösing's name crops up in various places, and at times it is difficult to keep track of his career. Born in Wilhelmshaven, he joined the Navy in 1924, making his way to the U-boat arm after its refounding in 1935, and becoming one of its early commanders. At the start of the war, Rösing commanded U-Flotilla 'Emsmann', which was renamed 7th U-Flotilla during the reorganization of October 1939. He then had another spell as a U-boat commander—a step that many people have interpreted as demotion. In fact, 'Vaddi' (Herbert) Schultze, the commander of *U48*, was taken ill and Dönitz quickly needed a tough replacement to control the U-boat's crew: *U48* had been in the thick of the action from the start, and

her men had earned the reputation of being "an uncontrollable wild bunch, who did not take kindly to inexperienced newcomers". Obviously, Dönitz thought Rösing the man for the job. After his spell of duty in *U48*, Rösing became Liaison Officer with the Flag Officer for U-boats in Bordeaux. In 1941, he took control of the 3rd Flotilla and later was made Commander of the Central Department (Zentral Abteilung). From July 1942 until the end of the war, he was Flag Officer for U-boats West (F.d.U. West), which had its headquarters first in France, then Norway and finally Germany.

Rogge, Bernhard   Vizeadmiral

1899-. Rogge was born in northern Germany, and was commander of the sail training ship *Albert Leo Schlageter*, and of the auxiliary cruiser *Atlantis*—with which he remained at sea for 622

days without putting into port. Rogge held several administrative posts after the sinking of *Atlantis* and, towards the end of the war, founded and commanded the Special Task Force 'Rogge', which operated in the eastern Baltic.

Ruckteschell, Hellmuth von   Kpt.z.S.

23.5.1890-1948. Born in Hamburg, Ruckteschell was commander of the auxiliary cruisers *Widder* and, later, *Michel*. He handed over command of *Michel* to Gumprich in May 1943, and then worked with the German Naval Attaché in Japan. Before serving on auxiliary cruisers he had commanded the minelayer *Cobra*.

Ruge, Friedrich   Vizeadmiral

25.12.1894-. Ruge was born in Leipzig, and his varied career spanned the following positions: Flag Officer for Minesweepers, Chief of a special staff for the Naval Group Command in Italy, Admiral with Army Group B and, towards the end of the war, Chief of the Armaments Office at the Supreme Naval Command. Ruge was made Commander-in-Chief of the Federal German Navy. Today he is a professor and prominent historian.

Schniewind, Otto   Generaladmiral
12.12.1887-26.3.1964. Born in the Saar Region, Schniewind joined the Navy in 1907. At the outbreak of the Second World War, he was both Chief of Staff to the Chief of Naval War Staff (SKL) and Chief of the Naval Command Office (Marinekommandoamt). He was made Fleet Commander after the sinking of the battleship *Bismarck* and, at the same time, held the office of Commander-in-Chief of Naval Group Command North. Schniewind briefly occupied several other posts before the end of the war, when he was arrested by the Allied Powers, tried for war crimes and found innocent.

Stohwasser, Hans   Vizeadmiral
1884-30.5.1967. He was Flag Officer for Minesweepers and later Commander-in-Chief for the security of the Baltic.

Thedsen, Otto   Konteradmiral
1886-11.2.1949. Born in Hamburg, Thedsen became Flotilla Engineer with the U-boat arm in 1935, and was later Chief of the Technical Division of the U-boat arm.

Thiele, August   Vizeadmiral
28.8.1893-. Thiele was commander of the heavy cruiser *Lützow* (ex-*Deutschland*) and, later, held the position of Sea Commander at Trondheim. Afterwards, he was made Admiral of the Norwegian North Coast. He was also Chief of Staff to the Fleet Command. Thiele founded and commanded the Special Task Force 'Thiele', a raiding force that operated in the eastern Baltic towards the end of the war.

Topp, Erich   Fregattenkapitän
2.7.1914-. Born in Hannover, Topp served as a U-boat commander, leaving the Navy in August 1945, having reached the rank of Fregattenkapitän. His commands included *U57, U552* and *U2513*. He was also Chief of the 27th U-Flotilla.

Topp held the Knight's Cross of the Iron Cross with Oakleaves and Swords.

Topp, Karl   Vizeadmiral
29.8.1895-. At the start of the war Topp worked at the Supreme Naval Command and, between February 1941 and February 1943, he commanded the battleship *Tirpitz*. The most important office he held after relinquishing command of *Tirpitz* was Chairman of the Shipbuilding Commission at Dr. Speer's Armaments Ministry.

Topp, Rudolf   Fregattenkapitän
1896-. A Rhinelander, Topp began the Second World War at the Naval School in Wilhelmshaven, but later held several other posts, including command of a battalion of naval marksmen. He was discharged in 1945.

Voss, Hans-Erich   Vizeadmiral
1897-1973. Born near Stettin, Voss commanded the heavy cruiser *Prinz Eugen*, after which he became Permanent Naval Representative at the Führer's headquarters—a position he held until the end of the war. He was then sent to a Russian prison camp, from which he was released towards the end of 1954.

Wagner, Gerhard   Konteradmiral
1898-. At the start of the war, Wagner held the post of Group Commander with the Supreme Naval Command. He became Head of the Operations Department of the Supreme Naval Command in June 1941, and later worked as Admiral with the Supreme Commander-in-Chief for a short time before becoming Permanent Representative to the Head of State. He was a member of the delegation that signed the surrender document at Lüneburg Heath in 1945.

Warzecha, Walter   Generaladmiral
1891-30.8.1956. Warzecha was Chief of the General Naval Office at the Supreme Naval Command and later Chief of the Naval Defence Department. He replaced Hans-Georg von Friedeburg as Supreme Commander-in-Chief of the Navy after von Friedeburg's suicide in 1945.

Wenneker, Paul   Admiral
Wenneker was commander of the pocket battleship *Deutschland* until November 1939, when he

became German Naval Attaché to Japan. He held this post from March 1940 until the end of the war.

Weyher, Kurt   Konteradmiral
Weyher was nicknamed 'The Singing Captain' by his cadets when he was commander of the sail training ship *Gorch Fock*. Afterwards, he commanded the auxiliary cruiser *Orion*. He then became First Admiralty Staff Officer with the Staff of the Commanding Admiral Aegean Region, after which he held a similar position with Naval Group Command South. He was moved to the Black Sea at the start of 1944 as Chief of the Security Forces. At the same time he was Chief of the German Naval Command at Constanta. He also served in Crete before returning to Germany to become Naval Commander of the East Fresian Region.

Witzel, Carl   Generaladmiral
1884-31.5.1976. Witzel was Chief of the Main Weapons Department with the Supreme Naval Command for most of the war.

Wurmbach, Hans-Heinrich   Admiral
Wurmbach was commander of the pocket battleship *Admiral Scheer*. He also held the positions of Commander of the Naval Station for the Baltic at Kiel and Chief of Staff to Naval Group Command East. After that he was first Commanding Admiral for the Black Sea and later Commanding Admiral for Denmark—a post that was renamed Commanding Admiral Skagerrak.

Zenker, Hans   Admiral
1870-1932. Zenker joined the Imperial Navy in 1889, commanding the small cruisers *Lübeck* and *Köln* before the First World War, when he also gained experience as departmental head in the Admiralty. During the war, he commanded the battlecruiser *von der Tann* and also held several other important posts. In 1920, he became Commander of the North Sea Naval Station and, in 1924, succeeded Paul Behncke as Commander-in-Chief of the Navy, a position that he held until Raeder was appointed in September 1928. Zenker retired in September 1928, and died in 1932, just five months before Hitler came to power. (Coincidentally, his son, Karl Adolf, was the first Commander-in-Chief of the Federal German Navy.)

Below: Vizeadmiral Friedrich Ruge (on left) with Konteradmiral Eberhard Godt at the headquarters of Admiral Burroughs R.N., near St. Germain, in May 1945. Ruge later became the first Supreme C-in-C of the Federal German Navy. (Photo: Imperial War Museum)

Below right: Konteradmiral Gerhard Wagner, Chief of the Operations Department with the Chief of Naval War Staff, later Admiral with the Head of State and a member of the delegation that signed the surrender document. (Photo: Imperial War Museum)

Features of the Atlantic U-Boat

Over six hundred Type VII U-boats were built, making them the largest class of submarines ever constructed. The first was launched in June 1936, the last in 1945, and they were the most important craft used by the Germans in the Battle of the Atlantic. The following boats were commissioned.

Type VIIA: *U27-U36.*

Type VIIB: *U45-U55, U73-U76, U83-U87, U99-U102.*

Type VIIC: *U69-U72, U77-U82, U88-U98, U132-U136, U201-U212, U221-U232, U235-U329, U331-U458, U465-U486, U551-U683, U701-U722, U731-U779, U821-U822, U825-U828, U901-U908, U921-U930, U951-U1032, U1051-U1058, U1063-U1065, U1101-U1110, U1131-U1132, U1161-U1172, U1191-U1210, U1271-U1279, U1301-U1308.*

Type VIIC-41: This was a slightly modified version of the ordinary VIIC produced towards the end of the war. (Their numbers are included with VIIC.)

Type VIID: *U213-U218.*

Type VIIE: None built.

Type VIIF: *U1059-U1062.*

Right: An early Type VIIC U-boat. There were two retractable bollards and an electric (or emergency manual) capstan on the bows. A cradle for lowering torpedoes is visible in front of the 88mm quick-firing gun. These large guns were removed from the vast majority of boats during the summer of 1943, and are a useful aid in dating photographs. The two parallel lines of rectangular vents just above the waterline and the four vents stepping upwards towards the bollards are typical of Type VII. Only Type VIIA differed slightly by having two rows of vents running almost as far as the anchor, without the four stepping upwards. Type A can be easily distinguished if the stern is visible, because it was the only U-boat of the Second World War with its rear torpedo tube above the waterline. Type D is also easily identifiable by a row of protruding mineshafts—a box-like structure—above the level of the deck, just aft of the conning-tower. The most difficult to recognize is Type F, but as only four boats were ever built, photos of them are quite rare. The deck space around the 88mm gun serves as a useful feature to distinguish between versions B and C: B had an enlarged deck protruding over the sides of the boat, like a platform. This was changed slightly for version C, where the sides of the hull curved outwards to run around the edges of the platform, instead of running underneath it. (Photo: MOD)

Left: A close-up of the 88mm quick-firing gun. A watertight tampion usually fitted over both ends of the barrel when the gun was not in use. Several of *U377*'s crew found some full bottles of whisky when the boat called at the deserted settlement of New Alesund on Spitzbergen. The external diameter of these bottles was a little less than the internal diameter of this gun and, unknown to the commander, they brought a barrel full of bottles home. (Photo: Author's Collection)

Below left: The pressure hull was a considerable distance below the planking of the upper deck, and it would only just break above the waterline when the boat was fully surfaced. Water could flow freely into this space through the vents along both sides and through the slats of the deck. This photograph, looking astern, was taken below the feet of the men in the photograph on the facing page. The pipe on the right was an air duct, and the circular hatch in the background could be used for loading the stern torpedoes. There was just sufficient space for a man to crawl along here on all fours. (Photo: Author's Collection)

Right: *U377* on 10 October 1943. The enlarged upper and additional lower gun platforms are clearly visible, as is the bulge in the deck where the large 88mm gun used to be. The large saddle-tank on the port side can also be seen. The AA armament consisted of two twin 20mm guns and one quadruple 20mm mounting. (Photo: Author's Collection)

Left: A typical conning-tower layout after the summer of 1943. The lower gun platform usually carried either one 37mm gun, as seen here, or one quadruple 20mm AA mounting. The upper, enlarged platform held two twin 20mm AA guns. The Hohentwiel or bedstead radar aerial is also visible beside the attack periscope. (Photo: Author's Collection)

Below left: A close-up of the 37mm AA gun. Magazines were inserted into the curved slots that can be seen sticking out above the breech; the dome-like lids of pressure- and water-resisting ammunition containers are also visible at deck level. Note the navigation light attached to the rails. (Photo: Author's Collection)

This page, left: One of the twin 20mm AA mountings as seen from deck level. (Photo: Author's Collection)

Top right: The rest of the conning-tower from deck level. The Hohentwiel, or bedstead radar aerial, could be used as a search device on one side and as a radar detector on the other. Just visible behind it is a small circular aerial for detecting radar waves. In the middle, in front of the attack periscope, is another water- and pressure-resisting ammunition container. The head lens of the navigation or sky periscope is covered by part of the 20mm gun. (Photo: Author's Collection)

Below right: Close-up of the aerials on the port side of the conning-tower. (Photo: Author's Collection)

Left: The conning-tower from keel level. The wind deflector, or upper edge of the conning-tower wall has been changed from earlier designs, where the lip was the other way round. The large bracket just below this lip on the right held the rigid schnorkel in the raised position. It could be lowered or raised from the inside of the boat, without the men having to surface. Also note the navigation light, radio aerial inlet and the fog horn; the latter can be seen just below a lip called the spray deflector. The foreward periscope would usually have had a much larger head than is shown in this photograph: this shows the head lens of an attack periscope. (Photo: Author's Collection)

Facing page:

Top: The torpedo-aimer in front and a magnetic compass behind. The iron rods at the top are part of a torpedo-loading device and these would usually be removed before the boat went to sea. A pair of special robust binoculars could be clipped on top of the torpedo-aimer and the target's bearing would be automatically transmitted below. (Photo: Author's Collection)

Below left: Close-up of the torpedo-aimer. (Photo: Author's Collection)

Below centre: The galley hatch just aft of the conning-tower. The locking wheel went straight through the lid and could be operated from both inside and outside. (Photo: Author's Collection)

Below right: Looking down from the conning-tower hatch into the commander's control room. Below it, through another pressure-resisting hatch, is the central control room. The commander would be locked in this small compartment inside the conning-tower during a submerged attack. His saddle by the periscope is just visible at the top of the photograph, next to the periscope well. Various instruments, such as the compass and engine telegraph, are situated on the wall, just to the right of the open hatch. The commander would usually have been assisted by one or even two men, who also squeezed into this frightfully small space. Orders were transmitted through a voice pipe to the central control room. (Photo: Author's Collection)

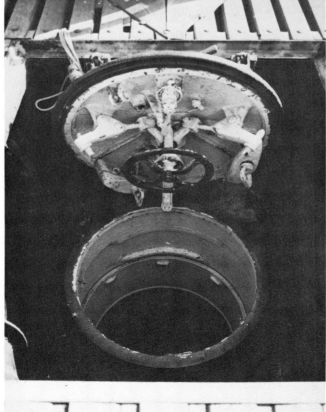

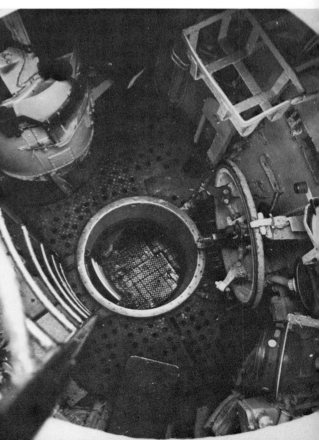

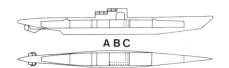

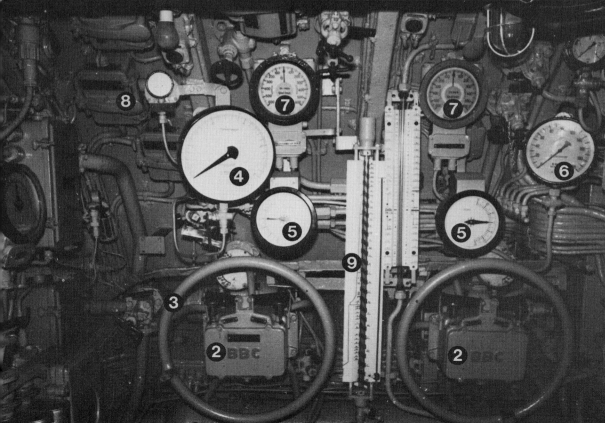

Opposite page (A): The central control room below the commander's compartment in the conning-tower. It is most difficult to understand or even photograph this space because so many items were fitted into such a small area. This photograph is looking forward and slightly towards the starboard side. The circular, pressure resistant door is in the middle of a thick bulkhead, and the arched sides of the pressure hull can be made out to the left of the loop hanging from the ceiling.

1, Rudder Control. There were two grips, which could be clasped firmly with each hand, and below each wrist was a button for working the electric steering motor. The emergency rudder, in case of power failure, was situated in the rear torpedo compartment.

2, Similar electric controls were provided for the bow and stern hydroplanes (for making the boat rise and sink), but these could also be operated manually by turning the two large wheels around the electric controls. The hydroplanes could also be operated from the torpedo compartments.

3, Speed indicator.

4, Navigation or sky periscope in the raised position. The rope below it would pull it down once the electric motor was switched on. (The attack periscope had a much smaller head lens, and could only be used from the commander's position in the conning-tower.) This sky periscope, used mainly for navigation, could only be used from the central control room.

5, Electric cable with socket and probably a microphone.
(Photo: Author's Collection)

This page, top (B): Looking forwards and upwards from the helmsman's position.
1, Wheels for operating the forward diving tanks.
2, Port and starboard engine telegraphs.
3, Speaking tube.
4, Loudspeaker.
5, Magnetic compass. The actual compass was situated above the level of the outside deck, in a small projection at the base of the conning tower, and this picture was transmitted down by light.
6, A 'slave' gyro compass.
7, Electric rudder controls.
8, Bottles for purifying the air; these only became standard fittings after the summer of 1943.
9, Indicator showing the position of the rudders. (The two rudders could only be operated in unison.)
(Photo: Author's Collection)

This page, bottom (C): The hydroplane controls, with depth gauges.
1, Compressed air bottles.
2, Electric hydroplane controls (bows on the left and stern on the right).
3, Wheel to operate hydroplanes manually.
4, Depth gauge for use when near the surface; this reads from 0 to 25m (approx. 82ft).
5, Indicators to show position of hydroplanes.
6, Depth gauge indicating 0 to 200m (approx. 656ft).
7, Telegraph to indicate engine revolutions (port and starboard engines).
8, Waterproof fuse boxes, with a telephone-like locking lever.
9, Depth gauges for use when the boat was at periscope depth. There was a diagram of an extended periscope on this gauge and mercury would rise up a tube to indicate the water level outside the boat. (Photo: Author's Collection)

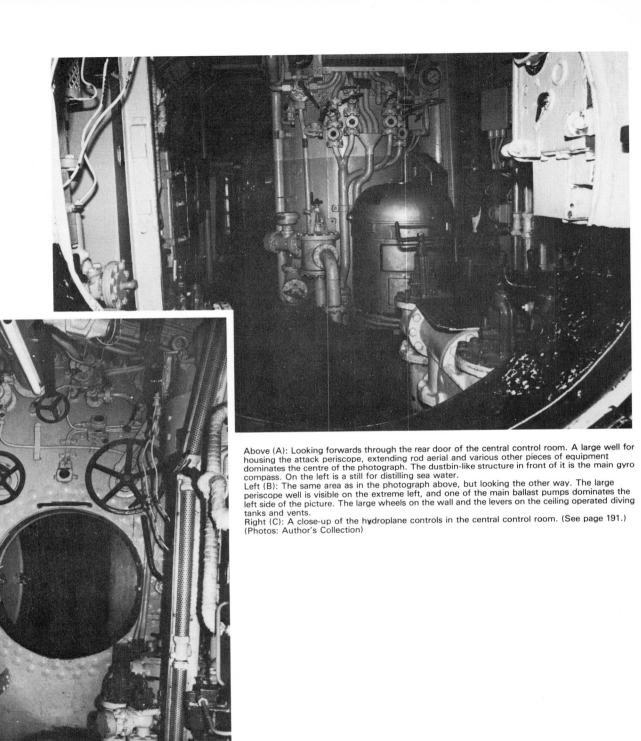

Above (A): Looking forwards through the rear door of the central control room. A large well for housing the attack periscope, extending rod aerial and various other pieces of equipment dominates the centre of the photograph. The dustbin-like structure in front of it is the main gyro compass. On the left is a still for distilling sea water.

Left (B): The same area as in the photograph above, but looking the other way. The large periscope well is visible on the extreme left, and one of the main ballast pumps dominates the left side of the picture. The large wheels on the wall and the levers on the ceiling operated diving tanks and vents.

Right (C): A close-up of the hydroplane controls in the central control room. (See page 191.)

(Photos: Author's Collection)

Left and below (A and B): The electro-control panel aboard a late Type VIIC. Earlier models were operated with levers instead of wheels. The port electric motor, most of it below floor level, can be seen at the base of the bottom picture. This could be used to propel the boat or to generate electricity for charging the batteries. (Photo: Author's Collection)

Right (C): The diesel compartment, looking forwards. (Photo: Author's Collection)

Far right (D): The diesel engine controls on the port side.

1, The starter handle and throttle.
2, Wheel for controlling the air flow to the engine.
3, Temperature control gauges, one for each cylinder and one for the exhaust.
4, Telegraph from the central control room.
5, Diesel engine.
(Photo: Author's Collection)

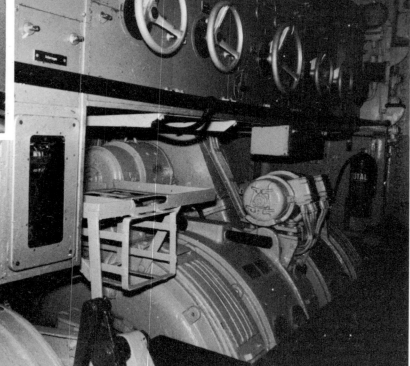

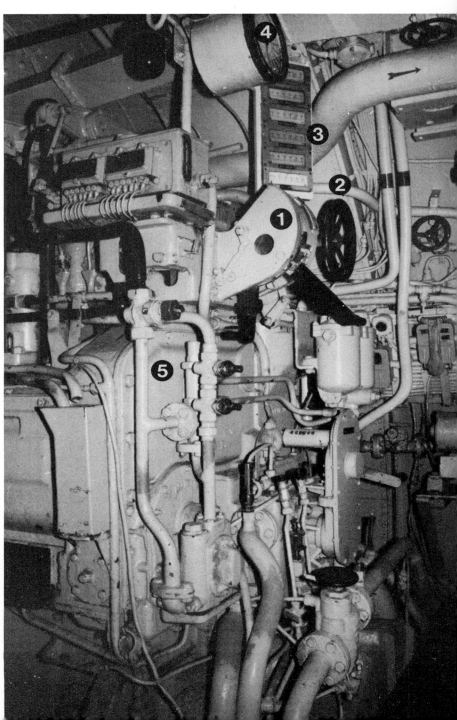

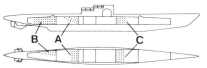

Left (A): The diesel engine controls on the roof of the engine compartment. (Photo: Author's Collection)

Below left (B): A close-up of the device for ejecting asdic 'foxers.' (Photo: Author's Collection)

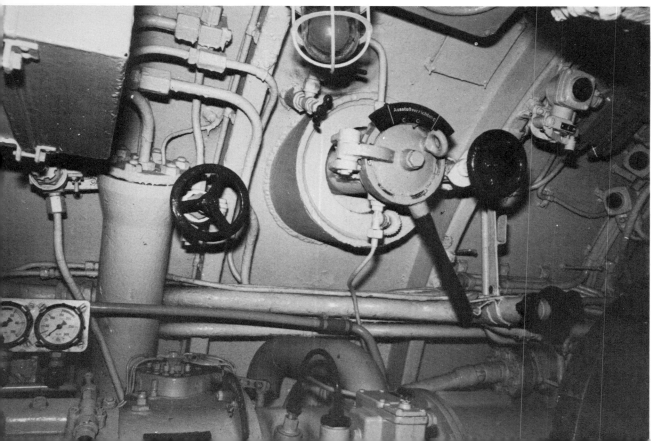

Left (C): The circular pressure door from the commander's 'cabin' into the central control room. There are some waterproof fuse boxes above the door, with telephone-like locking levers. The commander hardly had a cabin— just a small space that could be separated from the rest of the boat by a heavy curtain. (Photo: Author's Collection)

Below (A): The large clutch wheel between the diesel engine and the electric motors, starboard side. (Photo: Author's Collection)

Below right (B): The emergency rudder control, looking forwards. It was hinged at the top and could be swung into the middle of the boat when required. An indicator to show the position of the rudder was attached to the shaft, but the needle is missing in this photograph. Another 'slave' gyro compass can be seen to the left of the shaft. The control panel for the electro-motors is situated immediately behind this wheel. (Photo: Author's Collection)

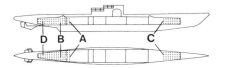

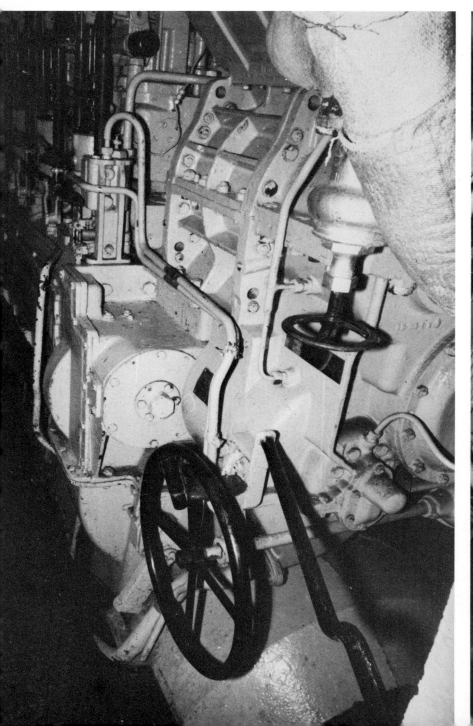

Left (C): The four bow torpedo tubes. (Photo: Author's Collection)

Below left (D): The stern torpedo tube. The door, opening towards the left, is hardly visible because it is pointing directly towards the camera. A torpedo would have been pushed into the tube and the piston (1) fitted in behind before closing the door. The tube would then be flooded and the outside doors opened; compressed air would be injected into this piston to force it along the tube and eject the torpedo.

2, Trim tank.
3, Compressed air cylinder.
4, Electric compressor.
5, Electric motor for rudder.
6, Device for ejecting asdic 'foxers'.
7, Torpedo 'mixer' to adjust the torpedo setting inside the torpedo tube.
8, Torpedo tank. There was another tank on the port side. The boat would become considerably lighter after torpedo-firing, and these tanks were filled with water to compensate for the difference in weight and to prevent the boat from rising. (Photo: Author's Collection)

Chronology

1919

28 June: Treaty of Versailles signed.

1920

10 Jan: Treaty of Versailles comes into effect.

1921

1 Jan: Foundation of the new German Navy, called Reichsmarine. (There had been great turmoil after the end of the First World War, with suggestions to scrap the Navy completely and put their few ships under command of the Army. Naval forces had been known as the 'Provisional Navy' (Vorläufige Reichsmarine) from 11 August 1919 until the end of 1920.)
11 April: Reichsmarine Ensign hoisted for the first time.
13 Dec: Washington Treaty signed.
31 Dec: Kaiser's Flag officially hauled down for the last time. However, it reappeared in later years, and was also flown during Hitler's time.

1925

7 Jan: Light cruiser *Emden* launched at Wilhelmshaven. She was the first large warship built in Germany after the First World War.

1926

1 Oct: The first post-First World War torpedo-boat, *Möwe*, commissioned.

1928

1 Oct: Erich Raeder made Commander-in-Chief of the Navy.

1929

17 April: Light cruiser *Königsberg* commissioned.
6 Nov: Light cruiser *Karlsruhe* commissioned.

1930

15 Jan: Light cruiser *Köln* commissioned.

1931

19 May: Pocket battleship *Deutschland* launched.
8 Oct: Light cruiser *Leipzig* commissioned.

1933

Early in year: German Naval Attachés appointed to London, Washington and Paris.
30 Jan: Adolf Hitler appointed Chancellor.
14 March: President of Germany, Paul von Hindenburg, orders a slight change in the Naval Ensign; the removal of the small canton in the upper left-hand corner.
1 April: Pocket battleships *Deutschland* commissioned and *Admiral Scheer* launched.
23 Nov: Motor torpedo-boat *S6* commissioned, the first post-First World War MTB to see service in the Second World War.

1934

3 June: Pocket battleship *Admiral Graf Spee* launched.
12 Nov: Pocket battleship *Admiral Scheer* commissioned.

1935

16 March: Hitler repudiates the Treaty of Versailles; National Conscription re-introduced.
21 May: German Navy was renamed Kriegsmarine.
18 June: Anglo-German Naval Treaty signed.
29 June: First of the new submarines, *U1*, commissioned.
18 Aug: *Leberecht Maass*, *Z1*, the first post-war destroyer, launched.
27 Sept: 1st U-boat Flotilla (Flotilla 'Weddigen') commissioned by Karl Dönitz (who had previously been commander of the light cruiser *Emden*).
2 Nov: Light cruiser *Nürnberg* commissioned.
9 Nov: New Ensign, with swastika, hoisted for the first time. (The young officer who carried it ceremonially through Kiel referred to it as a floor-cloth, and whispered out of the corner of his mouth, "It's not my idea to carry this red rag", as he passed friends on the parade.)

1936

6 Jan: Pocket battleship *Admiral Graf Spee* commissioned.
30 May: Great naval memorial at Laboe, near Kiel, officially opened. (The initial idea for a memorial was conceived by Obermaat* Wilhelm Lammertz, and the money was raised by members of the Marine Kameradschaft (Naval Comradeship Society)—quite an impressive feat when one considers that those were the years of the economic depression.)
3 Oct: Battlecruiser *Scharnhorst* launched. (The Germans categorized both *Scharnhorst* and *Gneisenau* as battleships.)
6 Nov: Germany joins London Submarine Protocol (Prize Ordinance)*.
22 Nov: *U18* sinks after a collision with the tender *T156*. This was the first U-boat to sink after the end of the First World War.
8 Dec: Battlecruiser *Gneisenau* launched.

1937

14 Jan: Destroyer *Z1* (*Leberecht Maass*) commissioned.
6 Feb: Heavy cruiser *Admiral Hipper* launched.
8 June: Heavy cruiser *Blücher* launched.

1938

4 Feb: Hitler appoints himself Supreme Commander-in-Chief of the armed forces, and soldiers take a new oath, swearing obedience to him.
13 March: The Austrian Anschluss; Austria becomes part of the Greater German Empire.
21 May: Battlecruiser *Gneisenau* commissioned.
22 Aug: Heavy cruiser *Prinz Eugen* launched.
Sept: The 'Z' Plan formulated.
1 Sept: *M1* commissioned, the first new minesweeper since the First World War.
29 Sept: The famous meeting in Munich, after which Neville Chamberlain returns to England waving a piece of paper and expressing confidence in "peace in our time".
Dec: Britain agrees to Germany increasing her submarine force.

1939

27 Jan: Hitler gives the 'Z' Plan highest priority.
14 Feb: Battleship *Bismarck* launched.
1 April: Battleship *Tirpitz* launched.
1 April: Erich Raeder promoted from General-admiral to Grand Admiral, a rank unused since the First World War.
27 April: Hitler repudiates the Anglo-German Naval Treaty.
29 April: *Admiral Hipper* commissioned.
18 Aug: German Naval High Command orders

*This international treaty was originally signed by the major naval powers in 1930, and sought to impose rules on submarine warfare. Surprise submerged attacks on merchant vessels were not permitted; instead, the submarine should surface, stop the ship and inspect its papers. The vessel could only be sunk if its cargo came under a specified list of contraband and the safety of the crew could be ensured. As lifeboats were not considered suitable accommodation on the high seas, the ship's crew was supposed to be taken aboard the submarine.

*Petty Officer in the Imperial Navy.

Below: *SS Hamburg* (22,117 tons) as a liner before the war. She was later moved to Danzig to serve as accommodation ship and headquarters of the 8th U-boat Flotilla. *Hamburg* was used to evacuate people from the eastern Baltic provinces towards the end of the war, and she hit a mine off Sassnitz during the night of 6/7 March 1945. (Photo: Author's Collection)

the previously planned 'Three Front War Programme' to come into effect as an emergency measure.

19 Aug: 14 submarines leave Germany and sail to their war stations in the North Atlantic.

21 Aug: Pocket battleship *Admiral Graf Spee* leaves Wilhelmshaven.

24 Aug: 2 more U-boats depart to their war stations; pocket battleship *Deutschland* (renamed *Lützow*) leaves Wilhelmshaven.

25 Aug: Warning telegrams of a possible war sent to German merchant ships not in German ports.

27 Aug: German merchant ships instructed to get home to Germany in four days or to run into the nearest neutral port.

1 Sept: 0445, start of the German attack on Poland.

3 Sept: Britain and France declare war on Germany. German ships start to lay mines in the North Sea, concentrating on the defence of the German Bight. Such mining operations continue throughout the year, and became one of the Navy's most important contributions to the war during its first winter.

7 Sept: Operational submarines withdrawn from the Baltic.

16 Sept: *U31*, commanded by Kptlt. Hans Habekost, is the first U-boat to attack a convoy.

17 Sept: British aircraft carrier HMS *Courageous* sunk by *U29*, commanded by Kptlt. Otto Schuhart.

20 Sept: Heavy cruiser *Blücher* commissioned.

25 Sept: Royal Navy starts to lay mines in the English Channel to block the route for enemy shipping. (These operations continue until the end of the year.)

4 Oct: The war against Allied merchant shipping intensified by the German Naval Command lifting various restrictions on the types of vessels that could be attacked.

13 Oct: U-boat War Badge instituted by Grand Admiral Raeder; *U47*, commanded by Günther Prien, penetrates the defences of Scapa Flow during the night of 13th/14th and sinks the battleship HMS *Royal Oak*.

29 Oct: German Naval High Command gives permission for passenger ships to be attacked if they are sailing with a convoy.

Oct: U-boats start to lay magnetic mines in British shipping lanes.

20 Nov: First mines dropped in British coastal waters by German aircraft.

23 Nov: A German magnetic mine dropped in shallow waters off Shoeburyness in Essex and defuzed by Lieutenant-Commander Ouvery; auxiliary cruiser HMS *Rawalpindi* sunk by battlecruiser *Scharnhorst*.

13/14 Dec: British submarine *Salmon* scores torpedo hits on cruisers *Leipzig* and *Nürnberg*.

15 Dec: The damaged *Leipzig* torpedoed again by HM Submarine *Ursula*.

13 Dec to 17 Dec: Battle of the River Plate and sinking of the pocket battleship *Admiral Graf Spee*.

1940

22/23 Feb: Destroyers *Leberecht Maass* and *Max Schultz* (commanded by Korvkpt. Fritz Bassenge and Korvkpt. Claus Trampedach), while trying to avoid attack from German aircraft, run on to mines laid by a British submarine.

31 March/1 April: Auxiliary cruiser *Atlantis* (commanded by Bernhard Rogge) leaves German coastal waters, the first auxiliary cruiser to do so.

3 April: Transports leave German ports for the invasion of Denmark and Norway.

6 April: *Orion*, under command of Kpt.z.S. Kurt Weyher, becomes the second auxiliary cruiser to leave Germany.

7 April: German warships leave German bases for the invasion of Norway and Denmark.

8 April: British destroyer HMS *Glowworm* sunk by *Admiral Hipper*.

9 April: Heavy cruiser *Blücher* sunk in Oslo Fjord.

10 April: Light cruisers *Karlsruhe* and *Königsberg* sunk in Norwegian waters.

11 April: First Battle of Narvik (Norway).

13 April: Second Battle of Narvik.

14 April: *U49* (commanded by Kptlt. Johann-Egbert von Gossler) sunk by HMS *Brazen* and HMS *Fearless*; secret documents, probably connected with the 'Enigma' cyphering machine, float to the surface and are captured.

10 May: German Forces invade Holland, Belgium and France.

15 May: Dutch forces capitulate.

24 May: Allied Supreme Command decides to evacuate Norway.

27 May: German auxiliary cruiser *Orion* passes Cape Horn on her outward voyage.

4 June: Destroyer Badge instituted.

5 June: Dunkirk evacuation completed.

8 June: British aircraft carrier *Glorious* sunk by *Scharnhorst* and *Gneisenau*.

10 June: Evacuation of British forces from Norway completed; Italy declares war on Britain and France.

17 June: First U-boats arrive in France, to use the

French Atlantic ports for refuelling.

22 June: Franco-German armistice concluded at Compiègne; auxiliary cruiser *Pinguin* passes through the Denmark Strait on her outward voyage.

25 June: Ceasefire in France comes into effect at 0135.

27 June: Britain announces a blockade of the Continent.

3 July: Auxiliary cruiser *Komet* leaves Gotenhafen in the Baltic for the Pacific Ocean, sailing, under command of Konteradmiral Robert Eyssen, around the North Cape of Norway and heading east via the Siberian Sea passage.

1 Aug: Heavy cruiser *Prinz Eugen* commissioned.

17 Aug: Germany announces a total blockade of the United Kingdom, and an area in which all ships are to be sunk without prior warning.

19 Aug: The Narvik Shield award instituted.

20 Aug: German High Command plans to capture Gibraltar (Operation 'Felix').

24 Aug: Battleship *Bismarck* commissioned.

27 Aug: Plan to mount an initially large-scale invasion of Great Britain abandoned in favour of landings on a small front from Eastbourne to Folkestone.

30 Aug: Invasion of Great Britain postponed.

31 Aug: War Badge for Minesweepers, Submarine-Hunters and Security Forces instituted.

9 Oct: Start of one of the most important and critical convoy battles—21 ships are sunk from convoy SC7 and another 12 from convoy HX79, making this also one of the most successful 'wolf pack' attacks.

23 Oct: Pocket battleship *Admiral Scheer* leaves Gotenhafen for the Atlantic under command of Kpt.z.S. Theodor Krancke. (Some of the heavy cruisers were classed as Pocket Battleships before the war.)

31 Oct: Auxiliary cruiser *Widder* arrives in Brest after a cruise in American waters.

18/19 Nov: First U-boat located by radar fitted in a Sunderland aircraft (but not sunk).

30 Nov: Auxiliary cruiser *Komet* returns to Hamburg after 516 days at sea.

3 Dec: Auxiliary cruiser *Kormoran* leaves Gotenhafen.

1941

4 Feb: 40 Fw 200 Condor long-range bombers

come under the direct control of the U-boat arm, to be used for reconnaissance purposes.

25 Feb: Battleship *Tirpitz* commissioned.

3 March: British capture 'Enigma'-type cypher machine from V-boat *Krebs*.

17 March: HMS *Vanoc* located U100 on the surface with radar, the first success with Type 286 radar, which leads to the sinking of U100 (Joachim Schepke) and U99 (Otto Kretschmer).

1 April: War Badge for Blockade-Breakers instituted.

23 April: Auxiliary cruiser *Thor* (commanded by Kpt.z.S. Otto Kähler) arrives in the Bay of Biscay after a successful cruise in the South Atlantic.

24 April: Auxiliary Cruiser Badge instituted.

30 April: Fleet War Badge instituted; auxiliary cruiser *Thor* arrives in Hamburg from France after 329 days at sea.

7 May: German floating weather station *München* sunk by a British cruiser force; men from the destroyer HMS *Somali* manage to get aboard her before she goes down, and capture valuable radio equipment, including a naval cypher machine of the 'Enigma'-type plus various important documents.

8 May: Auxiliary cruiser *Pinguin* sunk.

10 May: U110 (Fritz-Julius Lemp) captured by British forces; valuable secret material falls into British hands, including a working model of the secret cypher machine set up with the code of the day.

18 May: *Prinz Eugen* and *Bismarck* leave Gotenhafen for *Bismarck's* first and only war cruise.

24 May: Old British battlecruiser *Hood* sunk by *Bismarck*.

27 May: 1035, *Bismarck* goes down, with the Fleet Commander and the entire Fleet Command aboard.

30 May: Motor Torpedo-Boat Badge instituted.

4 June: German tanker *Gedania* is abandoned and scuttled when the British auxiliary cruiser *Marsdale* appears. Royal Navy personnel manage to get on board before the tanker sinks, and capture secret material relating to the secret cipher machine.

15 June: German supply ship *Lothringen* captured by the British cruiser *Dunedin*; once again, secret documents fall into British hands. (By this time, Britain had captured vital documents and machinery for understanding large proportions

of the German secret code.)

20 June: An incident occurs between USS *Texas* and U203 (Rolf Mützelburg); as a result, Dönitz forbids German submarines to attack American warships, even if they appear inside the blockade area around the British Isles.

22 June: U48, the most successful U-boat of the war, returns to port from her last operational war cruise. She was subsequently used for training. (It has been stated that U99 was the most successful U-boat of the war, but this is not correct: her commander, the famous Otto Kretschmer, was the most successful *commander*, but he commanded two different boats and U48 was responsible for sinking more tonnage than either of these two.)

24 June: Naval Artillery War Badge instituted.

End of June: German floating weather station *Launenburg* sunk in the North Atlantic; men from the British destroyer *Tartar* manage to get on board before she goes down, and they capture yet more secret documents.

June: During this month, U-boat Command begins to suspect that some Allied convoys are being deliberately routed around the German submarine 'wolf packs'.

5 July: U-boats start to operate in the Arctic seas.

23 Aug: Auxiliary cruiser *Orion* returns to France after a voyage lasting 511 days.

28 Aug: U570 captured by British forces. (She later became HMS *Graph*.)

Sept: U-boats experience noteworthy difficulties in finding and attacking enemy convoys.

Oct: H/F D/F sets (High Frequency Direction-Finders) are installed by the Allies in fairly large numbers.

14 Nov: British aircraft carrier *Ark Royal* sunk by U81 (Kptlt. Friedrich Guggenberger).

15 Nov: U459, the first purpose-built supply submarine, commissioned by Korvkpt. Georg von Wilamowitz-Möllendorf.

22 Nov: Auxiliary cruiser *Atlantis*, after a voyage lasting 622 days, is sunk by HMS *Devonshire*.

29 Nov: Auxiliary cruiser *Kormoran*, after 350 days at sea, is sunk by HMAS *Sydney*.

7 Dec: Pearl Harbor is attacked by Japanese forces and part of the United States Pacific Fleet destroyed.

11 Dec: Germany and Italy declare war on the United States.

Dec: A dramatic and very significant convoy

battle takes place in the Atlantic; Swordfish aircraft from the British escort carrier *Audacity* succeed in keeping U-boats away from convoy HX76. *U751* (Korvkpt. Gerhard Bigalk) manages to sink *Audacity* after a ferocious battle, but not before Dönitz has recorded in his war diary: "The risk of being sunk is greater than the possible success. The presence of aircraft make 'wolf pack' tactics impossible." U-boat High Command now issues standing directives to U-boat commanders telling them to make the location and destruction of aircraft carriers their prime objective; previously, the main aim of U-boats encountering convoys had been to shadow the enemy while calling in other boats.

1942

11 Feb: Start of the 'Channel Dash'; German warships sail through the English Channel from Brest (France) to Germany and Norway.

26/27 Feb: Battlecruiser *Gneisenau* put out of action by bomb hits; she remains in Kiel until 4 April, when she is moved to Gotenhafen.

13/14 March: German auxiliary cruiser *Michel* passes through the Strait of Dover on the outward voyage of her first operational cruise.

20 April: Motor torpedo-boats are given their own autonomous command under Kpt.z.S. and Kommodore Rudolf Petersen. (Previously, they had been under the jurisdiction of the Flag Officer for Destroyers.)

12 May: *Stier* leaves Kiel on her first war cruise as an auxiliary cruiser.

1 July: Battlecruiser *Gneisenau* decommissioned.

11 Aug: British aircraft carrier *Eagle* sunk by *U73* (Kptlt. Helmuth Rosenbaum).

12 Sept: Liner *Laconia* torpedoed and sunk by *U156* (Korvkpt. Werner Hartenstein).

27 Sept: Auxiliary cruiser *Stier* scuttled after damage caused by action with American armed freighter *Stephen Hopkins*.

28 Sept: Naval High Command, including leaders of the U-boat arm, meet Hitler in Berlin to discuss new trends in the Battle of the Atlantic and the deterioration of the U-boat impact on convoys.

8 Oct: Auxiliary cruiser *Komet* leaves Hamburg for her second war cruise, under command of Kpt.z.S. Ulrich Brocksien.

9 Oct: Auxiliary cruiser *Thor* arrives at Yokohama, at the end of her second cruise.

14 Oct: Auxiliary cruiser *Komet* torpedoed by a British MTB.

19 Nov: The Russians launch their attack on German forces at Stalingrad; this battle becomes one of the great turning points of the Second World War.

31 Dec: A battle off the North Cape of Norway; Hitler threatens to 'throw the surface fleet into the dustbin' as a result of the failure of the German North Norway Naval Squadron to drive home its attack on convoy JW51B (see p. 43).

1943

30 Jan: Grand Admiral Erich Raeder resigns as Supreme Commander-in-Chief of the Navy and is succeeded by Karl Dönitz.

2 Feb: The Battle of Stalingrad ends in a shattering defeat for the Germans.

12 Feb: 'Rotterdam Radar', from a crashed British aeroplane near Rotterdam in Holland, falls into German hands.

2 March: German auxiliary cruiser *Michel* arrives at Kobe in Japan to end her first war cruise.

16 March: The start of the largest convoy battle of war, with U-boats attacking convoys HX229 and SC122.

23 March to 8 April: Battle for convoy HX231, the first time since the fighting began that a convoy manages to cross the Atlantic and beat off all attacking U-boats, despite the 'air gap' still being 450 miles wide.

May: U-boat losses rise dramatically, and Grand Admiral Dönitz admits defeat in the Battle of the Atlantic by withdrawing U-boats from the troubled waters.

21 May: German auxiliary cruiser *Michel* leaves Yokohama in Japan, after fitting out.

31 May: U-boat construction is handed over completely to Dr. Speer's Department of Military Armament.

4 June: The last German auxiliary cruiser still operational, *Michel*, leaves Yokohama for her second war cruise, under command of Kpt.z.S. Günther Gumprich.

22 Sept: British midget submarines (*X*-craft) launch a successful attack on the battleship *Tirpitz* in Altenfjord.

17 Oct: *Michel*, the last German auxiliary cruiser on the high seas, is sunk by the American submarine *Tarpon*.

26 Dec: *Scharnhorst* is sunk in the Battle of the North Cape.

1944

15 Jan: *U377* (commanded by Oblt.z.S. Gerhard Kluth) torpedoed and sunk by a German acoustic torpedo fired from another German submarine. (*U972*, commanded by Oblt.z.S. Klaus-Dietrich König, suffers a similar fate during this same month.)

5 April: The British mount a large-scale air attack on the battleship *Tirpitz*, moored in Kaafjord.

13 May: Clasp for the Roll of Honour of the German Navy is instituted.

15 May: U-boat Clasp instituted.

May: Schnorkels, fitted to U-boats, come into widespread use.

6 June: Operation 'Overlord' (the Allied landing in Normandy).

11 June: Last remaining supply U-boat, *U490*, is sunk.

12 June: First electro-boat commissioned— *U2321*, of Type XXIII, a small coastal submarine carrying only two torpedoes.

27 June: First large electro-submarine commissioned—*U2501*, of Type XXI.

July: 'Versuchskommando 456' (Experimental Command 456) founded under Admiral Helmuth Heye to experiment with all types of midget craft.

15 Aug: *Tirpitz* again bombed in Kaafjord.

15 Oct: *Tirpitz* leaves Kaafjord for Haakoy Island, near Tromsö.

12 Nov: *Tirpitz* sinks at her anchorage, off Haakoy Island.

13 Nov: War Badge for Midget Weapons instituted (in seven grades).

19 Nov: Naval War Clasp (Marine Front Spange) instituted.

1945

Evacuation of Germans from the eastern provinces proceeds throughout early 1945 and continues until the end of the war.

30 April: Hitler commits suicide. Grand Admiral Dönitz becomes Head of State.

30 April: The first large electro-boat of Type XXI (*U2511* under command of Adalbert Schnee) leaves port for its first operational war cruise.

4 May: German delegation signs the surrender document at 1830 in Field Marshal Montgomery's headquarters at Lüneburg Heath (south of Hamburg).

1 Aug: German Minesweeping Administration founded.

Glossary

Abbreviation:	Full term:	Translation:
Abt.	Abteilung	Department; detachment; unit
	Abzeichen	Badge
	Abzeichen für Blockadebrecher	Blockade-Breakers Badge
	Adam	Midget submarines; entered production as Type Biber
	Administration	Verwaltung
	Admiral of the Fleet; Grand Admiral	Grossadmiral
	Admiral Nordmeer	Admiral Polar Seas
Asto	Admiralstabsoffizier	Admiralty Staff Officer
	Admiraltät. Used until August 1920, when it was replaced by Marineleitung. Later called Oberkommando der Marine (OKM)	Admiralty
	Airborne Forces	Luftstreitkrafte
	Aircraft spotter	Flugmelder
Akku	Akkumulator	Accumulator; battery
	Alberich Skin	A rubber-like skin for covering U-boats; used to absorb radar impulses
	Allgemeines Marine (haupt) amt. Later known as Seekriegsleitung (SKL)	General Naval Office
	Angle; rank chevron	Winkel
AA	Anti-aircraft	Flak; Fliegerabwehrkanone; Flugzeugabwehrkanone
	Aphrodite	German code-name for a radar 'foxer'. A hydrogen-filled balloon was anchored on the sea's surface by a 60m-long (65yds) cable attached to a heavy float. Three sheets of metal foil were fastened to the cable and reflected radar impulses.
	Armament	Rüstung
	Armed Forces	Streitkräfte
AF; AFP	Artilleriefährprahm	Artillery barge
	Artilleriemechaniker	Ordnance Engineer
AVK	Artillerieversuchskommando	Experimental Artillery Command
	Artillerist, see Schutze	
	Asdic	Allied Submarine Detection Investigation Committee
	Athos	German code-name for a radar detection device
	Auerhahn	German code-name for a railway train used briefly towards the end of the war as a headquarters for the Naval High Command

Abbreviation:	Full term:	Translation:
	Aufklärungsstreitkräfte	Reconnaissance Forces
AGRU-Front	Ausbildungsgruppe-Front	A technical branch for training men and testing new U-boats before they entered service
a.D.	ausser Dienst	Withdrawn from service; retired
	Auxiliary cruiser/raider	Hilfskreuzer; also see Handels-schutzkreuzer/Handel-störkreuzer
	Auxiliary cruiser badge, see	Kriegsabzeichen für Hilfskreuzer
	Aviso	Originally, a small, fast warship. Later, term also meant 'armed yacht'
Bb	Backbord	Port
	Bachstelze	A gliding helicopter towed by U-boats and used as a reconnaisance platform, mainly in the Indian Ocean
	Badge	Abzeichen
	Baltic	Ostsee
	Bandsman	Musikmaat
	Barge; punt; ferry	Fährprahm
	Battlecrüiser	Schlachtkreuzer
	Battleship	Linienschiff; later, Schlachtschiff
	Bauwerft	Shipbuilding yard
B-Dienst	See Funkbeobachtungsdienst	
	Bee (German slang)	Aircraft
	Befehlshaber	Commander-in-Chief
B.d.A.	Befehlshaber der Aufklärungs-streitkräfte	C-in-C for Reconnaissance Forces
B.d.K.	Befehlshaber der Kampfgruppe/ Befehlshaber der Kreuzer	C-in-C for Task Force/C-in-C for Cruisers
B.d.L.	Befehlshaber der Linienschiffe. An early term, later replaced by Befehlshaber der Schlachtschiffe	C-in-C for Battleships
B.d.P.	Befehlshaber der Panzer-schiffe	C-in-C for Pocket Battleship
B.d.S.	Befehlshaber der Schlacht-schiffe. (Also see Befehlshaber der Linien-schiffe)	C-in-C for Battleships
B.S.N.	Befehlshaber der Sicherung Nordsee	C-in-C for Security, North Sea
B.S.O.	Befehlshaber der Sicherung Ostee	C-in-C for Security, Baltic
B.d.Sich	Befehlshaber der Sicherungs-streitkräfte	C-in-C for Security Forces
B.S.W.	Befehlshaber der Sicherung West	C-in-C for Security, West
B.d.U.	Befehlshaber der Unterseeboote	C-in-C for U-boats

Abbreviation:	Full term:	Translation:
	Begleitschiff	Escort ship
	Beiboot	Ship's boat; long boat
	Beischiff	Tender
	Biber	One-man midget submarine; prototype was called 'Adam'
	Biscay Cross	A wooden-framed radar detector aerial fitted on U-boats. It was a makeshift structure that was later replaced by a purpose-built aerial
	Bismarck	Code-name of Naval Head-quarters in Eberswalde, near Berlin.
	Blockade; barrier; embargo	Sperre
	Blockade-Breakers Badge, see	Abzeichen fur Blockade-brecher
	Bluse	Pullover shirt
	Boatswain	Bootsmann
	Boatswain, Chief	Oberbootsmann
	Bold	An Asdic foxer used by U-boats. After ejection it formed bubbles, which reflected Asdic impulses.
	Bootsmann	Boatswain
	Bootmannsmaat	Petty Officer Boatswain
	Borkum	Name of radar detection equipment
BBC	Braun Boveri & Co	Firm of partly French origin (hence the non-German spelling of 'Co') that built electrical equipment. The initials 'BBC' can often be seen in photographs of U-boat equipment.
	Bronze alloy	Tombakbronze
BRT	Bruttoregistertonnen	Gross Registered Tonnage (GRT)
	Bundesmarine. This name was used between 1848 and 1852, and again after 1956.	Federal Navy
	Cadet/Midshipman	Fähnrich
	Captain	Kapitän zur see
	Carpenter	Zimmermannsmaat; Zimmermeister
	Chemist	Marineapotheker
	Chevron (denoting rank); angle	Winkel
	Clasp	Spange
	Cloak	Umhang; Spanier
	Coastal Commander	Küstenbefehlshaber
	Coastal Defence	Küstenschutz
	Coastal patrol boat	Küstenschnellboot
	Coastal Police	Marineküstenpolizei

Abbreviation:	Full term:	Translation:
	Command	Kommando
	Commander	Korvettenkapitän
C-in-C	Commander-in-Chief	Befehlshaber
	Commissioned	Indienststellung
NO	Communications Officer	Nachrichtenoffizier
	Conning tower	Kommandoturm
	Convoy	Geleit
	Deadlight, Operation	Code-name for the Allied sinking of German submarines after the war
	Dekan	Dean
	Delphin	A midget submarine; a few of these experimental craft were built towards the end of the war
	Demagnetizing Group	Entmagnetisierungsgruppe (EMG)
	Dentist	Marinezahnarzt
	Depth charges	Wasserbomben; Wabos (slang)
	Destroyer	Zerstorer
	Destroyer badge, see Zerstorer Kriegsabzeichen	
	Deutsche Bucht	German Bight
	Deutsches Kreuz	German Cross; medal introduced in 1941
DMRL	Deutsche Minenräumleitung	German Minesweeping Administration (GMSA), founded in August 1945
DeTe; DT Gerat	Dezimeter-Telephonie-Gerat; Drehturm Gerät	Radio rangefinder for artillery
	Dienst	Duty
	Dienstgrad	Rank
	Dienstjacke; Paradejacke	Uniform jacket
KVK	Distinguished Service Cross	Kriegsverdienstkreuz
	E-boat	English terms for an enemy motor torpedo-boat
	Eel (slang)	Torpedo
	Ehrentafel der deutschen Kriegsmarine	Roll of Honour of the German Navy
	Ehrentafelspange der Kriegsmarine	Clasp for the Roll of Honour of the Navy
I.O.	1. Offizier	First Officer
I.W.O.	1. Wachoffizier	First Watch Officer
EK1/EK2	Eisernes Kreuz	Iron Cross, 1st or 2nd Class
	Elefant, see Seeteufel	
	EMS	Experimental mine with periscope attached to top; the idea being that the Royal Navy would be prompted to ram it. EMS was probably never used operationally
	Engineer	Ingenieur

Abbreviation:	Full term:	Translation:
	Engineering Official	Seemaschinistenbeamter
	Enigma	German cypher machine. Naval version was called Schlusselmaschine 'M'
EMG	Entmagnetisierungsgruppe	Demagnetizing Group
EKK	Erprobungskommando für Kriegsschiffneubauten	Command for experimenting with new warships
E.-M.A.A.	Ersatz-Marineartillerie-abteilung	Naval Reserve Artillery Division
	Escort boat	Geleitboot
	Fahnrich zur See	Cadet/midshipman
	Fahrprahm	Barge; punt; ferry
FAT	Federapparat Torpedo; also, incorrectly, called Flächen-absuchender Torpedo. (See Lagenunabhängiger Torpedo)	Torpedo that would initially travel in a straight line and then start zig-zagging. It was used by U-boats against convoys
	Feindfahrt	Operational war cruise
	Feldbluse	Field grey tunic
FRG-Bt	Fernräumgerät-boot	Minesweeper with remote-control equipment
	Festungskommandant	Fortress Commander
	Flächenabsuchender Torpedo, see Federapparat Torpedo	
	Flag Officer; Commander	Führer
	Fleet	Flotte
	Fleet Commander	Flottenchef
	Fleet War Badge, see Flottenkriegsabzeichen	
	Fliege	Code-name for a radar detector
Flak	Fliegerabwehrkanone; Flugzeugabwehrkanone	Anti-aircraft gun
	Flotte	Fleet
	Flottenchef	Fleet Commander, C-in-C of the High Seas Fleet
	Flottenkriegsabzeichen	Fleet War Badge, introduced in April 1941
	Flottenstreitkräfte; Hochsee-flotte	High Seas Fleet
	Flottentrossschiffe	Fleet Supply Ships
	Flottille	Flotilla
	Flugmelder	Aircraft Spotter
Flak	Flugzeugabwehrkanone	Anti-aircraft gun
Fr-Fl	Flussräumflottille	River Minesweeper Flotilla
	FMB; FMC	Mines specially developed for rivers
	Forage cap	Schiffchen
	Fortress Commander	Festungskommandant
	Fregatte	Frigate
Fregkpt; FK	Fregattenkapitän	Captain (Junior)
	Freiherr	Baron
	Führer	Flag Officer; Commander

Abbreviation:	Full term:	Translation:
F.d.Luft	Führer der Luftstreitkräfte	Flag Officer/Commander for Airborne Forces
F.d.Minsch	Führer der Minenschiffe	Flag Officer/Commander for Minelayers
F.d.M.	Führer der Minensuchboote	Flag Officer/Commander for Minesweepers
F.d.Mot	Führer der Motorbootsver-bände	Flag Officer/Commander for Motor-Boat Units
F.d.S.	Führer der Schnellboote	Flag Officer/Commander for Motor Torpedo-Boats
F.d.T.	Führer der Torpedoboote	Flag Officer/Commander for Torpedo-Boats
F.d.U.	Führer der Unterseeboote	Flag Officer/Commander for Submarines
F.d.V.	Führer der Vorpostenboote	Flag Officer/Commander for Patrol Boats
F.d.Z.	Führer der Zerstörer	Flag Officer/Commander for Destroyers
	Funk	Radio telegraphy
B-Dienst	Funkbeobachtungsdienst	Radio monitoring service
	Funker	Radio operator
FuMB	Funkmessbeobachtung	Device for detecting radar waves
FuME	Funkmesserkennung	Radar recognition. This apparatus, which was fitted to German ships, picked up radar waves and sent them back in a magnified form to make it possible for the sender to distinguish between friendly and enemy ships
FuMG	Funkmessgerät	Radio rangefinder; radar apparatus
FuMO	Funkmessortung	Radio location; radar apparatus
	Funkpeilgerät	Radio direction-finder, used for determining the direction of radio signals
	Gehrock; later Rock	Frock coat
	Geleit	Convoy
	Geleitboot	Escort boat
G-Fl	Geleitflottille	Escort flotilla
Genadm; GA	Generaladmiral	A rank (not used in the Royal Navy) between Admiral and Admiral of the Fleet.
	German Bight	Deutsche Bucht
	German Cross	Deutsches Kreuz. Award introduced in 1941.
GMSA	German Minesweeping Administration, founded in August 1945	Deutsche Minenräum-leitung (DMRL)

Abbreviation:	Full term:	Translation:
	Gluckauf	Name of a Bureau founded during 1943 to develop new submarine designs.
	Goldbutt	An experimental torpedo
	Goldfisch	An experimental torpedo
	Goliath	German code-name for their huge radio transmitter, situated near Magdeburg
	Grand Admiral; Admiral of the Fleet	Grossadmiral
	Greatcoat	Mantel
	Grossadmiral	Admiral of the Fleet; Grand Admiral
GRT	Gross Registered Tonnage	Bruttoregistertonnen (BRT)
	Grundhai	A deep-diving submarine that was intended to be used as a rescue craft, but it was never built
	Gunner	Schütze; Artillerist
	Hafenkapitän; Hafen-kommandant	Port Commander
	Hafenschutz	Port protection
HS-Fl	Hafenschutzflottille	Port protection flotilla
	Hai	A midget submarine similar to the Marder Type.
Hs-Fl	Handelsschutzflottille	Convoy protection flotilla
HSK	Handelsschutzkreuzer, later Hilfskreuzer (see p. 93)	Auxiliary cruiser initially used for protecting merchant shipping, but later used for attacking it
HK	Hilfskreuzer	Auxiliary cruiser; raider
	Hochseeflotte; Flottenstreit-kräfte	High Seas Fleet
	Hoheitsabzeichen	German national emblem
	Hohentwiel	Radar equipment. The aerial resembled the springs of a bedstead
	Hohenzollern	The Kaiser's family name and also the name of the Imperial yacht
h.c.	honaris causa	Honorary title
	Huttenwerk	Steel or iron works
	Hydra	A small speedboat developed towards the end of the war. Only one flotilla became operational, in Holland
	Imperial Navy	Kaiserliche Marine
i.D.	Indienststellung	Commissioned
Ing.	Ingenieur	Engineer
	Ingolin	Name for hydrogen peroxide fuel used in experimental submarines and torpedoes

Abbreviation:	Full term:	Translation:
	Instructor	Lehrbeamter; Lehrer
	Jackett	Reefer jacket
	Justizbeamter	Justice official
	Kaiser	Emperor
KM	Kaiserliche Marine; the name was used between 1871 and 1919	Imperial Navy
	Kampfabzeichen der Kleinkampfmittel	Badge for Midget Weapons Unit; award introduced in November 1944
	Kampfgruppe	Task Force
Kaleu; Kaleunt; Kptlt; KL	Kapitänleutnant	Lieutenant-Commander
Kpt. z. S.; KS	Kapitän zur See	Captain
	Kleinkampfverband	Midget Weapons Unit
	KMA	German mine specially developed for shallow water; to be used on beaches against invasion forces
	Kommandierender Admiral. The chiefs of the Baltic and North Sea Naval Stations were known by this title. Later, heads of commands concerned with coastal defence were also given this title	Commanding Admiral
Kdo.	Kommando	Command
K.d.K.	Kommando der Klein-kampfverbände	Command for Midget Weapons Units
	Knight's Cross	Ritterkreuz, which see
Kdot	Kommandoturm	Conning tower
	Kommodore	Commodore
KA; Kadm.	Konteradmiral	Rear-Admiral
	Koralle	Code-name for naval head-quarters near Berlin
Korvkpt.; KK	Korvettenkapitän	Commander
	Kraftfahrer	Driver
	Kriegsabzeichen für Hilfs-kreuzer	Auxiliary cruiser badge; instituted in 1941
	Kriegsabzeichen für Minen-such, Ubootsjagd und Sicherungsverbände	Badge for Minesweepers, Submarine-Hunters and other Security Forces
KM	Kriegsmarine	Name of the German Navy, used between 1935 and 1945
	Kriegsabzeichen für Marine-artillerie	Naval Artillery Badge, instituted in June 1941
KMD	Kriegsmarine Dienststelle	Naval Headquarters
KMW	Kriegsmarine Werft	Naval shipbuilding yard
	Kriegsmetall	War metal
KVK	Kriegsverdienstkreuz	Distinguished Service Cross
KAS	Küstenartillerie	Coastal Artillery School
	Küstenbefehlshaber	Coastal Commander

Abbreviation:	Full term:	Translation:
KM-boot	Küstenminenboot	Small, fast coastal minelayer developed towards the end of the war
KS	Küstenschnellboot	Fast, coastal patrol boat
	Küstenschutz	Coastal defence
KSV	Küstensicherungsverband	Coastal Security/Defence Unit
LUT	Lagenunabhängiger Torpedo	A further development of Federapparat Torpedo, which see
L-fl	Landungsflottille	Landing flotilla
	Laufbahnabzeichen	Trade badges
	Launching	Stapellauf
	Lehrbeamter; Lehrer	Instructor
LAT	Leichter Artillerieträger	Light artillery barge
LS/LS Boot	Leichtes Schnellboot	Small speedboat, usually armed with small torpedoes
L.I.	Leitender Ingenieur	Chief Engineer
	Leiter	Leader; director
	Lerche	Name of a torpedo developed towards the end of the war. It could be guided by the thin wire it trailed behind
	Leutnant zur See	Lieutenant (Junior)
	Lieutenant-Commander	Kapitänleutnant
	Linienschiff	Early term for 'battleship', later replaced by 'Schlachtschiff'
	Linse	Small speedboat that carried explosives
	Lorient Shield	Lorientschild. Award to commemorate the stand of the Lorient garrison
	Maat	Petty Officer
	Machinist	Maschinist
MES	Magnetischer Eigenschutz; Magnet Eigenschutze	De-Magnetizing unit
	Mantel	Greatcoat
	Marder	Type of midget submarine
M	Marine	Navy
	Marineapotheker	Chemist
MA	Marineartillerie	Naval artillery
MAA	Marineartillerieabteilung	Naval Artillery Division
	Marineausrustungsstelle	Fitting-out base
	Marinebeamter	Naval administrative officials
	Marinedekan	Naval Dean
	Marineersatz	Naval Reserve
M. Fla. A.	Marineflakabteilung	Naval AA Division
M. Fla. R.; M. Flak. Reg.; M. Flak. Rgt.	Marineflakregiment	Naval AA Regiment
M. Fla. K. S.	Marine-Flugabwehr & Kustenartillerie Schule	Naval AA and Coastal Artillery School
	Marine Frontspange	Naval War Clasp, introduced

Abbreviation:	Full term:	Translation:
	Marinegruppenkommando	in November 1944 Naval Group Command (see p. 65)
	Marine-Hitlerjugend	Naval Hitler Youth
	Marine Inspektion	Naval Inspectorate
	Marinekommandoamt	Naval Command Office
	Marinekonstruktionsamt	Naval Construction Office
MKA	Marinekraftfahrabteilung	Naval Motor Vehicle Division (road transport)
	Marineküstenpolizei	Coastal Police
	Marinelehrabteilung or Marineunteroffizierslehrabteilung	NCO Training Division
	Marineleitung. Term used after the First World War, before it was called Oberkommando der Marine (OKM)	Supreme Naval Command
MNA	Marinenachrichtenabteilung	Naval Intelligence Division
MNHA	Marinenachrichtenhelferinnenausbildungsabteilung	Naval Intelligence Assistants (Female) Training Division
MNO	Marinenachrichtenoffizier	Naval Intelligence/Information Officer
MOK	Marineoberkommando. This should not be confused with Oberkommando der Marine. The just three MOKs were created in Feb. 1943, when the names of Naval Stations Baltic and North Sea and Commanding Admiral Norway were changed. Later, two more MOKs were added. Also see Marinestation der Ostsee/Nordsee and Stationskommando der Ostsee/Nordsee	Naval Station Baltic/North Sea
	Marinepfarrer	Naval Chaplain
	Marinestation der Ostsee/Nordsee; later renamed Marineoberkommando	
	Marineunteroffizierslehrabteilung, see Marinelehrabteilung	
	Marineverwaltungsamt	Naval Administration Office
	Marinewaffenamt	Naval Weapons Office
	Marinewehramt	Naval Defence Department
	Marinezahnarzt	Dentist
	Matrose	Ordinary Seaman
	Matrosen-Gefreiter	Able Seaman
	Matrosen-Hauptgefreiter	Leading Seaman (after 4 and a half years service)
	Marinestosstruppabteilung	Naval Assault Detachment
	Matrosen-Obergefreiter	Leading Seaman

Abbreviation:	Full term:	Translation:
	Matrosen-Stabsgefreiter	Leading Seaman
	Matrosen-Stabsoberge-freiter	Leading Seaman
	M-boat	Minesweeper
	Medical	Sanität
	Mess jacket	Messjacke
	Metox	Radar detector
	Midget Weapons Unit	Kleinkampfverband
	Midget Weapons Unit Badge, see Kampfabzeichen der Kleinkampfmittel	
	Midshipman; cadet	Fähnrich
MRS	Minenräumschiff; Minensuchboot	Minesweeper
	Minenschiffe; Minenleger	Minelayer
M-Fl	Minensuchflottille	Minesweeper flotilla
	Minesweepers, badge for: see Kriegsabzeichen für Minensuch, Ubootsjagd und Sicherungs-verbände	
	Molch	Midget submarine
	Monsoon Group	Long-range U-boats that ferried cargo from the Far East
MTB	Motor torpedo-boat	Schnellboot
	Motor torpedo-boat badge, see Schnellbootskriegsabzeichen	
	Musikmaat	Bandsman
NO	Nachrichtenoffizier	Communications Officer
	Narvik Shield	Narvikschild; award instituted in 1940 for men involved in the Battle of Narvik
NSDAP	Nationalsozialistische-Deutsche-Arbeiter-Partei	National Socialist Workers' Party
	Naval Anti-Aircraft Detachment	Marineflakabteilung
	Naval Artillery badge, see Kriegsabzeichen für Marineartillerie	
	Naval Artillery Detachment	Marineartillerieabteilung
	Naval Command, Supreme	Marineleitung, later changed to Oberkommando der Marine (OKM)
	Naval Group Command	Marinegruppenkommando
	Naval War Clasp, see Marine Frontspange	
	Naval War Staff	Seekriegsleitung (SKL)
	NCO Training Unit	Marinelehrabteilung
	Neger	Midget submarine
	Netzsperrflottille	Boom Defence Flotilla
	Neue Reichsmarine	New Navy: Reichsmarine
	Nordsee	North Sea
ObdM	Oberbefehlshaber der	Supreme Commander-in-

Abbreviation:	Full term:	Translation:
	Marine	Chief of the Navy
	Oberbootsmann	Chief Boatswain
	Oberfahnrich zur See	Sub-Lieutenant
OKM	Oberkommando der Marine	Supreme Naval Command; Naval High Command
OKW	Oberkommando der Wehrmacht	Supreme Command of the Armed Forces (No British equivalent)
	Oberleutnant zur See	Lieutenant (Senior)
	Obermaat	Chief Petty Officer
	Operationsabteilung, later called Ubootsführung	Operations Department
	Ordinary Seaman	Matrose
	Ordnance Engineer	Artilleriemechaniker
	Ortung	Radio location (radar); position-finding
	Ostsee	Baltic
	Panzerschiff	Pocket battleship
	Paradejacke, see Dienstjacke	
	Patrol boat	Vorpostenboot
	Petty Officer	Maat
	Petty Officer Boatswain	Bootmannsmaat
	Petty Officer, Chief	Obermaat
	Picket boat flotilla	Sicherungsflottille
	Port	Hafen
	Pullover shirt	Bluse
	Radio telegraphy	Funk
R-boot	Räumboot	Motor minesweeper; small vessel
R-Fl	Räumboot flottille	Motor minesweeper flotilla
	Rear-Admiral	Konteradmiral
	Reconnaissance Forces	Aufklärungsstreitkräfte
	Reich	Empire; nation
RM	Reichsmarine	Name of the German Navy between 1920 and 1935
Res.	Reserve	Reserve
	Ritterkreuz	Knight's Cross of the Iron Cross (unless specified, for there were other Knight's Crosses)
	Rock, see Gehrock	Frock coat
	Roll of Honour of the German Navy	Ehrentafel der deutschen Kriegsmarine
	Schiffchen	A small ship; also, a forage cap worn by officers and men
SAS	Schiffsartillerieschule	Ship artillery school
	Schiffsstammabteilung	Training detachment
	Schildbutt	Experimental torpedo powered by hydrogen peroxide
	Schirmmütze	Peaked cap
	Schlachtkreuzer	Battlecruiser
	Schlachtschiff	Battleship

Abbreviation:	Full term:	Translation:	Abbreviation:	Full term:	Translation:
	Schlepper	Tug		Sperre	Barrier; embargo; blockade
	Schlitten	Midget speedboat developed towards the end of the war		Sperrmechaniker	Mine engineer
				Stapellauf	Launching
	Schlusselmaschine 'M'	Naval version of Enigma		Stationskommando der Ostee/Nordsee. Name used after the First World War, until renamed Marinestation der Ostee/Nordsee	Naval Command Baltic/ North Sea
	Schnellbootskriegsabzeichen	Motor torpedo-boat badge; award instituted in 1941			
S-Boot	Schnellboot	Speedboat; Motor torpedo-boat			
	Schreiber	Yeoman		Steinbutt	Experimental torpedo powered by hydrogen peroxide; a further development of Steinfisch
	Schreiberobermaat	Chief Petty Officer			
	Schulschiff	Fleet training ship			
	Schütze; Artillerist	Gunner			
	Schwein	Experimental midget submarine that was never built		Steinfisch	German code-name for a high-speed torpedo with special walter turbine using hydrogen peroxide (Ingolin) as fuel
	Schwertwal	Fast midget submarine developed towards the end of the war. Only a few experimental craft were built			
			Stb.	Steuerbord	Starboard
				Streitkrafte	Armed Forces
				Submarine-hunter	Unterseebootsjager (UJ)
	Security Forces badge for: see Kriegsabzeichen für Minensuch, Ubootsjagd und Sicherungsverbände			Submarine-hunters, badge for: see Kriegsabzeichen für Minensuch, Ubootsjagd und Sicherungsverbande	
	Seehund	Midget submarine		Supply ship	Trossschiff
SKL	Seekriegsleitung	Naval War Staff. Directorate of the war at sea		Supreme Commander-in-Chief	Oberbefehlshaber
	Seelöwe	Sealion. Code-name for the invasion of the United Kingdom		Supreme Naval Command	See Oberkommando der Marine (OKM)
				T5 see Zaunkönig	
	Seemännischer Fahrzeugbeamter	Sea service official		Task Force	Kampfgruppe
	Seemaschinistenbeamter	Engineering official		Technischer Beamter	Technical Official
	Seeteufel; also called Elefant	Experimental midget submarine developed towards the end of the war. The vessel's caterpiller tracks enabled it to get from its transporter into the water		Telegrapher	Fernschreib
				Thetisboje	German radar 'foxer' consisting of a three-dimensional cross with wire strung between the supports, each of which had a small float attached to its tip. The idea was to float the cross on the surface and for the wires to reflect radar impulses
SMS	Seine Majestäts Schiff	His Majesty's Ship (HMS)			
	Shipyard Workers' Achievement Badge	Werftleistungsabzeichen			
Si-Fl	Sicherungstlottille	Picket boat flotilla			
	Sicherungsstreitkräfte	Security Forces		Tombakbronze	Bronze alloy
Sich. Vb.	Sicherungsverband	Picket boat unit	T-boot	Torpedoboot	Torpedo-boat
	Sonder	Special		Torpedomechaniker	Torpedo engineer
	Spange	Clasp	TEK	Torpedoerprobungskommando	Torpedo Trials Command. Also a sub-department of the TI, the TEK was founded in 1937 as an independent body for testing and evaluating torpedoes
	Spanish Cross	Spanienkreuz Award introduced during the Spanish Civil War			
	Speedboat; motor torpedo-boat	Schnellboot			
	Sperrbrecher	Barrier-breaking vessel; auxiliary minesweeper	TI	Torpedoinspektion	This Torpedo Inspectorate

Abbreviation:	Full term:	Translation:
		was founded in 1886 as an autonomous body to deal with all torpedo matters. It was responsible to the Supreme Naval Command, although personnel were administered by the Baltic and North Sea Naval Commands. The Inspectorate was amalgamated with several other bodies between Oct. 1919 and Oct. 1937
	Torpedokommando	Torpedo Command. Also under the jurisdiction of the TI these commands were part of the Torpedo Arsenals and were responsible for operational torpedoes used by any of the naval forces
TVA	Torpedoversuchsanstallt	Torpedo Experiment/Trials Institute. Operational as a sub-department of the TI since before the war, its function was to design, build, test and evaluate new torpedoes for the Navy
	Training ship, Fleet	Schulschiff
	Trossschiff	Supply ship
	Tug	Schlepper
	UA	Recognition mark of a submarine the Germans were building for Turkey before the War. The boat was never handed over, but commissioned instead in the German Navy
	UB	Recognition mark of HMS Seal, captured by German forces on 4 May 1940
	Überzieher	Pea jacket
	U-boat	English term, meaning German submarine
	Uboots Frontspange	U-boat clasp, introduced in May 1944
	Ubootsführung	U-boat Command
	Ubootskriegsabzeichen	U-boat badge; award instituted in 1939
UC		Norwegian submarines serving in the German Navy
UD		Dutch submarines serving in the German Navy

Abbreviation:	Full term:	Translation:
	UF	French submarines serving in the German Navy
	UIT	Italian submarines serving in German Navy
	Umhang; Spanier	Cloak
Uboot; earlier written as U-boot or U-Boot	Unterseeboot	Submarine of any nation
UJ	Unterseebootsjäger	Submarine-hunter
	Verband	Unit
	Versuch	Experiment; trial
	Versuchskommando 456	Experimental Command 456, founded by Admiral Helmuth Heye
	Verwaltung	Administration
	Verwaltungsbeamter	Administration official
VA	Vizeadmiral	Vice-Admiral
	von	Title of nobility
	Vorläufig	Provisional
	Vorläufige Reichsmarine	Provisional Navy. Name given to the Reichmarine's first few months
	Vorposten	Coastal defence (patrol boats)
	Vorpostenboot	Patrol boat for coastal defence
	VS5	Experimental submarine
	Wabos, slang for Wasserbomben	
	Wachoffizier	Watch Officer
	Wal	Midget submarine (never operational)
	Walter Boat	Submarine developed by Helmuth Walter (see p.34)
	War metal	Kriegsmetall
	Wasserbomben	Depth charges
	Welle	Wave; also propeller shaft
	Werftleistungsabzeichen	Shipyard Workers Achievement Badge
	Werkstattbeamter	Workshop official
	Weserübung	Code-name for the invasion of Norway and Denmark
WBS	Wetterbeobachtungsschiff	Weather ship
	Winkel	Angle; rank chevron
	Zaunbutt	Experimental submarine powered by hydrogen peroxide
	Zaunkönig (T5)	Acoustic torpedo
	Zentrale	Central control room
Z	Zerstörer	Destroyer
	Zerstörer Kriegsabzeichen	Destroyer badge; award instituted in June 1940, for men engaged in the Battle of Narvik
	Zimmermannsmaat; Zimmermeister	Carpenter

Select Bibliography

Air Ministry. *U-Boats 1939-45*. 4 vols. This is a part handwritten and part typed document dealing with the individual histories of U-boats. The work is most interesting, but it was compiled shortly after the war and parts of it are now slightly out of date. The only copy is in the Reference Library of the Imperial War Museum.

Almann, K. *Ritter der sieben Meere*. Erich Papel, Rastatt, 1963. A work dealing with some men who were awarded the Knight's Cross of the Iron Cross.

Angolia, J. R. *For Führer & Fatherland*. R. J. Bender, San José, 1976. Including naval war badges with citations.

Beesly, P. *Very Special Intelligence*. Hamish Hamilton, London, 1977; Doubleday, New York, 1978. This is the story of the British Admiralty's Operational Intelligence Centre between 1939-1945. A most interesting volume, important for anyone studying the history of the Second World War.

Bekker, C. *Flucht übers Meer*. Stalling, Oldenburg, 1959. The story of the evacuation of German people from the eastern Baltic during the last few months of the war.

— *The German Navy 1939-1945*. Hamlyn, London, 1974; Dial, New York, 1975. The photographs are interesting and they are supported by an easy-to-follow text. Specific ship types as well as various actions are covered. The book is well worth looking at for the photographs alone.

— *Hitler's Naval War*. Macdonald and Jane's, London, 1974; Doubleday, New York, 1974. Translated from *Verdammte See*, Stalling, Oldenburg, 1971. A most interesting book covering the main aspects of the war at sea.

Bensel, R. *Die deutsche Flottenpolitik von 1933-1939*. Mittler, Berlin, 1958. A study of ship construction in the light of Hitler's foreign policy.

Blundell, W. D. G. *German Navy Warships 1939-45*. Almark, London, 1972. This is a small, well-illustrated paperback giving essential details of the ships. Of very good quality and one of the best on the subject.

Bredemeier, H. *Schlachtschiff Scharnhorst*. Koehlers, Jugenheim, 1962.

Brennecke, H. J. *The Hunters and the Hunted*. Burke, 1958. Translated from *Jäger-Gejagte*. Koehlers, Jugenheim, 1956. A very good book about the U-boat war. The author outlines the events of the war at the start of each chapter and then describes specific U-boat operations in detail.

— *Die deutschen Hilfskreuzer im zweiten Weltkrieg*. Koehlers, Herford, 1976. The story of German auxiliary cruisers.

— *Ghost Cruiser HK 33*. William Kimber, London, 1954; US title: *Cruise of the Raider HK-33*. Crowell, New York, 1955. Translated from *Gespenster-Kreuzer HK 33*, Koehlers, Herford, 1968. The story of the auxiliary cruiser *Pinguin*, written with the co-operation of several crew members.

— *Schlachtschiff Bismarck*. Koehlers, Jugenheim, 1960.

— *Schlachtschiff Tirpitz*. Koehlers, Herford, 1975.

Brennecke, H. J. and Krancke, T. *Battleship Scheer*. Kimber, London, 1956. Translated from *Schwerer Kreuzer Admiral Scheer*. Koehlers, Jugenheim. Admiral Krancke was commander of *Admiral Scheer*.

Brown, D. *Tirpitz: the floating fortress*. Arms and Armour Press, London, 1977. Naval Institute Press, Annapolis, 1977. Contains a forty-page introduction, outlining the life of the battleship *Tirpitz*. Three-quarters of the book is devoted to an excellent collection of photographs.

Brustat, F. *Unternehming Rettung*. Koehlers, Herford, 1970. Deals with the rescue of Germans from the eastern Baltic region during the end of the war.

Buchheim, L-G. *U-Boat War*. Collins, London, 1978; Knopf, New York, 1978. Translated from *U-Boot-Krieg*. Piper, Zurich, 1976. This is an excellent pictorial account of the U-boat war. The photographs were taken by the author, who served as a war correspondent. Buried towards the end of the war, they were dug up again and form the backbone of this magnificent collection.

Busch, H. *U-boats at War*. Hamilton, London, 1954; Putnam, New York, 1954. An excellent account of life in U-boats. Busch served in the Kriegsmarine and came into contact with many U-boat men.

Davis, B. L. *Flags and Standards of the Third Reich*. Macdonald and Jane's, London, 1975; Arco, New York, 1975. Naval flags are included. There are some good colour plates.

Dollinger, H. *The Decline and Fall of Nazi Germany and Imperial Japan*. Odhams, London, 1965. This volume is packed with photographs of which only a few relate to the Navy. However, the work gives a good impression of the conditions under which Germans were living towards the end of the war, and it also helps to put naval minds into national perspective.

Dönitz, Karl. *Deutsche Strategie zur See im 2. Weltkrieg*. Bernard & Graefe, Frankfurt, 1972. The Grand Admiral answers forty questions. An interesting volume.

— *Mein wechselvolles Leben*. Muster-Schmidt, Göttingen, 1968. An interesting autobiography, dealing with those years not covered by *Ten Years and Twenty Days*.

— *Ten Years and Twenty Days*. Weidenfeld & Nicolson, London, 1959: World Pub. Co., 1959. Translated from *Zehn Jahre und Zwanzig Tage*, Athenäum, Frankfurt, 1958. Grand Admiral Dönitz's account of the U-boat war.

Elfrath, U. and Herzog, B. *Schlachtschiff Bismarck*. 1975. An account of the battleship in words and pictures.

Fock, H. *Schnellboote*. 3 vols. 1973. The first volume deals with the development of motor torpedo-boats until shortly before the Second World War. Volume Two covers the war years, and Three the post-war period.

Frank, W. *Sea Wolves: the story of the German U-boats at war*. Weidenfeld, London, 1955; Rinehart, New York, 1955. Translated from *Die Wölfe und der Admiral*. Stalling, Oldenburg, 1953. An interesting account of the U-boat war.

Frere-Cook, G. *The Attacks on the Tirpitz*. Allan, London, 1974. An account of the Allied attacks against *Tirpitz*.

Gabler, U. *Unterseebootsbau*. Wehr und Wissen, Bonn, 1964. Professor Gabler worked with Professor Walter on the new submarines during the war. This volume details German submarine construction before 1945.

Gasaway, E. B. *Grey Wolf, Grey Sea*. Arthur Barker, London, 1972. The story of *U124*.

Giese, F. *Die deutsche Marine 1920-1945*. Bernard & Graefe, Frankfurt, 1956. An account of the German Navy.

Giessler, H. *Der Marine-Nachrichten-und-Ortungsdienst*. J. F. Lehmanns, Munich, 1971. This is a most interesting account of German radio and radar development.

Görlitz, W. *Karl Dönitz*. Muster-Schmidt,

Göttingen, 1972. This small, inexpensive volume is part of a series called 'History and Personalities', and gives a good general introduction to Dönitz.

Gretton, Sir P. W. *Crisis Convoy: The Story of HX231.* P. Davies, London, 1974. The story of the first convoy to cross the Atlantic during the Second World War and fend off all attacking U-boats. The author was escort commander.

Gröner, E. *Die deutschen Kriegsschiffe 1815-1945.* J. F. Lehmanns, Munich, 1968. This is still the standard work on German warships. Most of the information is of a technical nature and illustrated with line drawings.

— *Die Schiffe der deutschen Kriegsmarine und Luftwaffe 1939-1945 und ihr Verbleib.* 8th edition, J. F. Lehmanns, Munich, 1976. This small volume gives the technical data of warships and their fate. There are also many line drawings.

Güth, R. *Die Marine des deutschen Reiches 1919-1939.* Bernard & Graefe, Frankfurt, 1972. An interesting outline of naval development before the war.

Hansen, H. J. *The Ships of the German Fleets, 1848-1945.* Hamlyn, London, 1975. Translated from *Die Schiffe der deutschen Flotten 1848-1945.* Stalling, Oldenburg, 1973. This is a pictorial work providing an introduction to some of the more interesting warships.

Harnack, W. *Die deutschen Zerstörer von 1934 bis 1945.* Koehlers, Herford, 1977. German destroyers from 1934 to 1945.

Herzog, B. *Die deutschen U-boote 1906-1945.* J. F. Lehmanns, Munich, 1959. A well-illustrated work about German submarines.

— *60 Jahre deutsche U-boote 1906-1966.* J. F. Lehmanns, Munich, 1968. A well-illustrated book with a vast variety of interesting information—most of it tabulated.

— *U-boats in Action.* Ian Allan, Shepperton. German edition *U-Boote im Einsatz 1939-45.* Podzun, Dorheim, 1970. This is a most interesting collection of photographs, with captions written in English and German.

Humble, R. *Hitler's High Seas Fleet.* Ballantine, New York, 1972. An account of battles fought by German surface ships.

Hümmelchen, G. *Die deutschen Seeflieger.* J. F. Lehmanns, Munich, 1976. An account of the Naval Air Arm.

Jones, G. *The Month of the Lost U-boats.*

William Kimber, London, 1977. An account of U-boat losses during May 1943.

— *Under Three Flags.* William Kimber, London, 1973. The story of *Nordmark* and the armed supply ships of the German Navy.

Kannapin, N. *Die Feldpostnummern der deutschen Kriegsmarine 1939-1945.* There are two volumes dealing with land forces and sea-going units. A list of postal numbers of the German Forces Post Office, published privately by the author in October 1974. Kannapin, Karolinger Str. 5, 221 Itzehoe.

Kennedy, L. *Pursuit: the chase and sinking of the Bismarck.* Collins, London, 1974; Pinnacle, 1975.

Kühn, V. *Schnellboote im Einsatz.* Motorbuch, Stuttgart, 1976. Motor torpedo-boats in action.

— *Torpedoboote und Zerstörer im Einsatz 1939-1945.* Motorbuch, Stuttgart, 1974. Torpedo-boat and destroyer actions during the war.

Kutzleben, K. von, Schröder, W. and Brennecke, J. *Minenschiffe 1939-1945.* Koehler, Herford, 1974.

Lenton, H. T. *German Warships of the Second World War.* Macdonald and Jane's, London, 1975; Arco, New York, 1976. The photographs are quite interesting.

Lewin, R. *Ultra Goes to War.* Hutchinson, London, 1978; McGraw, New York, 1978.

Littlejohn, D. and Dodkins, C. M. *Orders, Decorations, Medals and Badges of the 3rd Reich.* R. J. Bender, San José, 1967. Covers virtually all awards of the Third Reich, including naval awards.

Lohmann, W. and Hildebrand, H. H. *Die deutsche Kriegsmarine 1939-1945.* Podzun, Dorheim, 1956-64. This multi-volume work is the standard reference document on the German Navy. There are three volumes: I deals mainly with the Naval High Command, Naval Group Commands, the entire High Seas Fleet, the Security Forces and U-boats. II details important naval operations, Naval Stations for Baltic and North Sea and Naval Forces in occupied countries. There are also other interesting lists. III is a brief outline of the careers of the men mentioned in the other two volumes.

Lüdde-Neurath, W. *Regierung Dönitz.* Muster-Schmidt, Göttingen, 1964. This book does not deal directly with the German Navy. The author was Dönitz's last adjutant and he describes the

last days of the German High Command.

Lund, P. *Night of the U-boats.* W. Foulsham, Slough, 1973. A personal account of convoy SC7, as seen through the eyes of some survivors.

Macintyre, D. *U-boat Killer.* Weidenfeld & Nicolson, London, 1956; Norton, New York, 1956.

Middlebrook, M. *Convoy.* Allen Lane, London, 1977; Morrow, New York, 1977. A personal account of the battle for convoys SC122 and HX229, as seen through the eyes of some survivors.

Mollo, A. *German Uniforms of World War Two.* Macdonald and Jane's, London, 1976; Hippocrene, New York, 1976. Deals with German uniforms and insignia in chronological order of introduction.

— *Naval, Marine and Air Force Uniforms of WW2.* Blandford Press, London, 1975. Covers the basic naval uniforms of most countries. Includes only a few Kriegsmarine uniforms, but the work includes some variations which are not described in other books. Colour illustrations.

Peillard, L. *U-boats to the Rescue.* Jonathan Cape, London, 1963; US title: *The Laconia Affair.* Putnam, New York, 1963. The story of the *Laconia* rescue.

Peter, K. *Der Untergang der Niobe. Was geschah im Fehmarn Belt?* Koehlers, Herford, 1976. The sinking of the sail training ship *Niobe.*

Porten, E. P. von der. *The German Navy in World War II.* Arthur Barker, London, 1970. An interesting outline of the German Navy's activities during the war. The author lives in America and his book follows the classical Allied viewpoint.

Potter, J. P. *Fiasco.* Heinemann, London, 1970; Stein & Day, New York, 1970. The story of the 'Channel Dash', when German battleships left the French bases and sailed through the English Channel to Germany and Norway.

Price, A. *Aircraft versus Submarines.* William Kimber, London, 1973; Naval Institute Press, Annapolis, 1974. This is an excellent and most interesting volume dealing with the war against submarines.

Prochnow, G. *Deutsche Kriegsschiffe in zwei Jahrhunderten.* Ernst Gerdes, Preetz/Holstein, 1966. This is a good series of small, pocket size books providing the basic mechanical details and the fate of German warships.

I: Schlachtschiffe, Schlachtkreuzer, Flugzeugträger.
II: Leichte und Schwere Kreuzer.
III: Torpedoboote und Zerstörer.
IV: Unterseeboote.
V: Kanonenboote, Geleit und Minensuchfahrzeuge, Schnellboote, kleine Kampffahrzeuge.
VI: Versuchs & Hilfsschiffe.
Profile Publications, Windsor, England. This publisher has produced several small, inexpensive, but excellent books including *U107, Prinz Eugen* and *Admiral Graf Spee*.

Raeder, E. *My Life*. US Naval Institute, 1960. Translated from *Mein Leben*. Schild, Munich, 1956.

—*Struggle for the Sea*. William Kimber, London, 1959. Raeder's account of the war at sea.

Range, C. *Die Ritterkreuzträger der Marine*. Motorbuch, Stuttgart, 1974. There is a brief history of the Iron Cross, followed by a photograph of almost every recipient of the Knight's Cross, together with brief biographical details.

Rasenack, F. W. *Panzerschiff Admiral Graf Spee*. Koehler, Biberach, 1957.

Robertson, T. *The Golden Horseshoe*. Evans, London, 1966. The story of Otto Kretschmer.

Rogge, B. and Frank, W. *Under Ten Flags*. Weidenfeld & Nicolson, London, 1957. Translated from *Schiff 16*. Heyne. The story of the auxiliary cruiser *Atlantis* as told by her commander to Wolfgang Frank.

Röhr, A. *Deutsche Marinechronik*. Stalling, Oldenburg, 1974. An interesting volume, which lists naval historical events in chronological order.

Rohwer, J. and Hümmelchen, G. *Chronology of the War at Sea*. Ian Allan, Shepperton, 1974; Arco, New York, 1975. Translated from *Chronik des Seekrieges 1939-45*. Stalling, Oldenburg, 1968. Volume I: 1939 to 1942; Volume II: 1943 to 1945. This is an excellent, well-indexed study of the war at sea, giving essential details of many actions. There is no chatty text.

Rohwer, J. and Jacobsen, H. A. *Decisive Battles of World War II*. Andre Deutsch, London, 1965. Translated from *Entscheidungsschachten des 2. Weltkrieges*. Bernard & Graefe, Frankfurt, 1960. An account, from the German viewpoint, of decisive battles during the Second World War.

Rohwer, J. *Die U-Boot-Erfolge der Achsenmächte*. J. F. Lehmanns, Munich, 1968. This excellent book consists of a table which lists the successes of Axis Powers' submarines in chronological order. The table also lists interesting additional material such as times, positions, how sunk, ship types, etc. There is also a good index.

— *Eine Chronik in Bildern*. Stalling, Oldenburg, 1962. There are numerous pages of explanatory text and an interesting collection of photographs.

— *The Critical Convoy Battles of 1943*. Ian Allan, Shepperton, 1977. Translated from *Geleitzugschlachten im März 1943*. Motorbuch, Stuttgart, 1975. This is an excellent, detailed account of the battle for convoys SC122 and HX229. There is a good bibliography and the text is supported by photos, maps and tables. The author also provides an interesting introduction to the U-boat war, covering important aspects from the beginning of the war until 1943. These are not eye-witness accounts, instead, the author has consulted many British, American and German documents and he has described what went on during these battles.

Roskill, S. *The Secret Capture*. Collins, London, 1959; Collins, New York, 1959. The story of how *U110* was captured.

Rössler, E. *Geschichte des deutschen Ubootbaus*. J. F. Lehmanns, Munich, 1975. An excellent history of German submarine development from the first U-boat built in 1850 to the boats of the present day. The book is illustrated with photos and with many excellent plans, many drawn by Fritz Köhl.

— *U-Bootstyp XXI; U-bootstyp XXIII*. J. F. Lehmanns, Munich, 1967. These two books provide an interesting study of the electro-submarines.

Ruge, F. *Sea Warfare, 1939-45: A German Viewpoint*. Cassell, London, 1957. US title: *Der Seekrieg* (the German Navy's story, 1939-45), US Naval Institute, Annapolis, 1957. Translated from *Der Seekrieg 1939-45*. Koehlers, Herford, 1954. An excellent account of the war at sea, written by a German admiral.

Salewski, M. *Die deutsche Seekriegsleitung 1939-1945*. Bernard & Graefe, Frankfurt, 1970.
Volume 1: 1935 to 1941.
Volume 2: 1942 to 1946.
Volume 3: Denschriften und Lagebetrachtungen.

Schaeffer, H. *U-boat 977*. William Kimber, London, 1952. The career of *U977* told by her commander, including her escape to Argentina after the war.

Schmalenbach, P. *Die deutschen Hilfskreuzer 1895 bis 1945*. Stalling, Oldenburg, 1977. The development of German auxiliary cruisers, their mode of operations, equipment carried, life on board and their successes are included in this volume.

Schofield, B. B. *Loss of the Bismarck*. Ian Allan, Shepperton, 1977.

Showell, J. P. M. *U-boats under the Swastika*. Ian Allan, Shepperton, 1973; Arco, New York, 1974. An introduction to German submarines, 1935 to 1945, illustrated with maps, plans and well over 150 photos, many of which have not been published elsewhere. The work deals with a brief history up to the start of the war, with radar, boat types, administration of the U-boat arm, captured U-boats, the men, and there is a table of technical data plus other sections.

Taylor, J. C. *German Warships of World War II*. Ian Allan, Shepperton, 1966; Doubleday, New York, 1968.

Waddington, C. H. *OR in WW2*. Paul Elek, London, 1973. Operational Research against the U-boat during the Second World War. This is a most interesting, but also highly technical account.

Wagner, G. *Lagevorträge des Oberbefehlshaber der Kriegsmarine vor Hitler 1939-1945*. J. F. Lehmanns, Munich, 1972. This vast volume has over 700 pages and is an interesting and important record of meetings between Hitler and the Supreme Commander-in-Chief of the Navy. The editor, Gerhard Wagner, was Admiral in the Supreme C-in-C's staff.

Waters, J. M. *Bloody Winter*. Van Nostrand Reinhold, London and New York, 1967. An interesting account of the battles in the Atlantic during the winter of 1942/43.

Watts, A. J. *Axis Submarines*. Macdonald and Jane's, London, 1977; Arco, New York, 1977. Technical data, losses and some brief comments make up this small, inexpensive volume. It is illustrated with an excellent collection of interesting photographs.

— *The Loss of the Scharnhorst*. Ian Allan, Shepperton, 1970; Naval Institute Press, Annapolis, 1971. A detailed account, together with information of the ship's movements, dealing with the sinking of the famous battle-cruiser. Compiled from action reports and from

Below: The staggered rear 150mm turrets of *Karlsruhe's* main armament. (Photo: Author's Collection)

contemporary documents, it covers convoy JW55B, technical data, etc.
— *The U-boat Hunters.* Macdonald and Jane's, London, 1976. An excellent account of the weapons used to combat U-boats, including ships, aeroplanes and small items such as depth charges. The author describes the various phases of the war as well as the techniques used to fight U-boats.

Watson-Watt, Sir R. *Three Steps to Victory.* Odhams, London, 1957. The development of British radar and 'similar' inventions.

Werner, H. A. *Iron Coffins.* Arthur Barker, London, 1970; Holt, New York, 1969. German edition *Die eisernen Särge.* Hoffmann and Campe, Hamburg, 1970. A personal account of the German U-boat battles of the Second World War.

Winterbotham, F. W. *The Ultra Secret.* Weidenfeld and Nicolson, London, 1974; Harper Row, New York, 1974. The story of breaking German secret codes at Bletchley Park by the Chief of the Air Department of the Secret Intelligence Service 1930-1945.

Witthöft, H. J. *Lexikon zur deutschen Marinegeschichte.* Koehlers, Herford, 1977. Volume 1: A to M. Volume 2: N to Z. This is an excellent encyclopedia of German naval history.

Zienert, J. *Unsere Marineuniform.* Helmuth Gerhard Schulz, Hamburg, 1970. An interesting account of the history of German naval uniforms from the beginning to the present day. Illustrated.

Appendices

'ENIGMA' (Schlüsselmaschine 'M')

Germany's armed forces used a machine known as 'Enigma' to encode most of their day-to-day secret communications. 'Enigma' was such a complex piece of apparatus that it was thought the codes could not be broken. Yet the Polish Secret Service knew about 'Enigma' some ten years before the start of the war, and their knowledge was passed on to the British shortly before the Germans entered Warsaw. British cryptologists, working in conjunction with mathematicians and scientists, continued the work started by the Poles. They reconstructed an 'Enigma' machine and, by mid-1941, were able to break the majority of German secret codes. Initially, they were able to decode German signals for up to two to three days a week, but the decodings became more frequent as time passed. Consequently, the British High Command knew almost every move the Germans were about to make. Obviously, it did not tell them everything, but it did give them a pretty good idea of German positions, and what they were doing. It must have given them the locations of many secret meeting places in isolated parts of the Atlantic and enabled British forces to surprise and then destroy German ships while they were refuelling and taking on fresh provisions. So, deciphering 'Enigma' did play a very important role in the war.

Schlüsselmaschine 'M' (Cypher Machine 'M'), used only by the German Navy, worked on the same principle as the 'Enigma' machine used by the Army and Air Force. It was usually housed in a small portable box, about the size of an office typewriter. It had a typewriter keyboard, above which was a set of small windows. If one of the keys were pressed, this would light up the relevant letter of the alphabet. Above the windows were three (later four) wheels rotating inside the box, with their outside edges just visible through the holes in the cover. These wheels rotated in the same way as a typewriter roller and could be set manually in any position; a set of serrations protruded above the surface of the box for this purpose. Each wheel had fifty-two electrical contacts: twenty-six on one side wired up to another twenty-six on the other side. The wiring pattern differed on each wheel. When a key was depressed, an electrical contact would be made to any one of the first wheel's twenty-six terminals and the electric current would flow through the wiring of all three wheels, pass through a system of complicated loops at the end and return through the wheels to light up a bulb in one of the windows above the keyboard. Meanwhile, one of the wheels would rotate by one position, so that when the same key was depressed a second time, the electric current would follow a slightly different circuit and light up a different letter of the alphabet.

To make matters more complicated, there was a switchboard at the back that had to be wired up correctly with the 'code of the day' before the set could be used. Later on in the war, the Navy had a choice of four wheels from a total of eight. These could be shuffled around to fit any position, and the starting position of each wheel was pre-set by hand according to that day's code. It was, therefore, almost impossible to break the code manually. Even with a captured machine, it would have been necessary to know the switchboard settings at the back, which wheels to insert, the order of these wheels and their starting positions. A modern computer could crack a complicated problem like this, but such advanced electronics were not available in 1939—although Britain did construct the first modern computer to help break the code.

The details of how this was done are dealt with in two books included in the Bibliography: one by Patrick Beesly and the other by F. W. Winterbotham. Jürgen Rohwer also gives a valuable insight into radio telegraphy and the workings of Schlüsselmaschine 'M' and how German models were captured, in his book *The Critical Convoy Battles of 1943*.

The cracking of the German's secret radio code enabled the British to know the approximate positions of German forces. And, later on in the war, high frequency direction-finders made it possible for them to get bearings on even the shortest radio signals, thus informing naval commanders of the direction of imminent U-boat attacks. U-boats habitually radioed back to their bases at the start of an attack, and this gave convoy commanders some idea of the direction and time of incoming U-boats. It was then possible for them to cover the area with radar and wait for the enemy to close in. Once the submarine had been forced underwater, asdic would then be used to locate it, and a variety of weapons utilized to sink it.

GERMAN NAVAL CHARTS

Standard German naval charts were based on a system of artificial squares covering the earth's surface. The actual size of each square on the ground differed slightly because the maps were drawn to Mercator's projection: the same area of ground was represented by squares that gradually decreased as they neared the equator. Furthermore, some areas were a little irregular to enable the pattern to be used more conveniently.

Each large square, of about 900km (486 nautical miles) each side, was identified by two letters: 'EG', 'EH', 'EQ', 'ER' and so on. These letters followed a consecutive sequence over the earth's surface. The square was then subdivided into 9 further squares—as shown in 'ER'. The numbers given in 'ER' were featured as the first digit in 'EH', and each smaller square was numbered by adding another digit. The four squares numbered 49, 57, 73 and 81, which are part of 'EG', are also shown enlarged: each of these squares was subdivided into 9 smaller squares, which were further subdivided as shown in square 49. As practical examples, the positions on the diagrams can be written as follows.

A: EG 8137; E: EG 7364; B: EG 8165; F: EG 7345; C: EG 8176; G: EG 7322; D: EG 8199; H: EG 7376.

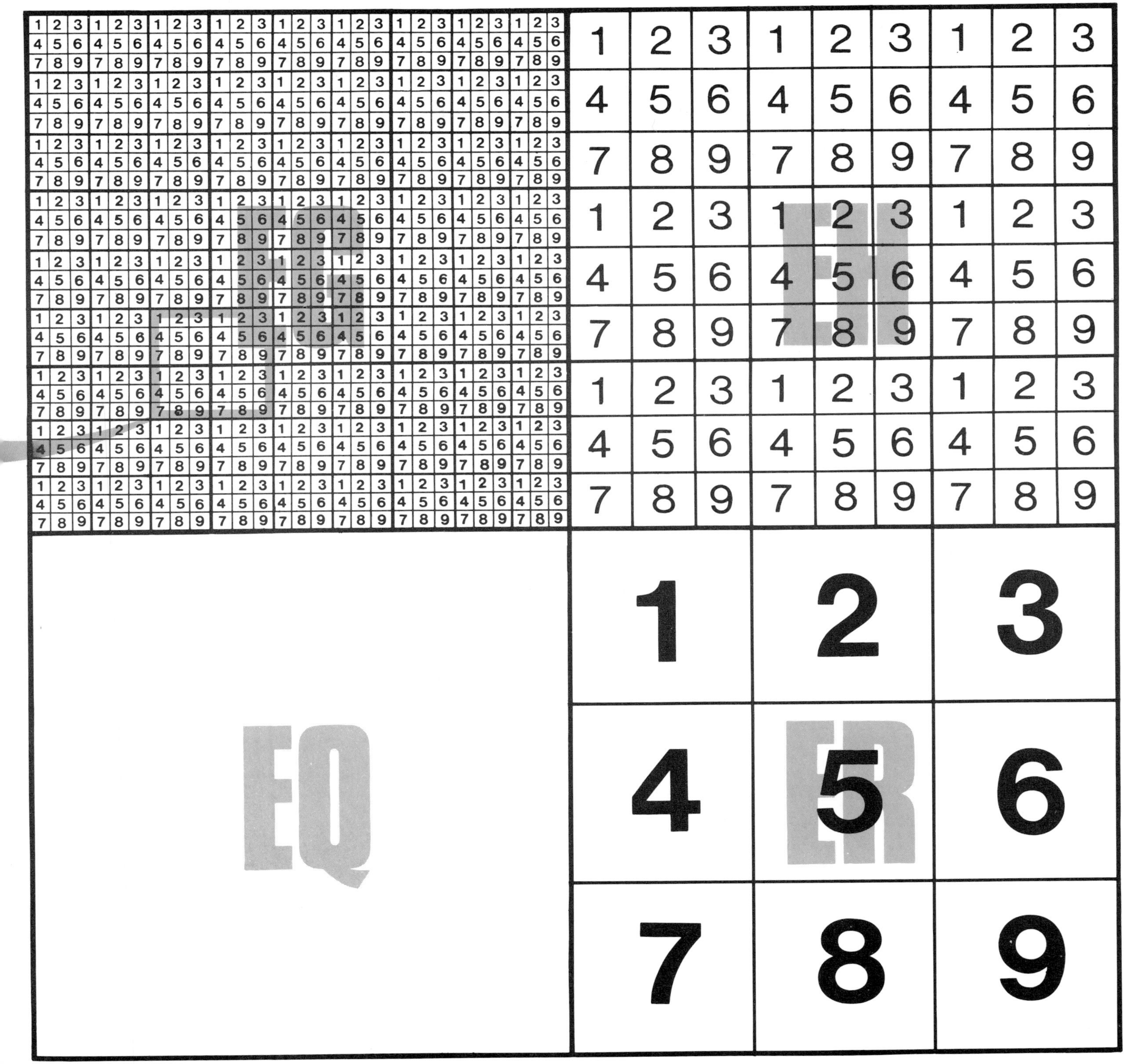
EG
EH
EQ
ER

Below: One of the small Rhine patrol boats on an exercise in 1940. There is a large inland waterway network along the Rhine estuary, and such fast patrol boats were used for a variety of duties. Some of them were manned by Army personnel. The flag flying at the mast, had two functions: it was the Flotilla Commander's Pennant (Flottillenstander) when it was attached to the top of the mainmast, and marked the boat of a Group or Unit Commander when it was flying from the signal mast or from a yardarm. There was a similar flag (also with small Iron Cross), but much longer, called the Kommandanten or Kommandowimpel (Commander's or Command Pennant), which was flown on warships when they were under command of a commissioned officer: examples can be seen on pages 36 and 49. (Photo: Bundesarchiv, Koblenz)

FLAGS

The Grand Admiral's Flag

The flag for the Grand Admiral was introduced in 1939, at the same time that the rank was re-introduced into the German Navy. (Previously, the Supreme Commander-in-Chief of the Navy had held the rank of Generaladmiral.) The Flag consisted of a white square with a large black iron cross, edged in white. Behind the iron cross were two admiral batons crossed, and a gold eagle with swastika was superimposed on the cross.

Flag for Commander-in-Chief of the Navy

This flag was introduced in 1935 to be flown from vessels, shore establishments, and vehicles in which the Commander-in-Chief was travelling. It consisted of a white square with a large black iron cross, edged in white and superimposed upon two golden-yellow coloured crossed swords.

Command Flags

Command flags were flown from the flagships of various admirals to indicate their presence on board—they were also flown at shore bases and from the wing of the admiral's car. This flag was in a miniature form on vehicles and it was either flown from a small staff on the wing or was painted directly on to the wing itself. These vehicle flags were about 30cm (12in) square. The flag featured a black disc in the upper and lower staff-side hand corners for Konteradmiral; only one disc for a Vizeadmiral; a full admiral had a cross without any discs; and a Generaladmiral had a pair of crossed swords in the lower staff-side corner.

Flags for Naval Land Units

The first flag awarded to a naval land unit was presented during September 1936. Similar Army flags utilized a variety of different colours and patterns for various units, but the Navy only produced one pattern. This was a blue square with a white central disc carrying a black swastika. The disc was edged in gold-wire embroidered oak-leaves. Gold-edged white 'wedges' ran from the centre to each corner, and there were black and silver iron crosses in the top right and bottom left hand corners. The opposing corners showed gold, fouled anchors. The reverse of the flag was similar, but with a black and silver iron cross in the centre and a gold eagle in place of the iron cross.

Pennants

Whereas the command flags, mentioned before, were flown from, or painted on to, the right hand wings of vehicles, other officer ranks flew a blue triangular pennant. These blue pennants were edged in gold, and had the national emblem, also in gold, in the centre. Admirals flew a similar pennant, but theirs had more elaborate edging in gold wire and there was a woven swastika design.

Command Pennant

Admiral's Pennant

Generaladmiral's Flag

Admiral's Flag

Vizeadmiral's Flag

Konteradmiral's Flag

Index

INDEX OF SHIP NAMES

Acknowledgments

Gordon Wiliamson has been responsible for writing the sections on ranks, uniforms, badges and flags, which he has illustrated with his own drawings. I would like to thank him for all the other help he has given me.

Special thanks must go to Otto Köhler for devoting many hours to sorting out information, verifying facts and checking through the manuscript; it would have been most difficult to have completed this project without his help. Also many thanks to his wife, Erika, for putting up with the vast untidy piles of paper in their lovely flat and for looking after me so well while I was working with Otto in Munich.

I am most grateful to 'Ajax' Bleichrodt for talking with me about his wartime experiences; and I wish to thank his son, Dr. Wolf-Heinrich Bleichrodt, for kindly helping me after Ajax's tragic death.

Heinrich Böhm, the first torpedo mechanic of U377, has been a most willing helper by clarifying details, providing some excellent photographs and a fair volume of new information—all of which has been greatly appreciated.

Thanks also to the Deutscher Marinebund e.V.; especially to Kurt Reimers and the staff of U995 for making it possible for me to have two special tours of the boat. Their explanations have been a great help. (U995 is now a museum next to the Naval Memorial at Laboe near Kiel, and is well worth a visit.)

Old photographs have been identified with help from Peter Cremer; Walter Lüdde-Neurath; Bernhard Rogge; Walter Richter; Professor Friedrich Ruge; and Adalbert Schnee.

Jack and Hanni Fletcher, Klaus and Anneliese Mallmann, Karl and Adele Prawitt and Heidi Prawitt have helped with numerous administrative problems, which has been a tremendous help. Neville Button and my wife, Imke, read through the manuscript before it went to press.

I am also indebted to many people and institutions who have kindly helped me in the past. It would be difficult to mention everybody by name, but all support has been deeply appreciated, and I should like to thank everyone who has taken an interest in my project. Each of the following has made a direct contribution: Ing. Franz Albert; Rudolf Bahr; Patrick Beesly, R.N.; Henry Birkenhagen; Wilhelm Brauel; Bundesarchiv, Koblenz, especially Dr. Haupt and his staff; Buchhändler Vereinigung, particularly Waltraut Schütte; Michael Cooper; Kpt.z.S. a.D. Hans Dehnert; Roel Diepeveen; Commodore J. F. van Dulm of the Royal Netherlands Navy; Trevor Dart; Admiral Kurt Freiwald; Professor Ulrich Gabler; Kpt.z.S. a.D. Helmuth Giessler; Konteradmiral Eberhard Godt; Kpt.z.S. a.D. Rolf Güth; Korvkpt. a.D. Jan Hansen-Nootbaar; Günther Heinrich; Geoffrey Jones; Fritz Köhl; Flottillenadmiral a.D. Otto Kretschmer; David Lees; Heinrich Lehmann-Willenbrock; David Littlejohn; Kpt.z.S. a.D. Hans Meckel; Peter Nops; Commander F. C. van Oosten of the Royal Netherlands Navy; Arthur Pitt, R.N.; Richard Reskey; Donald Ream; Konteradmiral Hans Rösing; Professor Dr. Jürgen Rohwer; Daniel Rose; Helmut Schmoeckel; Kpt.z.S. a.D. Herbert Schultze; Flottillenadmiral Dr. Werner Schünemann; Franz Selinger; Mr. R. E. Squires; Tom Stafford; Hans Staus; Frederick J. Stephens; Wrekin Photo Services; Commander Craig Waller, R.N.; Captain J. J. Wichers of the Royal Netherlands Navy; and Garry York.

J.P.M.S.